VIOLENCE IN CHILDREN

Other titles in the

Forensic Psychotherapy Monograph Series

Violence: A Public Health Menace and a Public Health Approach
Edited by Sandra L. Bloom

Life within Hidden Walls: Psychotherapy in Prisons
Edited by Jessica Williams Saunders

Forensic Psychotherapy and Psychopathology: Winnicottian Perspectives
Edited by Brett Kahr

Dangerous Patients: A Psychodynamic Approach to Risk Assessment and Management
Edited by Ronald Doctor

Anxiety at 35,000 Feet: An Introduction to Clinical Aerospace Psychology
Robert Bor

The Mind of the Paedophile: Psychoanalytic Perspectives
Edited by Charles W. Socarides

Violent Adolescents: Understanding the Destructive Impulse
Lynn Greenwood

VIOLENCE IN CHILDREN
Understanding and Helping Those Who Harm

Edited by

Rosemary Campher

Foreword by

Donald Campbell

Forensic Psychotherapy Monograph Series

Series Editor
Brett Kahr

Honorary Consultant
Estela Welldon

KARNAC

Chapter 1, "Early Life Trauma and the Psychogenesis and Prevention of Violence", by P. Fonagy, reproduced by permission from: Annals of the New York Academy of Sciences, 1036 (2004): 181–200.

First published in 2008 by
Karnac Books
118 Finchley Road
London NW3 5HT

British Library Cataloguing in Publication Data

A C.I.P. for this book is available from the British Library

ISBN: 978–1–85575–477–5

Edited, designed, and produced by Communication Crafts

Printed in Great Britain

www.karnacbooks.com

To: All those who are attempting to help traumatized and violent children

CONTENTS

ACKNOWLEDGEMENTS

I would like to thank the following people for their support, collaboration, and encouragement while planning, preparing, writing, and editing this book:

My husband, Richard Cushing, for his support and encouragement

My son, Lucas, who is a constant source of inspiration and joy

Brett Kahr, for his collaboration, understanding, encouragement, and support.

Donald Campbell, for his ongoing excellent supervision and support and for writing the Foreword to this book.

All the contributing authors for their extensive and intensive work of writing such inspiring chapters: Peter Fonagy, A. H. Brafman, Roderick Macleod, Camilla Sim, Stella. M. Acquarone, Clare Keogh, and Valerie Sinason.

The New York Academy of Sciences for granting permission to reprint Peter Fonagy's paper, "Early Life Trauma and the Psychogenesis and Prevention of Violence"; and for Ralph W. Brown's help in this matter.

SERIES FOREWORD

Brett Kahr

Centre for Child Mental Health, London
and
The Winnicott Clinic of Psychotherapy, London

Throughout most of human history, our ancestors have done rather poorly when dealing with acts of violence. To cite but one of many shocking examples, let us perhaps recall a case from 1801, of an English boy aged only 13, who was executed by hanging on the gallows at Tyburn. What was his crime? It seems that he had been condemned to die for having stolen a spoon (Westwick, 1940).

In most cases, our predecessors have either *ignored* murderousness and aggression, as in the case of Graeco–Roman infanticide, which occurred so regularly in the ancient world that it acquired an almost normative status (deMause, 1974; Kahr, 1994); or they have *punished* murderousness and destruction with retaliatory sadism, a form of unconscious identification with the aggressor. Any history of criminology will readily reveal the cruel punishments inflicted upon prisoners throughout the ages, ranging from beatings and stockades, to more severe forms of torture, culminating in eviscerations, beheadings, or lynchings.

Only during the last one hundred years have we begun to develop the capacity to respond more intelligently and more humanely to acts of dangerousness and destruction. Since the advent of psychoanalysis and psychoanalytic psychotherapy, we now have access to a much deeper understanding both of the aetiology of aggressive acts and of their treatment; and nowadays we need no longer ignore criminals or abuse them—instead, we can provide compassion and containment, as well as conduct research that can help to prevent future acts of violence.

The modern discipline of forensic psychotherapy, which can be defined, quite simply, as the use of psychoanalytically orientated "talking therapy" to treat violent, offender patients, stems directly from the work of Sigmund Freud. Almost one hundred years ago, at a meeting of the Vienna Psycho-Analytical Society, held on 6 February 1907, Sigmund Freud anticipated the clarion call of contemporary forensic psychotherapists when he bemoaned the often horrible treatment of mentally ill offenders, in a discussion on the psychology of vagrancy. According to Otto Rank, Freud's secretary at the time, the founder of psychoanalysis expressed his sorrow at the "nonsensical treatment of these people in prisons" (quoted in Nunberg & Federn, 1962, p. 108).

Many of the early psychoanalysts preoccupied themselves with forensic topics. Hanns Sachs, himself a trained lawyer, and Marie Bonaparte, the French princess who wrote about the cruelty of war, each spoke fiercely against capital punishment. Sachs, one of the first members of Freud's secret committee, regarded the death penalty for offenders as an example of group sadism (Moellenhoff, 1966). Bonaparte, who had studied various murderers throughout her career, had actually lobbied politicians in America to free the convicted killer Caryl Chessman, during his sentence on Death Row at the California State Prison in San Quentin, albeit unsuccessfully (Bertin, 1982).

Melanie Klein concluded her first book, the landmark text *Die Psychoanalyse des Kindes* [*The Psycho-Analysis of Children*], with resounding passion about the problem of violence in our culture. Mrs Klein noted that acts of criminality invariably stem from disturbances in childhood, and that if young people could receive access to psychoanalytic treatment at any early age, then much cruelty could be prevented in later years. Klein expressed the hope that: "If every child who shows disturbances that are at all severe were to be analysed in good time, a great number of these people who later end up in prisons or lunatic asylums, or who go completely to pieces, would be saved from such a fate and be able to develop a normal life" (1932, p. 374).

Shortly after the publication of Klein's transformative book, Atwell Westwick, a Judge of the Superior Court of Santa Barbara, California, published a little-known though highly inspiring article, "Criminology and Psychoanalysis" (1940), in the *Psychoanalytic Quarterly*. Westwick may well be the first judge to commit himself in print to the value of psychoanalysis in the study of criminality, arguing that punishment of the forensic patient remains, in fact, a sheer waste of time. With foresight, Judge Westwick queried, "Can we not, in our well nigh hopeless and overwhelming struggle with the problems of delinquency and crime, profit by medical experience with the problems of health and disease? Will we not, eventually, terminate the senseless policy of sitting idly by until misbehavior occurs, often with irreparable damage, then dumping the delinquent into the juvenile court or reformatory and dumping the criminal into prison?" (p. 281). Westwick noted that we should, instead, train judges, probation officers, social workers, as well as teachers and parents, in the precepts of psychoanalysis, in order to arrive at a more sensitive, non-punitive understanding of the nature of criminality. He opined: "When we shall have succeeded in committing society to such a program, when we see it launched definitely upon the venture, as in time it surely will be—then shall we have erected an appropriate memorial to Sigmund Freud" (p. 281).

In more recent years, the field of forensic psychotherapy has become increasingly well constellated. Building upon the pioneering contributions of such psychoanalysts and psychotherapists as Edward Glover, Grace Pailthorpe, Melitta Schmideberg, and more recently Murray Cox, Mervin Glasser, Ismond Rosen, Estela Welldon, and others too numerous to mention, forensic psychotherapy has now become an increasingly formalized discipline that can be dated to the inauguration of the International Association for Forensic Psychotherapy and to the first annual conference, held at St. Bartholomew's Hospital in London in 1991. The profession now boasts a more robust foundation, with training courses developing in the United Kingdom and beyond. Since the inauguration of the Diploma in Forensic Psychotherapy (and subsequently the Diploma in Forensic Psychotherapeutic Studies), under the auspices of the British Postgraduate Medical Federation of the University of London in association with the Portman Clinic, students can now seek further instruction in the psychodynamic treatment of patients who act out in a dangerous and illegal manner.

The volumes in this series of books will aim to provide both practical advice and theoretical stimulation for introductory students and for senior practitioners alike. In the Karnac Books Forensic Psychotherapy Monograph Series, we will endeavour to produce a regular stream of high-quality titles, written by leading members of the profession, who will share their expertise in a concise and practice-orientated fashion. We trust that such a collection of books will help to consolidate the knowledge and experience that we have already acquired and will also provide new directions for the upcoming decades of the new century. In this way, we shall hope to plant the seeds for a more rigorous, sturdy, and wide-reaching profession of forensic psychotherapy.

As the new millennium begins to unfold, we now have an opportunity for psychotherapeutically orientated forensic mental health professionals to work in close conjunction with child psychologists and with infant mental health specialists so that the problems of violence can be tackled both preventatively and retrospectively. With the growth of the field of forensic psychotherapy, we at last have reason to be hopeful that serious criminality can be forestalled and perhaps, one day, even eradicated.

References

Bertin, C. (1982). *La Dernière Bonaparte.* Paris: Librairie Académique Perrin.

deMause, L. (1974). The evolution of childhood. In: Lloyd deMause (Ed.), *The History of Childhood* (pp. 1–73). New York: Psychohistory Press.

Kahr, B. (1994). The historical foundations of ritual abuse: an excavation of ancient infanticide. In: Valerie Sinason (Ed.), *Treating Survivors of Satanist Abuse* (pp. 45–56). London: Routledge.

Klein, M. (1932). *The Psycho-Analysis of Children,* trans. Alix Strachey. London: Hogarth Press and The Institute of Psycho-Analysis. [First published as *Die Psychoanalyse des Kindes.* Vienna: Internationaler Psychoanalytischer Verlag.]

Moellenhoff, F. (1966). Hanns Sachs, 1881–1947: the creative unconscious. In: F. Alexander, S. Eisenstein, & M. Grotjahn (Eds.), *Psychoanalytic Pioneers* (pp. 180–199). New York: Basic Books.

Nunberg, H., & Federn, E. (Eds.) (1962). *Minutes of the Vienna Psychoanalytic Society. Volume I: 1906–1908,* trans. Margarethe Nunberg. New York: International Universities Press.

Westwick, A. (1940). Criminology and Psychoanalysis. *Psychoanalytic Quarterly,* 9: 269–282.

EDITOR AND CONTRIBUTORS

Stella M. Acquarone is the Director of the Parent Infant Clinic and School of Infant Mental Health in London and of its branch in the United States. She is a practising adult and child psychotherapist and has worked for thirty-one years in the NHS. She is a member of the British Psychological Society, the Association of Child Psychotherapists, and the London Centre for Psychotherapy. She has pioneered studies in early infant clinical research and development and lectures internationally on all aspects of infant–parent development and psychotherapy. She has written extensively in professional publications and journals, as well as chapters in books. Her book *Infant–Parent Psychotherapy: A Handbook* was published in 2004, and she edited *Signs of Autism in Infants* in 2007. Another book, *Ayudando a los ayudan* [Helping the helpers], is to be published shortly in Argentina. She has taught infant observational studies and new clinical strategies in working with disturbed children, especially those with autism, and in the prevention in the first year of life of the evolution of mental disorders in childhood.

A. H. Brafman is a psychoanalyst and child analyst. He worked in the NHS as a Consultant Child and Adolescent Psychiatrist, where, besides his ordinary clinical work, for many years he ran a group for under-5s and their parents. He has been involved in the teaching programmes of several psychodynamic training societies. He is particularly interested in child development and the mutual influences between children and parents. This has led to his close involvement with teaching programmes of infant observation and to the publication of several papers on this subject. He has also published a book, *Untying the Knot* (2001), describing his work with children and parents, and more recently *Can You Help Me?* (2004), in which he answers questions put to him by parents facing problems with their children. He was also until recently an Honorary Senior Lecturer at the Psychotherapy Department of University College Hospital.

Donald Campbell is a training analyst for child, adolescent, and adult analysis and former President of the British Psychoanalytical Society. He worked for thirty years as Principal Child Psychotherapist at the Portman Clinic where he also served as Chair. He was formerly Secretary General of the International Psychoanalytical Association. He has published on the subjects of violence, suicide, child sexual abuse, delinquency, perversion, and adolescent development.

Rosemary Campher is a practising UKCP-registered psychotherapist, working with children and adults. She lectured on psychology and psychotherapy at the British American College in London and works in private practice with children, adults, and supervisees. She has worked for fifteen years with children in various contexts: children's homes, schools, and private practice. Her special interests include psychoanalysis, child therapy, and early intervention and prevention programmes, particularly for infants and children and infant/child–parent relationships.

Peter Fonagy is Freud Memorial Professor of Psychoanalysis and is Director of the Sub-Department of Clinical Health Psychology at University College London; Chief Executive of the Anna Freud Centre, London; and a consultant to the Child and Family Program at the Menninger Department of Psychiatry at Baylor College of Medicine, USA. He is a clinical psychologist and a training and supervising analyst in child and adult analysis in the British Psychoanalytical Society. His clinical interests centre around issues of borderline psychopathology, violence, and early attachment relationships. His work attempts to integrate empirical research with psychoanalytic theory. He holds a number of important positions, including Co-Chair of the Research Committee of the International Psychoanalytical Association and Fellowship of the British Academy. He has published over two-hundred chapters and articles and has authored, co-authored, or edited several books, including *Attachment Theory and Psychoanalysis* (2001); *Affect Regulation, Mentalization, and the Development of the Self* (2002); *What Works For Whom? A Critical Review of Treatments for Children and Adolescents* (2002); *Psychoanalytic Theories: Perspectives from Developmental Psychopathology* (2003); *Psychotherapy for Borderline Personality Disorder: Mentalization Based Treatment* (2004); and *What Works For Whom? A Critical Review of Psychotherapy Research* (2004); *Mentalization-Based Treatment for Borderline Personality Disorder: A Practical Guide* (2006); *Handbook of Mentalization-Based Treatment* (2006); *Reaching the Hard to Reach: Evidence-Based Funding Priorities for Intervention and Research* (2006); *and Developmental Science and Psychoanalysis: Integration and Innovation* (2007).

Clare Keogh is a Chartered Counselling Psychologist registered with the BPS. She also has a Masters degree in Research Methods and Psychological Assessment. Clare works at a family centre, in schools, and in private practice. She works with children, adolescents, families, couples, groups, and individuals; she specializes in working with children. She is also a clinical supervisor (individual and group). She has worked in many inner-city schools, and while previously working in a children's charity, she built up and expanded a therapeutic school-based project providing therapy for children. She does personal, social, and health education for 11- to 18-year-olds and is also a university lecturer. She has experience teaching Psychology and also Child and Adult Psychotherapy at undergraduate level (BACL at Regent's College) and presently teaches at City University (Postgraduate Certificate in Counselling Psychology).

Roderick Macleod started to train in the field of psychotherapy in his mid-thirties after a career in the television industry. He has worked in a number of clinical and school settings as a trainee psychotherapist and as an in-school counsellor. He trained at Regents College in Integrative Psychotherapy & Counselling and is currently studying at Birkbeck College for an MSc in Psychodynamic

Counselling for Children and Adolescents. His clinical interests include the development of in-school psychotherapy programmes and the challenges that these bring to the established frame of working with young children.

Camilla Sim is a UKCP-registered child and adult psychotherapist. She started working with children in 1992 and has worked for Kids Company and Place2Be, both of which are charities that provide counselling in schools. She now works in schools in Hammersmith and Fulham and also works privately as a therapist and supervisor. Her work has developed since writing her chapter in 2004 and has a more relational focus based on her understanding of attachment theory.

Valerie Sinason is a child and adult psychotherapist and an adult psychoanalyst registered with both the BPC and the UKCP. She is Director of the Clinic for Dissociative Studies, one of only three UK clinics focusing on dissociative identity disorder (DID). She is Hon. Consultant Psychotherapist for the Cape Town Child Guidance Clinic, University of Cape Town. She was a Consultant Research Psychoanalyst at St George's Medical School's Psychiatry of Disability Department until December 2007 and previously was Consultant Child Psychotherapist at the Tavistock Clinic, where she worked from 1987 to 1999, and a Consultant Psychotherapist at both the Anna Freud and Portman Clinics from 1994 to 1997. She specializes in disability, trauma, and abuse and is regularly used as an expert in court cases. She has written extensively on psychotherapy, disability, and abuse, with over seventy published peer-reviewed papers, chapters, and books. Her recent publications include two edited books: *Memory in Dispute* (1998) and *Attachment, Trauma and Multiplicity: Working with Dissociative Identity Disorder* (2002). She is also a widely published and anthologized poet, with two full-length collections.

FOREWORD

Donald Campbell

This is a rare book. Although much has been written from a psychoanalytic point of view about aggression, very little has been written about violence, and even less about violent children. This book goes some way to redressing that imbalance. Every chapter in Rosemary Campher's book *Violence in Children: Understanding and Helping Those Who Harm* is written by a psychoanalyst or child psychotherapist who has worked therapeutically with violent children. Their work is built upon a psychoanalytic orientation that ensures a stable technique and provides a resource for insight. For the reader, this shared psychoanalytic perspective contributes to an authenticity and continuity of thinking in the research, theoretical, and clinical contributions. The reader will be helped to think about both why some children rely on violence to deal with internal conflicts and developmental deficits and what it is like to treat violent children. The book will increase the reader's understanding of violent children and the value and vicissitudes of their psychoanalysis and psychoanalytic psychotherapy.

Resistance to thinking about violence

Freud never underestimated the individual's propensity to exercise aggression or the power of its physical manifestation in violence. Neither did he minimize the need for the individual to repress and control aggressive instincts, which are so prominent in childhood, in the interests of adapting to a communal life. He also recognized our ambivalent relationship with violence. On the one hand, power and sadism associated with some aggressive acts are nearly irresistible. For instance, we are often drawn to violence and unable to overcome our curiosity about real violent acts or imagined ones (such as in horror films) and the perpetrators; or, we cannot resist projecting our own aggressive instincts onto the perpetrators and then reviling and attacking them; or, we find ourselves secretly or openly identifying with an aggressor. On the other hand, to counter these impulses we may try to repress pleasure derived from the power and sadism associated with the exercise of aggression. When this ambivalent and often unconscious relationship to our own violence and violent fantasies is unacceptable, efforts to understand the perpetrator of a violent act as a human being, in some ways not unlike ourselves, provoke strong resistance.

Many people feel that it is difficult, even dangerous, to distinguish between a violent act and the person who commits it. Any effort to go beyond apprehension and incarceration to attempt to understand violent acts by children inevitably revives anxieties about our own children's physical safety, on the one hand, and helplessness regarding our incomprehension, on the other. For those outside the mental health field, a common solution to this dilemma is to demonize the child who kills and to see that child as "evil". This kind of thinking puts the child killer outside the pale and beyond anything that the observer could identify as "me".

However, a psychoanalytic point of view does not split off and project unacceptable or unthinkable violent actions; rather, it sees all of us as having entertained murderous fantasies and accepts that in circumstances where we believe our survival is at stake, all of us are capable of acting on those fantasies. Psychoanalysts would also understand that our survival could be threatened physically as well as psychologically. Someone who tries to rob us at gunpoint can threaten our physical survival. Our survival as a coherent, self-respecting human being can also be threatened psychologically by a humiliating insult. Either of these threats to physical safety or psychic well being may provoke a violent response in certain individuals.

Some problems encountered in psychotherapy with children who harm

A critical feature that distinguishes the child patient from the adult patient is the child's use of physical activity as the primary medium for communication of internal conflicts, whether it takes the form of play, or fighting, or running away. As a consequence, child analysts and psychotherapists are often forced to think on the run, literally. Child psychotherapists will be familiar with the effect of the intensity and immediacy of a child's actions on the therapist's capacity to think about the child.

By bringing together case histories of psychoanalytic psychotherapy with violent children, Rosemary Campher demonstrates the reality of working therapeutically with children, especially children who rely upon action to deal with internal conflicts, developmental deficits, and environmental pressures. Those who are interested in what really goes on in psychotherapy sessions with children who have been violent will read about colleagues who are trying to contain acting out and violent attacks, understand their meaning, and develop interpretations that can be accepted by their young patients.

This book is about children who act with the specific intention to hurt others. As Rosemary Campher states in the title, this book is about children who harm. These are children who have attacked others and are likely to physically attack the therapist with the aim of inflicting pain or injury. Child psychoanalysts and psychotherapists expect that their violent patients will try to harm them. As a consequence, working with a violent child adds unique dimensions to the treatment relationship—namely, the therapist's fear of being hurt and the experience of pain.

The reader will see that the authors use the transference–countertransference as the primary medium for understanding the violent children they are working with in psychotherapy. Many aspects of the patient–therapist relationship contribute to the nature and function of the transference and countertransference. I would like to address only one aspect, but one that is particularly germane for therapists working with violent children—namely, the impact that the therapist's fear of being hurt and the experience of pain has upon the countertransference and as a source of understanding the internal world of the violent child.

Physical pain

Most of the children referred to in this book were subjected to bodily pain through physical or sexual abuse. The clinical studies feature the child psychotherapists' efforts to understand and interpret the psychic consequences for their child patients of their experiences of physical or sexual abuse. One of the consequences of physical pain is that, by its nature, pain destroys language and defies communication. Severe pain reduces us to the non-symbolic communication of screams, cries, and groans. Language, which enables us to communicate self-experience to others, is replaced by sounds that pre-date speech. The irony is that for the person in pain there is nothing so vibrantly certain as their pain. However, in spite of the sufferer's certainty, the observer may imagine, but can never know, the victim's pain.

Those who most often inflict pain upon children (parents, relatives, and friends) are the ones the child is most likely to depend upon for comfort and understanding. Tragically, the perpetrators are also most likely to deny a child's pain in order to defend against shame and guilt. The child's sense of betrayal and shattered trust is re-enacted in the transference via splitting and projective identification. Action not words will be the medium for the projection of pain. The child will try to turn the passive experience of pain into an active one by hurting the therapist, in the mistaken belief that in this way the therapist can be made to experience the child's pain.

Sadly, pain is idiosyncratic. Physically traumatized children are, to some extent, alone with the painful residue of past abuse and are dependent on the therapist's belief that they are *in* pain and the therapist's willingness or capacity to *imagine* the nature of their pain. This is not an easy task when the child is inflicting pain on the therapist by kicking, hitting, or biting. The child not only projects his or her experience of pain, but recreates the experience of being with a trusted object who is preoccupied with his or her own pain, confused, and perhaps even angry, and, therefore, unable to imagine the child's pain. By turning the expectation of a passive experience into an active one, the child controls his or her fear of being left utterly alone.

Not surprisingly, the violent child will resort to physical attack to overcome his or her feeling of isolation and attempt to break through to something personal in the therapist by inflicting pain. Consequently, violent patients stimulate real fears about our personal—that is, bodily—safety, and this impacts on our capacity to think. The therapist's experience of pain, especially when being kicked by a child, draws the violent child and the therapist into more personal, intimate contact.

I imagine that other child therapists who have been kicked by their patients will remember that this often occurs when we are out of touch with what the child is thinking or feeling. In the subjective, bodily experience of pain, I might grimace, or reflexively pull away, or say, "Ouch". I hasten to add that my spontaneous reflexive reactions do not come from me in my role as the child's analyst, but from me with a hurting shin. Being kicked by a child often triggers a self-protective reaction, which aims to stop the kicking, so the therapist can feel physically safe enough to return to thinking about the child. When I am able to return to that moment when the child hurt me, I can recognize with my patient that he or she can affect me in a real way, in the here-and-now.

Violent children hunger for a real response to their aggression that recognizes them as distinct and separate. They are yearning for a reaction that takes them into account without negating them or retaliating, but one that is reparative in the way that understanding can be. The therapist's real but non-retaliatory reaction to being hurt is the beginning of a new experience for children who often experience others as reacting intrusively or by withdrawing. When the therapist returns to that earlier moment of pain to think about what might have motivated the child, the therapist develops further that new experience with the child in the immediacy of the therapeutic relationship. One such moment will not be enough, but it can be built upon. Just as the children in this book repeat earlier traumas in order to communicate them and to master them, the therapist has new opportunities to reflect upon the traumas that are recreated in the treatment relationship. By reflecting and not retaliating, the therapist offers the child alternatives to the original traumas—that is, a new experience in the immediacy of the present moment and a new relationship to internalize.

Rosemary Campher's book invites the reader into the physicality and reflectiveness of the therapeutic relationship to learn about what makes these children violent and how to help them.

VIOLENCE IN CHILDREN

Introduction: the therapeutic work and theoretical framework

Rosemary Campher

This book explores various aspects of violence and the attendant emotional, psychological, biological, and social features that may be found to accompany these states in children. It highlights the importance of prevention and early intervention and the implicit use of therapy to help children who are in these vulnerable and dangerous states of mind and body. Interdisciplinary research is also advocated as a research tool to help us to obtain as complete an understanding as possible of violence and its vicissitudes in children.

Because violence may have many antecedents and consequences in the mind, the provision of psychoanalytic psychotherapy is a very useful and elucidative method to use as a form of intervention. This book rests on fundamental psychoanalytic principles and processes as well as on something very simple that we all know yet tend to lose sight of, in the need to fulfil budget requirements and in the context of under-resourced clinics and agencies that deal with vulnerable and psychologically at-risk children: that children and parents who have increased social and emotional support in our society are less likely to develop pathological ways of coping with the various stressors and strains that are in part an inevitable element of living in the twenty-first century and may also be at times an inherent part of our psychobiological make-up.

Clinical material[1] in all the chapters also provides supporting evidence for how useful psychotherapy can be for children who have *already* developed coping strategies that are pathological, particularly in relation to violence. Research done by Cavadino and Allen (2000) found that too many obstacles are actually placed in the way of allowing violent children receive the necessary treatment that could help them to overcome their violent tendencies.

The visible forms of the violent child

The *WHO Report on Violence and Health* (WHO, 2002a) highlights the fact that "Violence by young people is one of the most visible forms of violence in society" (p. 25), and Karr-Morse and Wiley (1997) confirm that within the United States, children are found to be the fastest-growing section of the criminal population. The role played by the broadcast media and newspapers that highlight youth violence daily make this form of violence more visible to us. Fonagy, in the conclusion to his chapter, "Early Life Trauma and the Psychogenesis and Prevention of Violence" (chapter 1, this volume), proposes that it is both the "glamorization and the demonization of violence" that actually prevents us from understanding the violent mind. Fonagy further proposes the need to enter into the subjective world of the violent person, so that we may facilitate an understanding that helps us in both our preventative and our therapeutic/treatment measures.

All the analysts and psychotherapists who have contributed to this book have entered very deeply into the complex and multilayered subjective world of the violent child or children and have written about these therapeutic processes here. These clinicians all began their psychotherapeutic work from the same central starting point—that of attempting to understand the child or infant who has been identified as "violent". What we see, when the child's subjective world has been entered, is that beneath the violence lies extreme vulnerability and need.

* * *

The individual contributions of the clinicians to the book are introduced below. This is followed by a review of various important concepts, theories, and questions that are raised within the overall context of the book and within the theoretical and clinical context of the violent child.

An introduction to the chapters

Peter Fonagy, in "Early Life Trauma and the Psychogenesis and Prevention of Violence" (chapter 1), explores the role played by trauma in the psychogenesis of violence, and he addresses important aspects of prevention. Fonagy proposes a developmental approach to violence and suggests that violence is not exactly the "learnt" phenomenon that we had previously thought it was; he suggests, rather, that it is "unlearned"—that is, that it is an indication of the absence of normal developmental phenomena that leads to its formation. Fonagy suggests (with detailed supporting research information) that the answer to the "riddle" of understanding how individuals may become violent lies "in what is ordinary rather than extraordinary: *normal human development*". Fonagy discusses the relevance of attachment theory, mentalization, trauma and the inhibition of mentalization, psychosocial factors, neurocognitive vulnerability, genetic susceptibility, and preventative measures in relation to the psychogenesis of violence.

A. H. Brafman, in "Violence in Children" (chapter 2), begins by exploring the importance of taking into account the subjectivity and multiplicity involved in interpreting various acts of violence. Brafman explores many complex aspects of understanding and treating violence in children from a psychoanalytic perspective. This exploration begins with Aichhorn's work with "troubled adolescents", proceeds to Winnicott's clinical work and relevant conceptual formulations (the antisocial tendency seen as a sign of hope and the importance of a good-enough environment that survives the child's aggressive tendencies), and then continues with differing psychoanalytic views in relation to the origination of violent behaviour.

Brafman refers to his concept of a "mutually reinforcing vicious circle" (Brafman, 2001) in relation to the complexity inherent in attempting to determine what is cause and what is effect in relation to the violent child and his or her family. Vivid clinical examples are used to clarify ideas and ask questions; these range from baby observation studies to clinical psychoanalytic vignettes taken from both individual and family therapeutic processes.

Brafman also importantly explores two fundamental questions that need to be addressed during an assessment of a violent child; these pertain to attempting to determine the child's capacity to change his/her violent behaviour and the therapist's "preparedness to cope" with the challenge of working therapeutically with a violent child. Brafman explores central problems that we face in relation to understanding and treating violence in children, and he proposes that at the centre of these difficulties lies a theoretical dilemma—that despite the *prospective* language used, in essence our attempts at explanation are theoretical constructs that attempt *retrospectively* to explain our clinical work.

Brafman concludes by acknowledging significant psychosocial factors that may be involved in understanding violence in children, and he further advocates the possibility of the existence of innate physical factors (which are as yet unidentifiable) that may make a child vulnerable to developing violent tendencies and behaviour when these find themselves in interaction with violent parents or peers.

Roderick Macleod details in "The Kick of Life" (chapter 3) a very intense and challenging therapeutic relationship with a violent 9-year-old child called "Sarah", which took place over a two-year period. Macleod explains how Sarah was one of his first clients whom he saw in a clinical placement that related to the beginning of a clinical training programme. Macleod is honest and frank in his portrayal of this very moving and challenging therapeutic process. As with all the other detailed clinical "one-child case studies" documented in this book, Macleod writes about what works and what doesn't work in his dedicated therapeutic endeavours.

Macleod links Sarah's extreme behaviour, emotional distress, and violent behaviour to "fundamental difficulties in thinking" and refers to Perelberg's proposal that violent acts may be seen as attempts to rid the mind of intolerable states. Macleod also views aspects of Sarah's violence as indicative of her "will to live", and he connects this to Boston and Szur's concept of the "fighting spirit" being associated with being alive as opposed to an "emotional deadness". Macleod explains and details the complexities inherent in the transference and countertransference dynamics that he encounters, and he gives many examples of the role played by using interpretations amid these complex and profound experiences.

Macleod interconnects his clinical work with theoretical working concepts from Bion, Klein, Winnicott, Grinberg, Anna Freud, and Willock to provide a containing conceptual–clinical context from which he attempts to understand his therapeutic work with Sarah. Macleod's clinical work highlights the importance of using play as a therapeutic tool, alongside the use of verbal interpretations that attempt to contain the work and assist the process of understanding, and he shows how difficult and challenging this task can be at times—that is, the child therapeutic task of "playing *and* thinking".

Stella Acquarone writes about "Violence and Babies" (chapter 4) and explores, explains, and documents cases of the earliest possible form of therapeutic intervention in relation to the violent child within the context of infant–parent psychotherapy. Acquarone presents her model of infant–parent psychotherapy alongside discussing important aspects of attachment theory, innate psycho-biological factors ("unknown sensibilities"), neurobiological research, and historical thoughts about violence (including Freud's instinct theory) and by also presenting detailed case studies where early intervention was used. Acquarone presents four models of attachment that may be evidenced within the parent–infant sphere and explores these in detail with the presentation of case studies: (1) caregiving, as in normal development; (2) scare-giving, as in hypervigilant development; (3) little or no caregiving, as in delayed development; and (4) vulnerable infant, as in deficient development.

Acquarone maintains that the prevention of the development of violence in small children is possible by early intervention. Acquarone presents her early methods of intervention, which are aimed at interrupting cycles of abuse; these methods rest on acknowledging both the parents' and the babies' needs and then aiming to facilitate healthy separate development of the self in both the parents and the infants.

Camilla Sim chronicles in "Non-Retaliation: Surviving a Violent 5-Year-Old" (chapter 5) a long and challenging therapeutic process with a 5-year-old boy called "Dan", who also had difficulties in thinking and tended to use violence when experiencing unbearable anxieties. Sim refers to Winnicott's idea that when a child is unable to think, he or she is usually encountering "unthinkable anxiety". It was Sim's clear aim from the start of the therapy with Dan to attempt to keep thinking and understanding Dan without "reacting or retaliating". Sim describes how difficult the process of therapy was at times.

Dan was known to be part of a family where there was regular domestic violence. Sim analyses the impact that this has had on Dan's development, especially prenatally, as the domestic violence may actually have increased during this time, and she refers to Brown's research in relation to this concept. Sim understands aspects of Dan's behaviour from an attachment-based perspective and proposes that Dan could be seen as having a "disorganized attachment" and thus would be more at risk for the development of various psychopathologies. Dan's extremely disruptive, distressed, distressing, and disorganized behaviour is portrayed very clearly by Sim, as she details aspects of the therapeutic work from the beginning to the end.

The work with Dan took place in a specialist behavioural unit that was attached to a school, and Sim gives examples of how the usual containing function of the therapeutic framework came under threat many times. Sim discusses her strong countertransference feelings in a very honest way and details how she was able at times to use these feelings to help Dan understand his feelings. The strong transference that developed from Dan to Sim is described amid the multilayered play and the violence. The transference–countertransference dynamics changed considerably when Sim introduced her pregnancy to Dan. The work that follows to the conclusion of the therapeutic process shows fluctuations within Dan from violence, to concern, and then finally towards reparation and recovery. Sim contains the intense therapeutic work at this stage beautifully as she continued to think with Dan about his internal world and the real world of the therapy room and the school. Sim explores important aspects of his psychosexual development as he displayed various features of a gender identity disorder. Sim discusses Dan's confusions and anxieties around his sexuality in relation to the role played by the emotionally absent and yet physically violent father and his depressed mother.

Sim also explores very painful aspects of Dan's experience which were indicative of neglect, and she describes how these entered into the therapeutic relationship in a very powerful way.

Sim refers to working concepts from Brown, Freud, Winnicott, Fonagy and Target, Panksepp, and Sunderland, among others, which helped her to understand and work with this very challenging child and produce a chapter that is well integrated both clinically and theoretically.

Clare Keogh details in "A Little Boy Left Alone" (chapter 6) the therapeutic process with a 5-year-old boy, "Sam", over an eighteen-month period. Sam's violence is thought about within the context of early maternal deprivation and domestic violence. Keogh refers to attachment theory and object relations theory within psychoanalysis to comprehend Sam's challenging and complex behaviour. The importance of the therapist's containment of the child, both physically and psychologically, is highlighted, and Keogh refers to instances where this function is seriously challenged. Sam's regressive behaviour and violent acting out are also considered in relation to Glasser's core complex and the ideas of Fonagy and Target about mentalization. The clinical work vividly depicted here again highlights what appears to be a very common feature of the violent child—that beneath the violence and uncontained aggression lies extreme vulnerability, helplessness, and unresolved dependency needs.

Rosemary Campher describes in "Neutralizing Terror" (chapter 7) the therapeutic process of a violent 8-year-old boy, "Tim", over a three-year period. Theoretical concepts in relation to both normal and abnormal development are explored, as are the development of violent tendencies and their use as a defence against extreme vulnerability, helplessness, and terror. Campher discusses various complexities that are involved with working with a violent child, and explores the role played by countertransference feelings and thoughts. The importance of a secure therapeutic frame is explored within the context of an inner-city school. Campher also refers to Tim's difficulties in thinking by referring to Fonagy and Target's work on mentalization, and she relates his violence to thinking difficulties, the absent father, and feeling overwhelmed by fear. Glasser's core complex is discussed to highlight Tim's fear of engulfment and abandonment. The importance of playing is explored within the context of Tim's developmental process, alongside thinking about how violence often replaced playing and thinking and was indicative of a failure to use normal transitional phenomena, and, finally, how violence appeared to attempt to have a transitional (albeit unhealthy) function in relation to separation difficulties.

Valerie Sinason writes in "Finding Abused Children's Voices: Junior-School Living Nightmares" (chapter 8) about violent children. Sinason demonstrates how both individual and group therapy can be facilitating therapeutic contexts, which help children to find words and a voice for their trauma and difficulties. We see how Sinason skilfully and sensitively helps the children to find their true voices, within the context of violence, learning difficulties, and physical difficulties and in trauma-related emotional difficulties.

Sinason introduces the children and her therapeutic work within the context of explaining how trauma can profoundly affect a child's "finding, seeking, and attaching experiences" and disrupt the "seeking and finding system" that is an integral part of our neurobiological system. Sinason details aspects of the therapy of four individual children who were seen in individual therapy and two groups of children who were seen in group therapy.

Bion's concept of "nameless dread" is highlighted to explain the terror that children may experience if there is a failure in Winnicott's idea of a "good-enough environment" and difficulties in the early phase of separation that an infant has to manage in relation to the mother.

Sinason also refers to the importance of humour, sensitivity, responsivity, and play within the mother–child relationship (especially within the hide-and-seek game), which assist the child in gaining mastery over separation anxieties, and she explains how things can also go wrong at this stage.

Sinason gives therapeutic space to allow the voices of traumatized violent children to be heard, and we read how they may "smear, wet, fight, self-harm, cannot concentrate, sexualize, cut off their voices, and scream" and how they may also be "excluded, moved on and on" and at times finally thrown to the "vagaries of the care system". Sinason demonstrates how effective therapy can be in helping these vulnerable children who are at risk and who put other people at risk, and she notes that long-term work is needed. The children's voices and the specific words that you will hear as you read this chapter are a further testament to the reality that beneath the veneer of violence in the child lies extreme sensitivity and potential for growth and concern if an optimal therapeutic environment is provided.

Definition of violence

Glasser (1979) offers a descriptive definition of violence which proposes that violence is the "intended infliction of bodily harm on another person". There are a number of ways that children may express violence towards others—kicking, biting, pushing, spitting, throwing things, attacking, bullying, assault, and homicide—and towards themselves—self-harming behaviour (head banging, scratching, or cutting) and suicide.

Increases in youth violence

Sadly, despite many valuable advances that we have made in our society, there is still a very high rate of childhood disorders and suffering in our children. Violence in children is seen to be only one facet of the multiplicity of challenges that children may experience emotionally and that also poses excessive problems and strains on the environment. While research shows that the pattern and emergence of homicide by children is broadly stable, the rate of juvenile violence is on the increase—the figure for children who were cautioned or convicted for violent offences in England and Wales in 1994 was 580 per 100,000; since 1997 this rate has increased yet again, with figures showing that 87% of males under the age of 14 and 55% of males between the ages of 14 and 18 were cautioned for violent acts committed against the person (Cavadino & Allen, 2000). The increase in youth violence over the last decade has prompted the United Nations to publish a detailed study called "Youth Violence" (WHO, 2002a, chap. 2), within which it highlights the need both for a more complete understanding of youth violence (for prevention and treatment) and also to increase our support/help to those children in their dangerous states and those also affected by them. In the Foreword to the UN report, Nelson Mandela speaks the words we need to hear: "We owe our children—the most vulnerable citizens in any society—a life free from violence and fear" (WHO, 2002a, p. ix), and he concludes by stressing the need to address the roots of violence.

The summary of the UN's detailed and comprehensive report (WHO, 2002b) raises the important point that "Raising awareness of the fact that violence can be prevented is, however, only the first step in shaping the response to it" and claims that the purpose of the report "is to challenge the secrecy, taboos and feelings of inevitability that surround violent behaviour, and to encourage debate that will increase our understanding of this hugely complex phenomena" (WHO, 2002b, p. 1).

The report details how in the year 2000, deaths caused by young people (between the age of 10 and 29) towards other young people reached an estimate of 199,000 (a rate of 9.2 per 100,000), and that "For every young person killed by violence, an estimated 20–40 receive injuries that require hospital treatment" (WHO, 2002b, p. 13).

Acting out unresolved trauma in a criminal way

Maltreatment and violence

Children who find themselves in dangerous, abusive, neglectful, and vacant internal and external environments are faced with innumerable challenges and dilemmas—especially in relation to emotional and psychological development. Renn (2000), in his clinical research as a probation officer, consolidates the link that has already been established by many researchers and clinicians that "young offenders show a history of maltreatment and loss in up to 90% of the sample population" (Renn, 2000, p. 71). Renn explains that the acting out of unresolved trauma in a criminal way is a consistent feature in the behaviour of the young offenders with whom he works.

There are few choices open to the child who has no way of getting what he or she may need. There is, of course, depression, withdrawal, learning difficulties, anxiety, sleep problems, eating disorders, behavioural and emotional difficulties, and—the most neglected area of all—violence. Children who are violent have turned their vulnerability in on themselves and encapsulated themselves in a self-protected world that is based on fear, aggression, and violence, yet this is still based on extreme need, painful dependencies, and helplessness. As therapists we are naturally interested and concerned with a child's inner world, but also within the context of the real world and the therapeutic relationship. Psychic reality has power, but so does social reality. A violent child is not some figment of a therapist's inner world or an illusionary aspects of the child's—violence is a very real, powerful, and extremely painful state that the child finds him/herself in when other doors and paths that could have provided a means of escape have been closed to him or her. This includes both internal and external avenues. A child who has chosen violence over depression has done so in order to survive. If the latter has been chosen, the child may become an unfortunate victim of the ultimate act of violence—violence against the self in the form of suicide.

Suicidal ideation

Thompson et al.'s research (2005) found that maltreated children and those exposed to violence at home and in the community are at increased risk of suicidal ideation, even by the age of 8 years. Strong predictive factors that were linked to suicidal ideation among a large group of young children (9.9% in a group of 1, 051 maltreated children) included variables such as chronicity of maltreatment, the existence of multiple types of maltreatment, and the severity of physical abuse experienced (Thompson et al., 2005).

Bullying

School bullying is a form of aggressive behaviour that can be linked to violence, in that there is an "intention" involved. Many of the children written about in this book did in fact engage in serious bullying of other children, and in some instances they too were bullied. Olweus (1993) distinguishes between two types of bullying: "direct bullying—with relatively open attacks on the victim—and indirect bullying, which may take the form of social isolation and exclusion from the group" (Cowie, p. 140). Cowie explains that some bullying includes the use of physical violence such as hitting, kicking, and pushing, while bullying that uses indirect aggression (such as spreading rumours, gestures, social exclusion) still has a very damaging effect on the child being bullied.

Children who kill and who are killed

While none of the children written about in this book actualizes their murderous thoughts and feelings, it is important to think about those children who do indeed commit the most violent of crimes and commit murder. There are obviously multiple causations and complex interactions among various causal factors in the disturbing area of the child that kills. Cavadino and Allen (2000) list these contributory factors. They include: "serious physical abuse, sexual abuse, emotional abuse or neglect, exposure to repetitive or extreme violence (including witnessing such violence), parental mental illness, parental abandonment, rejection by parents and others, traumatic loss, neurological abnormalities, conduct disorder, substance abuse, and in a few cases, mental illness" (p. 5).

Fatal child abuse

According to the 2002 WHO report summary, in the year 2000 there was a worldwide estimate of 57,000 homicides committed among children under the age of 15, and the figures show that the younger the child the greater the risk of him or her being murdered: "homicide rates among children aged 0–4 years are more than twice those among children aged 5–14 years (5.2 per 100 000 compared with 2.1 per 100 000)" and "The most common cause of death is head injury, followed by abdominal injuries and intentional suffocation" (WHO, 2002b, p. 16).

How do we help?

We do not like to think of violence in children, perhaps partly because it reflects our own hidden and repressed violent tendencies and also because it threatens to dispel the myth that is inherent in every aspect of our society—that children are supposed to be happy, adaptable, well behaved, and polite. But the crucial question is, "What about those children who are not happy, who are not able to adapt and cannot, despite at times an effort of will, behave in ways that make their place in their social system easier to take?" There are many of these children in our social world, children who need to be helped by being understood on a deep level of psychic and social reality—children who need specialized psychological treatment. In order for this help to be forthcoming, we need adults who are well trained and educated in all aspects of child development and therapy. Ideally, for every violent child, we need a well-contained adult who can help that child to understand his or her violence and find alternative ways of coping with the enormous internal and external stressors that the child may be experiencing. Working with and understanding the violent child within both the subjective and psychic internal world *and* the external, social world of the child will shed light on his or her violent tendencies and facilitate the process of change.

Beneath the multifaceted veneer of violence

In each chapter of this book you will find a connecting thread that appears to create a very specific and painful pattern. This pattern relates to evidence that shows that beneath the multifaceted veneer of violence in these children lies extreme vulnerability, pain, and helplessness, which needs to be contained through understanding and the provision of a stable, consistent, reliable, and trustworthy relationship(s). Working therapeutically with violent children has a lot to offer, not only to the vulnerable child, but also to the distressed and frightened surrounding community. Inevitably, the therapist, too, will learn a lot about human nature, development, relationships, and all the complexities inherent in these vital areas of human nature. Perhaps, too, the juvenile courts and the police and prison services will find that if funding is given to the correct therapeutic help, they will find less of a strain on their services and their budgets.

On knowing and not knowing, and yet still helping

Not all of the complexities and questions related to violence in children will have definite resolutions, however, nor will there be an easy provision of absolute answers to the dilemmas involved with the violent child. We all have to sustain not being able to hold on to certainty at this stage in the evolution of thought, theories, and interventions that are designed around the important attempts to understand violence and its vicissitudes in children.

Throughout this book, you will read about simple and complex dynamics that are woven into each and every child's history. The central underlying thread within all the therapeutic works undertaken and written about here is the intention of every therapist or analyst to *understand* the child. When this understanding approximates accurately the truth of the child's experience, we sometimes see small moves in the direction of emotional and psychological development. Sometimes this movement seems to be imperceptible or extremely slow, and thus the relevance of the therapist's capacity to survive and to remain in touch with his or her thinking capacity is vital. In many of the cases that are presented here in this book, we see how, in time, thinking does indeed replace violent action.

Research

Humphreys, Sharps, and Campbell (2005) highlight the fact that research has indeed changed how we conceptualize both the causes and the consequences of violence, and yet despite these advances there are still many unanswered questions and areas of research that have been overlooked—infants and young children being just two of these. Humphreys, Sharps, and Campbell (2005) note, however, both the beginnings and the benefits of longitudinal and intervention-based research, and they stress the need for both ongoing research and intervention. Fonagy et al. (2002) also detail many aspects of research and of intervention programmes and their effectiveness. In this book, research, intervention, and collaboration are highlighted within the complex arena of working with violent children.

How do we promote an understanding of the violent child that helps?

Attempts at solutions

We may think of violence and its various vicissitudes in the child as being an attempt to provide a solution—albeit a "pathological solution" (Fonagy & Target, 1995a, 1999; Fonagy et al., 2002)—to unbearable anxieties, painful thoughts and feelings, and disturbing environments and also as a "defence against breakdown" (Campbell, 1995, 1999, 2000). Although many people may prefer to think of children in terms of being safe, protected, sane, healthy, and living in healthy home environments, we are still faced with the challenge of having to think about, and help as best we can, those children who are in social, political, and emotional environments that are inherently unhealthy, damaging, and dangerous. All of these environments are written about in this book. Many of the children in the above-mentioned contexts do not have the internal resources to cope with the type of danger and deprivation that they encounter, and they are also not usually in close proximity to adults who can provide support and offer them the use of their own resources. This may be due to a deficit in the adults, or to the adults becoming depleted and affected by the child's repeated disturbing and damaging behaviour.

Not *all* of the children written about here, however, come from damaging, abusive, traumatic, or depriving backgrounds. The violent children in this category pose even more unanswered questions as to the origin, perpetuation, and manifestation of violence. Fonagy and Target (1999) find that violent patients who, despite living in environments that "appear to be relatively benign (Weiss, et al., 1960; Blackman, Weiss, & Lamberti, 1963)", may actually have had "certain forms of violence" done to their "psychological self", and yet in these instances these forms of violence "were more subtle, hard to pinpoint in external relationships, and usually only become clear in an intensive personal encounter, such as Psychoanalysis" (Fonagy & Target, 1999, p. 54).

Internal and external factors in the aetiology of violence

Complex issues pertaining to the interaction between inherent, internal factors and external, environmental factors come into play when we begin to attempt to understand aetiological factors linked to violence. There is thus a need to clarify and integrate, on the one hand, all theories that pertain to attempting to understand internal, predisposed constitutional and neurobiological phenomena (innate drives and instincts, inherited traits, genetic make-up, etc.) with, on the other, all the rich and varied theories and research findings we have on nurturance and psychosocial development (i.e. early infantile experience within the mother–child and father–child dyads, identifications, mentalization, the development of the mind, the development of the self, the capacity to manage attachments and separations, etc.).

"Despite increasing knowledge of social and biological risk factors for antisocial and violent behaviour, we know surprisingly little about how these two sets of risk factors interact" (Raine, 2002,

p. 311). Raine's research includes 39 empirical examples of biosocial interaction from areas of research within genetics, psychophysiology, obstetrics, brain imaging, neuropsychology, and neurology and studies of hormones, neurotransmitters, and environmental toxins. Raine found the emergence of two main themes:

> First, when biological and social factors are grouping variables (*independent variables*) and when antisocial behaviour is the outcome, then the presence of both risk factors exponentially increases the rates of antisocial and violent behaviour. Second, when social and antisocial variables are grouping variables and biological functioning is the outcome, then the social variable invariably moderates the antisocial–biology relationship such that these relationships are strongest in those from benign home backgrounds. [p. 311]

As a result of these important findings, Raine (2002) proposes that biosocial research is essential if we are to establish "a new generation of more successful intervention and prevention research" (p. 311). The important above-mentioned research also highlights how social factors can moderate violent behaviour, even when there are strong constitutional factors in play.

We appear to be approximating new territory in relation to the age-old nature-versus-nurture controversy. For many decades now, in most scientific fields, there has been a movement away from thinking in terms of either/or in this fundamental area of research, to thinking about the complex interactions that do indeed exist between these two vital and necessary realities. Ridley (1993) has proposed the term "nature via nurture", to exemplify the necessity of taking this interaction seriously.

Research evidence has given us new information about both the "nurture" and the "nature" side, and hopefully with interdisciplinary communication between these two fields, our knowledge base can be more firmly embedded in an effective conceptual context. Peter Fonagy (chapter 1) proposes that "Only through careful studies of the objective and subjective environment will we understand how genetic influences create biological risks for the human organism".

Interesting research is currently being undertaken in the field of epigenetics where there is confirmation of Freud's main thesis about how important the first few years of life are for later development. Epigenetics is the study of *epigenetic inheritance*, which refers to a set of *reversible* heritable changes in gene function or other cell phenotypes that occur *without* a change in DNA sequence (genotype) (*Wikipedia—The Free Encyclopaedia*). One aspect of epigenetic research is looking into the effect of maternal care on the genetic, behavioural, emotional, and chemical systems in the body, and the research confirms a critical period for development. Meaney and Szyf's (2005) research on maternal care confirms how early maternal experience has significant correlates with behavioural experience in adulthood.

Cross-cultural research

Another research variable that needs considering and integrating into current and future research (genetic-biological and psychosocial) is cross-cultural research. Rashid (2000) maintains that there are at least four theoretical approaches that need to be considered when trying to understand violence in children—the psychological, the sociological, the anthropological, and the historical, with overlaps occurring between each approach. Rashid's research focuses on the "complex relationships between youth violence and the social and cultural settings in which it occurs" (p. 169). Rashids cross-cultural research sheds an interesting light on understanding the growing problem of violence in children within a global world context. Rashid maintains that while there is no one theoretical approach that can currently explain all the complexities of violence in children, "each offers insights and explanations at a particular level" (Rashid, 2000, p. 182). Rashid proposes that there is a need to integrate research and different approaches that attempt to explain violence in children, as this will not only assist in "theoretical completeness", but also help to "address and prevent the growing problem of violence in young people across the world" (p. 182).

Research from many different areas (discussed above) has clearly shown us that it is possible to both *predict and prevent* violence. Recent psychotherapy research with violent children has also demonstrated that it is possible to *therapeutically help* violent children. This book includes valuable resources that we can learn from in order to help violent children therapeutically. The primary prevention of violence, however, will not occur without personal, interpersonal, and social change (Ryan, 2005).

Psychoanalytic literature on aggression and violence

Perelberg (1999) has done an excellent and extensive review of the literature within the field of psychoanalysis pertaining to the debates surrounding complex questions and theories to do with aggression and violence. Her important review covers explanations and theories on both sides of the equation—whether aggression is an innate predisposition or whether it is reactive to the environment. Perelberg follows Freud's ideas and formulations about drive theory with an analysis of developments in Britain, North America, and France regarding thoughts about aggression, violence, and developmental factors. I shall not summarize the review here as it is lengthy, but I strongly recommend that you take a look at this work. I do, however, present important concepts and thoughts that have direct relevance to the violent child and to the chapters in this book.

Death drive

Freud's (1920g) advocation of the existence of an aggressive drive as an autonomous entity, also known as the death instinct or Thanatos, came after his hypothesis that aggression was linked to attempts made by the individual to gain mastery over his or her sexual drives (1905d). Freud (1920g) proposed that this re-evaluated non-sexual aggressive drive was innate and had the function of "unbinding connections" and was in direct contrast to the innate life instinct or Eros, whose function was seen to be one of "binding". By redefining the existence of the aggressive drive, Freud (1920g) links functions of the aggressive drive to its attempts at maintaining a homeostatic balance within the ego.

In the past, debates appeared to focus on whether or not the aggressive drive is innate—that is, an instinctual drive—or whether it actually originates from the environment in relation to frustrating experiences. Migone and Rabaiotti (2003) propose that we dismiss this dichotomy as it has its origins within an outdated conceptual framework pertaining to the development of the mind, and they emphasize instead current neurobiological research that shows the continuous interaction that is evident from birth onwards between environmental factors and neurological factors.

Bell (2004) proposes that the concept of the death drive still remains controversial, and according to Diamond and Marrone

(2003), "Heinz Kohut believed that aggression is not rooted in the *death instinct* but based on the need to defend a threatened self" (p. 105).

Campbell (2004) maintains that there is no substantial evidence to support Freud's instinct theory, and refers to Glasser's (1998) and Hartmann, Kris, and Lowenstein's (1949) views on this subject. Campbell additionally refers to Britton's (2003) ideas about Freud's diffidence in relation to the death instinct, and he quotes some interesting thoughts written by Freud in 1937 in a letter to Princess Marie Bonaparte: "I beg you not to set too much value on my remarks about the destructive instinct. They were made only at random and would have to be carefully thought over before being published" (Freud, 1930, p. 63).

Black (2001) notes that Freud's hypothesis of a death drive had its early origins in evolutionary theory, and Freud then subsequently attempted to support it from a neuroanatomical point of view. Black's extensive analysis of these two supporting arguments leads him (Black) to conclude that neither are persuasive and thus to maintain that the death drive has no future within psychoanalysis.

Aggression vs violence

Glasser (1985) presents definitions of aggression and violence that assist in clarifying the difference between the two terms; he proposes that violence be defined as "the intended infliction of bodily harm on another person" (p. 3), whereas aggression is seen to be an innate part of our biological systems that functions in a reactionary way to danger. Glasser links the two terms by proposing that "violence is the bodily actualisation of aggression which aims to negate the danger" (p. 3).

Glasser (1998) makes a further distinction between self-preservative violence and sadistic violence and maintains that, in self-preservative violence, the perpetrator feels anxiety and/or fear, and the aim is to negate the danger that is felt or to eliminate anything that is a threat to his or her survival. Glasser (1998) maintains that in sadistic violence the aim changes to controlling and inflicting pain and suffering in the object and in preserving rather than eliminating the object and that this violence is accompanied by excitement and pleasure, not anxiety. Dermen (2002) suggests that ultimately sadism is a defence against the more primitive, self-preservative aggression.

Can nurturance modify violence?

Shengold (1999) highlights the current controversy between internal and external explanations in some research realms: "No one worthy of serious study doubts the existence of aggression as an internal force central to understanding psychic conflict, defence and motivation; or of violence as a seemingly uncontrollable and ineradicable human characteristic" (p. xiii). Furthermore, he states, ever since instinct theory has been seriously questioned, the actual origin itself of aggression has been the subject matter of much debate and controversy. He continues by writing that no uncertainty surrounds the theories that pertain to the "*experiential e*vocation of aggression—aggression as a response to frustration, deprivation, pain, overstimulation" (p. xiii). Shengold ends his discussion by asking if it is possible for nurturance to modify destructive aggressiveness, even though it (destructive aggression) may be part of what is innate in us.

In this book, *Violence in Children: Understanding and Helping Those Who Harm*, there is supporting evidence to perhaps propose an answer of "Yes" to this very important question—holding in mind that psychotherapy may be seen as a special form of nurturance in and of itself.

Early maternal and paternal influences

Extensive research has been done on the importance of the early maternal relationship and the need for protection and care in order that a child develops as naturally as possible across the various developmental milestones and emotional continuums (Bion, 1962; Bowlby, 1969; Erikson, 1959; Fairbairn, 1952; A. Freud, 1936a, 1965; Freud, 1914c; Klein, 1932; Kohut, 1977; Mahler, 1968; Mahler, Pine & Bergman, 1975; Spitz, 1965; Stern, 1985; Winnicott, 1958, 1965c, 1971a). More recently Campbell (1995, 1999, 2000), Fonagy (1991), Fonagy and Target (1995a, 1999), and Glasser (1979; 1992) have proposed the important role that is played by the father or the absent father within the aetiology of violence.

One of the most memorable facts that I learnt about as a student in one of my early psychoanalytic seminars was the idea that Freud had a very strong desire to change the face of pedagogy, and yet he has often been criticized for underestimating the effect of the early environment (Leowald, 1969).

The concept of a "good-enough mother" (Winnicott, 1965c) is a widely acknowledged and significant term to denote optimal—not perfect—care of the baby. Here, the mother (or significant carer) offers the infant psychological, emotional, and physical care that is consistent, reliable, continuous (at the beginning), and dependable. It is the later task of the mother to slowly "fail" the infant as she introduces more adaptation to reality to her infant. This adjustment period is as crucial to a child's development as the almost constant early nurturance. The baby has to learn to deal with the frustrating aspects of reality—not having mother available 24 hours a day, having to sometimes wait a bit for food or for the mother to understand what the baby is communicating, and so forth. This transition—from an almost symbiotic type of care towards being in relation to the mother in a different way—helps the child to overcome its omnipotence and other unconscious phantasies (Winnicott, 1965c).

Campbell (1999) introduces the concept of a "good-enough father" who is vital in fundamental ways to the development of the child in terms of separation, identity, and the formation of identifications. Fonagy and Target (1999) suggest that "The father's capacity to present the child with a reflection of his place in relationships then becomes essential to the child's developing capacity to perceive himself in relation to the object" (Fonagy & Target, 1999, p. 67). Campbell also proposes that, "In normal development, both pre-oedipal parents represent to the child the world outside the exclusivity of the mother–infant relationship, e.g. the realities of time and place and objects" (Campbell, 1999, p. 81).

Mentalization and the reflective function

The process of "mentalization" (Fonagy, 1991; Fonagy & Target, 1999; Fonagy, Gergely, Jurist, & Target, 2002) helps the infant to adapt through the development of using representational states of mind that are, in turn, facilitated by the "reflective" mode of the mother. These relational patterns are then integrated, if all goes well, into the psycho-neurobiological system, where they continue to help a child in various fundamental ways.

Fonagy et al.'s (2002) research is fundamental when attempting to understand the mind of the violent child in terms of the development of the capacity to think, the process of mentalization, and how pathological solutions may develop if there is an inhibition or failure in the process of mentalization. Extensive research illustrates that violence may be linked to failures in the capacity to mentalize (Fonagy, 1991; Fonagy et al., 2002).

Fonagy et al. (2002) propose that mentalization is intricately related to the development of the psychological part of the self. They have proposed four main propositions that arise from their clinical perspective. The first proposition relates to two modes of internal functioning and relating: the psychic equivalence mode and the pretend mode. Within the former, subjectivity has a strong role to play in the child's expectation that his or her internal reality (and that of others) corresponds to external reality. The second mode of internal functioning involves a child's capacity to play, where "the child knows that internal experience may not reflect external reality . . ., but then the internal state is thought to have no relationship to the outside world and to have no implications for it (pretend mode)" (Fonagy et al., 2002, pp. 56–57).

The second proposition maintains that within the normal process of development an integration of these two modes may occur, which results in the child's arrival "at the stage of mentalization—or reflective function—in which mental states can be experienced as representations" (Fonagy et al., 2002, p. 57). This stage implies that a child has the capacity to link internal and external reality without the use of equation or dissociation (Fonagy et al., 2002, p. 57).

The third proposition hypothesizes that "mentalization normally comes about through the child's experience of his mental states being reflected on, prototypically through the experience of secure play with a parent or older child, which facilitates the integration of the pretend and psychic equivalence modes, through an interpersonal process that is perhaps an elaboration of the complex mirroring of the infant by the care-giver" (Fonagy et al., 2002, p. 57).

The fourth proposition pertains to the complex effect that trauma has on a child's capacity to integrate the above-mentioned two modes of psychic functioning, resulting in aspects of the modes becoming confused (Fonagy et al., 2002).

All the above-mentioned propositions have important implications for understanding most of the children in this book, as abuse, trauma, violence, and difficulties in thinking appear to be related to many of their worlds. "The abused or traumatized child, evading or entangled in the mental world, never acquires adequate regulatory control over the representational world of internal working models" (Fonagy et al., 2002, p. 479).

Glasser's core complex

Glasser's concept of the "core complex" as a universal, normal developmental process is presented within the context of a model of psychic homeostasis, which proposes that the ego has a dynamic role to play in maintaining psychic homeostasis (Glasser, 1996). Aggression, violence, and difficulties in negotiating the core complex are understood within the context of anything that threatens this homeostasis (Glasser, 1996). Glasser (1996) proposes a human *capacity* for aggression. Campbell (2004) elaborates on Glasser's ideas on aggression and violence and their link to psychological and biological responses by noting that Glasser differentiated "aggression as a *psychological* response, from violence as a physical expression of aggression, that is a *behavioural*, therefore observable, response" (Campbell, 2004, p. 2).

Glasser's (1979, 1992) core complex has its origins in normal developmental phenomena "and begins with the infant's wish to merge with an idealised, omnipotently gratifying mother as an early solution to anxieties of loss engendered by its own moves towards separation and individuation" (Campbell, 2004, p. 4). Problems arise for the infant within this developmental process if there is a mother or father present who is unavailable or narcissistically orientated, which may in turn give rise to "annihilation anxieties about engulfment and abandonment arising from a failure to successfully negotiate the *core complex*" (Campbell, 2004, p. 4).

Optimal neurobiological and emotional development

Optimal neurobiological and emotional development has been linked by Schore (1994, 1996) to early good contact that the infant or child has with an adult who utilizes a thinking mind in relation to the child, and thus this research adds significant support to Fonagy et al.'s (2002) hypothesis about mentalization and the development of the self. Schore's (2003b) research highlights the importance of optimal early experience and development and links this to significant research that arises from current neurobiology, which refers to the "social construction of the human brain". Schore (2003b) describes an optimal environment for the overall development of an infant as one in which the infant is able to become attached to a caregiver who is attuned to the infant psycho-biologically. With such an optimal experience, the primary caregiver reduces as much as possible an infant's experience of negative affect and correspondingly attempts to increase the infant's experience of positive affect.

Attachment and its implications

Fonagy (2001a) highlights the fact that a high degree of attachment security experienced by a child serves as an important "protective factor against psychopathology, and that it is associated with a wide range of healthier personality variables such as lower anxiety . . ., less hostility, greater resilience . . ., and greater ability to regulate affect through interpersonal relatedness . . ." (Fonagy, 2001a, p. 33). Fonagy (2001a) links disorganized attachment to three specific clinical problems: "Childhood aggression, dissociation, and relationship violence" (pp. 39–40). Schore's (2003a) research found that the majority of children who are maltreated or abused end up forming disorganized attachments. Gerhardt (2004) notes that "Many children with disorganised attachments will have experienced this poisonous concoction of love combined with harm" (p. 146).

Understanding attachment theory and its links to psychosocial development and psychoanalytic thinking is particularly important in relation to attempting to understand the development of violent tendencies and actions in children. Fonagy et al. (2002) propose that "Research on the social development of infants has probably been the most influential advance in empirical science for psychoanalysis" (p. 469). Attachment theory provides a good model for integrating "early childhood experience with later development, particularly the development of psychopathology" (p. 44). De Zulueta (1993) notes that all too often the seeds of violence are planted very early on in life—as early as infancy—and thus a preventative approach to reducing violence in our society calls for a campaign that stresses the attachment needs of the individual.

Blumenthal (2000), in reviewing the developmental and attachment literature on violence, considers the origins of violence to lie within damaged "internal working models" of relationships, whereby the damage has been caused by childhood trauma. Blumenthal (2000) views the actual perpetration of violence within the context of three main conceptual frameworks: identification with the aggressor, obliterating thought processes, and the repetition of early childhood trauma. Campbell (1995, 1999, 2000) has also added important ideas that pertain to viewing violence as a defence against breakdown and to the role played by the father in the child's development.

Antenatal attachment

Early risk factors of the antenatal period and infancy have been increasingly linked to various psychological, emotional, and behavioural problems in children and adults. Mäki's (2003) research found a link between early separation and maternal depression and the development of violence in the offspring. The aim of Mäki's research was to study the associations between very early parental separation and maternal depressed mood in pregnancy, on the one hand, and schizophrenia and criminality in the offspring in adolescence and adulthood, on the other. Research findings indicated that there was no connection between early separation and maternal depression to the development of schizophrenia in the children, and yet connections were found to the development of criminal behaviour, especially the development of violent criminality in men (Mäki, 2003).

Maternal antenatal emotional attachment to the foetus has been proposed as an important factor for the emergence of harm to the unborn child (Pollock & Percy, 1999, p. 1345). Pollock and Percy's findings have important "implications for understanding difficulties which may emerge in mother–foetus bonding and the identification of interventions for mothers who report an intention to harm the foetus" (p. 1345).

Karr-Morse and Wiley (1997) acknowledge the complexity inherent in understanding the related causalities linked to the origins of violence, yet they propose, following extensive research, that abuse that occurs towards a child within his or her first 33 months threatens three key components that usually act as a protective measure against the later development of violent behaviour. These three protective factors—intelligence, trust, and empathy—are also under threat from various precursors to violence, such as toxins that may originate from chemical, emotional, or social processes (Karr-Morse & Wiley, 1997).

Chamberlain (1995) points out that despite current scientific research's demonstration of the fact that babies (from gestation to birth and beyond) show high sensitivity and reactivity, alongside the fact that they are "impressionable participants", this view is still held in the minority within the fields of both psychology and medicine. Chamberlain demonstrates, with the support of research findings, how "exquisitely sensitive" babies are to their surrounding experiences while in the womb. Chamberlain refers to research done by Correia (1994) in which measurements were made of the effect that a mother's brief viewing of a violent film had on the fetus. The results demonstrated that both mother and fetus were upset and affected by the violence, which implies that fetuses do in fact share the world of emotions (Correia, 1994).

Chamberlain (1995) proposes that we reassess our understanding of the roots of violence and refers to research done by Ianniruberto and Tajani (1981) in which ultrasound scans revealed specific affectionate and aggressive behaviours displayed by twins in utero: at 24 weeks in utero, a pair of monoamniotic twins were filmed having a "boxing match" where striking actions were made with their hands. Chamberlain (1995) also acknowledges that most of the "in utero violence" that occurs is both silent and invisible, and its effects are usually detected only much later on in development. Chamberlain (1995) includes two significant sources to this category of violence: the first refers to the effect that attitudes can have on causing psychic damage, and the second refers to how neglect can result in brain damage.

Early psychic development and what we still need to know

It seems that the most called-for current research is that which aims to clarify the different strands and interactions between both internal and external factors. The very early development of this interaction appears also to be of vital importance: We know that all experience is encoded into very specific neurological pathways; if we can avoid or reduce the integration of highly disorganized and disorganizing experiences into the formative psycho-neuronal patterns, we may have more chance of understanding the implicit and necessary role of prevention and remediation.

It appears that more research and clarification is needed on the imbalances that may occur in the early stages of psychic development, first between the libidinal and aggressive tendencies and their relationship to the environment (especially the mother–child and father–child dyads) and, second, the developmental problems (violence being one) that can arise during the early separation–individuation phase.

A particular aspect of early psychic development that needs clarification is whether at the very early stages libidinal and aggressive drives or tendencies are undifferentiated from one another or are differentiated (Perelberg, 1999). Perelberg (1999) refers to, among others, Hartmann, Kris, and Lowenstein's (1949) proposal that in the early stages of development libido and aggression exist in an undifferentiated state, where it is difficult to distinguish one from the other. Perelberg (1999) additionally refers to Spitz's (1953, 1965) proposal that the differentiation of the drives only occurs as a result of development, and that the way that the infant modifies and expresses its aggressive behaviour is specifically related to the infant's early love relationships.

The containing context of therapy: serious play

Klein (1932) and Anna Freud (1927) both developed methods of understanding children based upon their play. The essence of this analytic understanding rested on the belief that in play, children expressed what was in, or on, their minds. This is a commonly held working hypothesis among psychotherapists working with children in a therapeutic setting.

Play is understood as being the child's natural capacity for expressing thoughts, feelings, and experiences and attempting to work through these. It is interesting to note that features of play have been observed via ultrasound scan within the first few months of prenatal development (the inter-uterine baby playing with the umbilical cord, turning somersaults, etc.), implying perhaps how *innate* the capacity for play actually is. It is also a well-known fact that the actual absence of playing in a child is indicative of inhibited development and poses serious obstacles to development itself. While the capacity to play may be innate, it does take a significant carer to ignite this capacity to play, once the child has been born.

The importance of play in relation to a child's development has been well documented in relation to cognitive development (Piaget, 1945); intellectual and language development (Vygotsky, 1933, 1978); as a means to assist the development of the ego and self-esteem (Erikson, 1950, 1959, 1977b); as a form of thinking and learning (Segal and Adcock, 1981); in relation to creativity, problem solving, language learning, and the development of social role (Garvey, 1977); in child development and evolution (Bruner, Jolly, & Sylva, 1976); as a way of gaining mastery over the internal world, and as an aid to adapting to reality (Freud, 1920g); as a symbolic way of controlling anxiety (Anna Freud, 1927, 1936a); as a means of assisting psychological and emotional development (Klein, 1925, 1932 ; Winnicott, 1965c, 1971a); as a therapeutic tool (A. Freud, 1927; Freud, 1920g; Klein, 1925; Winnicott, 1965c; Erikson, 1950); and as a way of facilitating mentalization and secure attachment patterns (Fonagy et al., 2002). More recently, Flaxman (2000) has summarized many of the benefits that playing has for children and links these functions to: (1) muscular control and development, fine motor skills, and hand–eye coordination; (2) speech development; (3) social development; (4) language development; (5) problem solving and creative thinking; (6) increased awareness in relation to understanding events; (7) therapeutic value; (8) opportunities for self-talk; (9) development of self-confidence; and (10) learning cooperation and value.

It is clear that play has many important functions within the overall development of a child and that it particularly assists in the development of cognitive, social, psychological, biological, and emotional functioning. The process of therapy with children rests centrally upon this process of expression and its functioning as a working-through process, within a specific type of environment—a containing, therapeutic context. In this book we see many examples of play taking place within various therapeutic environments, and we are able to consider the multifaceted functions of play for the child.

Freud (1920g) stresses the importance of play in children with regard to attempting to master the internal world; thus, for Freud, the importance in play lies in how the child attempts through the process of play to change a passive experience in reality—over which the child may not have had any control—into an active experience. For Sigmund Freud, Anna Freud, Melanie Klein, and

Donald Winnicott, play in children was understood to be a deeply serious business. This is the view that is still held among child psychotherapists.

Winnicott (1971a) looked at both the content of the child's play as well as the actual process of playing itself. For Winnicott, there is something vital to the actual process of playing that is as important as the content of the play, and this led him to propose that playing in itself could be considered to have enormous therapeutic value. Winnicott (1971a) linked the child's capacity to be able to play with the parent's capacity (or that of the person present with the child) to be playful. Winnicott's (1971a) views on play and creativity led him to propose that it is through these two vital processes that the child discovers the self. Bruner, Jolly, and Sylva (1976) maintain that play offers children a whole range of possible responses, aimed primarily at attempting to adapt to the various challenges that the world offers them.

The therapeutic work between the therapist and the child takes place mostly in the form of play in the room. But it is play of a very serious nature, for here the child is perhaps able to bring his or her innermost thoughts, feelings, and experiences, which the child may be experiencing as threatening, stressful, and difficult and which may be contributing to him or her feeling isolated, alone, and unable to communicate in any other way but through the use of violence. It is a known fact that creativity and development flourish in a place that is safe and that is based on the acceptance of the child's various states of mind.

Creativity—and specifically playing—in the child therapy context introduces a way of attempting to symbolize internal experiences (anxiety, depression, frustration, jealousy, envy, anger and rage, etc.) or complex external experiences (poverty, abuse, refugee experiences, trauma, maternal deprivation, care issues, violence, etc.). The capacity to use symbols is an achievement in development, as well as something that fosters development itself.

Playing and "thinking through things" introduces the idea that something can be done about a situation that is perhaps very difficult—hope replaces despair, creativity replaces destructive tendencies—and this allows for a thinking through and a working through of these emotional obstacles, which can result in the child living a freer, more constructively creative life: at school, at home, and in the other various play places. The capacity to symbolize, and to do this through play, evokes a deep sense of "there is something I can do" or "there is something that can be done" (D. Campbell, personal communication, 1998). This is a very important idea in the development of the child—to have a sense that he or she can have some control over his or her destiny, as opposed to being a helpless victim of life's struggles—both internal and external.

Often a child in despair will use some form of violence as a "defence against breakdown" (Campbell, 2000). The violence replaces the vulnerability of feeling that "things are falling apart" inside and outside. In the therapy room there is an opportunity for these feelings of vulnerability to be explored. A safe, containing place offers the possibility of change and a relief from psychological pain.

Understanding is important to the child, and one of the main therapeutic tasks is for the therapist to understand the child. This will, hopefully, eventually result in a sense of internal containment. For the child, being within the room, playing, and being listened to in a safe, contained space also ushers in the feeling of "being inside something good" (Britton, 1992b).

Winnicott (1958) talks about this therapeutic space as a "facilitating environment", which can make the child feel as though he or she is being "psychologically held". The therapeutic space has the potential to facilitate growth on many different levels.

A relationship within this space is encouraged which is reliable, consistent, and continuous, and thus there is an attempt to engender trust by what is done, not just by what is said. The frame and boundaries are vital to a healthy and effective therapeutic process. Other features that are important to aspects of child therapy work with violent children in clinic or school settings are the importance of communication between professionals and for support to be given to parents or the family or to the teachers in the schools dealing with violent children.

The frame and boundary conditions

Implicit in the psychoanalytic context is the function of the therapeutic frame or the setting. There exists a continuum of beliefs about how the secure frame or the frame in psychotherapy should be managed.

Freud's "Papers on Technique" (1911–1915) are concerned primarily with the ground rules of psychoanalysis. Freud attempted to create an atmosphere of safety for his patients that would enable them to express some or all of their innermost thoughts and feelings. Freud was thus one of the first clinicians to express his recommendations as to how therapy or analysis should be conducted.

In 1954 Winnicott presented ideas about the frame, which associated the frame to the maternal function (Winnicott, 1958). Essentially, within psychodynamic therapy, the frame, or boundary conditions, attempts to provide a secure foundation within which the therapeutic work can progress. The frame thus has important contributions to make to the therapeutic holding environment. The frame, alongside the interpersonal therapeutic relationship, contributes to the containing context, which facilitates therapeutic processes:

> the most obvious condition is that the child has the toys and the adult for himself—no sudden interruptions to disturb the unfolding of his play intentions. For to "play it out" is the most natural self-healing measure childhood affords. [Erikson, 1977b, p. 200]

There is general agreement within therapeutic practices that the frame relates to specific conditions/boundaries pertaining to the clinical setting that need to have important elements of reliability, consistency, and continuity. Central features of the frame in psychoanalytic therapy pertain to total privacy; the use of free association or play activities; the therapist's anonymity and neutrality; the absence of physical contact; confidentiality; a fee; set frequency and duration of sessions; and the patient's responsibility for termination of therapy.

Note

1. Throughout the book, in clinical material all names and some details have been changed in order to protect confidentiality.

CHAPTER ONE

Early life trauma and the psychogenesis and prevention of violence

Peter Fonagy

Violence is extreme aggression, perhaps distinguished by the implicit intent to cause injury or death. Young offenders (under 20) account for more than half of violent crimes in the UK. Statistics on the onset of serious and violent delinquency show us that about half of persistent juvenile offenders are "active" by ages 12–13 and only a couple of years later over 80% of those who will be offenders have begun to commit serious delinquency. Prevalence peaks between ages 17 and 18, but most serious delinquent offenders have started their offending careers much earlier.

Adolescents possess both the means (physical strength, cognitive competence), the opportunity (greater freedom from supervision and more access to resources), and the motive (they feel pressured to perform at school, in terms of a career, in sexual relationships). This undoubtedly explains why adolescence is the phase when individuals are most likely to resort to violent behaviour. The Dunedin Study was a detailed longitudinal study of a birth cohort of 1,037 young people followed from ages 3 to 26

Paper presented at Scientific Approaches to Youth Violence Prevention: A New York Academy of Sciences Conference, 25 April, 2004.

(Moffitt, Caspi, Harrington, & Milne, 2002). This showed that most adolescents will commit some delinquent act, but most of these are minor infractions. Only a small proportion of these (around 6%) are the persistent offenders who account for the majority of violent acts. Tracing the development of these young people's aggression has been a major challenge to the field.

This chapter considers the development of violence with particular reference to family factors in violence such as the quality of parent–child attachment. Taking a developmental approach to violence, we attempt to establish a link between the maltreatment of children in an attachment context and the risk of violence via the child's capacity to envision mental states in the other. We attempt to bring evidence from epidemiology and neuroscience to bear on this link. We finally consider studies of prevention of violence likely to enhance attachment and mentalizing.

The risk of violence

Over the last decades we have learnt that the risk factors associated with antisocial behaviour in general and violence in particular are evident from relatively early childhood. The findings from reviews (Farrington, 2003; Loeber, Green, & Lahey, 2003; Rutter, Giller, & Hagell, 1998) and from some of the best-known longitudinal studies, including the Cambridge Study (Farrington, 1995), the Pittsburgh studies (Loeber, Stouthamer-Loeber, et al., 2002), and the Dunedin Study (Moffitt et al., 2002) have been fairly consistent. Repeatedly reported personality and temperament individual risk factors include: (1) uncontrolled temperament observed at age 3 years leading to adult aggression (e.g. Caspi, 2000), (2) impulsive traits at age 8–10 associated with adult offending (e.g. Farrington, 1995), (3) hyperactive traits at age 13 linked to adult violence (e.g. Klinteberg, Andersson, Magnusson, & Stattin, 1993), (4) callous traits at age 7–12 predicting antisocial personality disorder in maturity (e.g. Loeber, Burke, & Lahey, 2002), and (5) low IQ and poor academic achievement predicting being arrested and charged (Moffitt, 1993). The risk of an adult antisocial personality disorder diagnosis has been shown to be increased by a range of childhood psychiatric conditions: (1) major depression at age 14 (e.g. Kasen et al., 2001), (2) oppositional defiant disorder diagnosed age 7–12 (e.g. Loeber, Burke, & Lahey, 2002), (3) conduct disorder diagnosed age 9–16 (e.g. Harrington, Fudge, Rutter, Pickles, & Hill, 1991), and substance abuse observed age 7–12 (e.g. Loeber, Burke, & Lahey, 2002). Particular features of parenting and parents have also been good predictors of later offending and violence including: (1) antisocial diagnosis and/or behaviour in the parent when the child is age 8–10 (e.g. Smith & Farrington, 2004), (2) poor supervision of 8-year-olds (e.g. Farrington, 1995), (3) abuse when the child is under age 12 (e.g. Widom, 1989), and (3) early or late exposure to domestic violence, which appears to predict not just violence but also violence to the individual's own child (e.g. Moffitt & Caspi, 2003). In addition, of course, wider social factors have also been shown to play a part, including obvious risk factors such as association in adolescence with a deviant peer group (e.g. Lipsey & Derzon, 1998) and being in a high-delinquency school (e.g. Farrington, 1995).

Knowledge of risk factors on its own is only of limited value. Risk factors that clearly have causal significance and are open to modification as part of prevention are of greatest practical relevance. Unmodifiable risk factors (e.g. gender) or modifiable risk factors that antedate the problem of violence but are not part of a causal process such as peer delinquency are of limited value. For example, peer delinquency may be as much a consequence of a delinquent and violent predisposition as its cause (Farrington, Loeber, Yin, & Anderson, 2002). Broadly speaking, the greater the number of risk domains that are entailed in the history of a particular case, the higher the risk of violent antisocial behaviour (Loeber, Stouthamer-Loeber, et al., 2002). Violence is the end product of a chain of events over the course of a child's development, where risks accumulate and reinforce each other (Maughan & Rutter, 2001). So, for example, low IQ will place a child at increased risk of experiencing problems at school, which in turn can create major problem behaviours that lead to exclusion, and failing to graduate can lead to employment problems that in turn increase the risk of persistent antisocial behaviour. This is the argument for ensuring that violence-prevention programmes must simultaneously target multiple risk factors. There is further valuable epidemiological information to be gained from understanding why certain factors appear to moderate the impact of risk factors. These characteristics, usually termed protective factors (Garmezy & Masten, 1994), appear to interrupt the causal chain of risk. For example, in the case of risk factors for violence, we know that characteristics such as shyness and inhibition, intelligence, a close relationship with at least one adult, good school or sporting achievements, and non-antisocial peers can positively moderate the impact of risk factors (Losel & Bender, 2003).

The developmental approach to violence

Developmental approaches to violence share the basic assumption that correlates of violent behaviour contribute to the developmental process that permits the emergence of violence. A range of family factors are implicated in the risk process of violence. These include inadequate monitoring or supervision, abuse and neglect by parents, exposure to family violence (intragenerational transmission of abuse), parental drug or alcohol abuse (particularly maternal), problems in attachment to parents or caregivers, absent fathers, family disruption, and harsh or erratic discipline. The prevalence of violent delinquency peaks at around the age of 17 or 18, but more than 50% of persistent juvenile offenders are already "active" by the age of 12 or 13. Most adolescents will commit some delinquent act, but the vast majority of these are minor infractions; only around 6% of adolescents who are persistent offenders account for the majority of violent acts (Moffitt et al., 2002). Tracing the development of the aggression of these young people is clearly the key to prevention.

The little-known brilliant developmentalist who was also Piaget's statistician, A. R. Jonckheere, was fond of cautioning the unwary that most developmental trends tended to disappear once foot size was included in a statistical model. The same applies to violence. Recent epidemiological data has clarified that if children are followed from school entry to the end of adolescence, the frequency with which they are likely to resort to physical aggression, as reported by parents, teachers, peers, or themselves, decreases with age (foot size) (Tremblay, 2000; Tremblay, Japel, & Perusse, 1999). While physical aggression (violence) decreases, indirect aggression (same intent but no "harm" done) increases, particularly for girls. It seems that physical aggression peaks around perhaps the second year of life, but then in different individuals shows distinct developmental trajectories.

It may seem surprising, but until very recently there has been a dearth of statistical techniques for identifying the typical trajectories. The highly influential proposal of Terrie Moffitt (Moffitt et al., 2002) differentiated between life-course persistent offenders, whose antisocial behaviour begins in childhood only to worsen thereafter, versus adolescence-limited offenders, whose antisocial behaviour begins in adolescence and who desist in young adulthood. Very recent methodological advances have now enabled researchers to move beyond the "ad hoc" categorization procedures for studying developmental trajectories to statistical approaches that allow us empirically to identify clusters of individuals who share common pathways. The first study to apply this technique looked at teachers' observations of aggression in over 1, 000 boys and girls in Montreal, rated annually between the ages of 6 and 15, and identified four typical trajectories (Nagin & Tremblay, 2001): 17 percent were never aggressive; 4% showed high physical aggression from 6–15 years; 28% started with high levels of aggression and became less and less physically aggressive; and the largest group had relatively low aggression, which nevertheless decreased with maturity. The group whose level of aggression stayed high were more likely to have teenage mothers and mothers with low education.

A further study from Pittsburgh of developmental trajectories of 284 low-income boys from 2 to 8 years yielded similar clusters, with 14% always low, 6% always high, 38% high but decreasing, and 43% moderate and decreasing, in parental reports of violence (Shaw, Gilliom, Ingoldsby, & Nagin, 2002). Children who failed to show a decrease in their aggression did not differ in their IQ, maternal age or education but had shown more fearlessness at age 2 and had had more rejecting mothers compared to the group who were also initially highly aggressive but whose aggression declined over the six years of the study. Maternal depression also played a role. Children who followed the chronic or the initially high then gradually declining trajectories both had mothers with a high level of depression. Thus, children who do not desist from violence are more likely to have been fearless at age 2 and to have had teenage mothers with low education who are more rejecting and to have high levels of depression.

While in the original Montreal study there was no suggestion of a significant group of children who showed physical aggression in adolescence having successfully inhibited physical aggression throughout childhood, in a more recent report looking at impulsivity rather than physical violence, and with a larger sample, a group of boys were identified whose impulsivity became marked after age 9 years continuing to rise to age 12 (Cote, Tremblay, Nagin, Zoccolillo, & Vitaro, 2002). Furthermore, a self-report study exploring Moffitt's hypothesis of delinquency trajectories into adulthood found an adolescence-limited group of delinquents (33%), a persistent group of delinquents who remained delinquent through to young adulthood (7%), and a further group whose delinquency increased from age 12 steadily to age 31 (13%) (White, Bates, & Buyske, 2001). Moffitt's own report of the follow-up at age 26 of the Dunedin cohort (Moffitt et al., 2002) succeeded in differentiating the early-onset life-course persistent from the adolescent-onset groups but disappointingly found that violent offences remained significantly elevated both in terms of self-report and convictions among the so-called adolescence-limited offenders.

These initial findings have been more or less entirely confirmed by reanalysis of six sets of longitudinal data (Broidy et al., 2003). Data from six sites and three countries examined the developmental course of physical aggression in childhood and analysed its linkage to violent and non-violent offending outcomes in adolescence: (1) the Montreal sample of 1,161 boys, recruited at age 6, assessed annually from ages 10 to 17 years; (2) the Quebec provincial sample of about 1,000, including both girls and boys who had yearly assessments from 6 to 12 years interviewed at age 15; (3) the Christchurch Health and Development Study (New Zealand), which was a birth cohort of 1,265 children (635 boys and 630 girls) assessed at birth, at 4 months, annually from age 1 to age 16, and at age 18; (4) the Dunedin Multidisciplinary Health and Development Study (New Zealand) of 535 boys and 502 girls, assessed since the children were 3 years old, with the latest assessment at age 26; (5) the Pittsburgh Youth Study of 1,517 boys, who initially were in Grades 1, 4, or 7, regularly followed up over 12 years; and (6) the Child Development Project, which is a multi-site US longitudinal study of 585 families (52% boys), assessed on a yearly basis children, parents, and teachers. The simultaneous analysis of the six samples by Broidy et al. (2003) led the authors to conclude that there appears to be a continuity in problem behaviour from childhood to adolescence and that such continuity is especially acute when early problem behaviour takes the form of physical aggression. Chronic physical aggression during the elementary-school years seems specifically to increase the risk for continued physical violence as well as other non-violent forms of delinquency during adolescence. This was true, however, only for boys, because the results indicate no clear linkage between childhood physical aggression and adolescent offending among female samples.

Violence is unlearned, not learned

The new data from the clustering of developmental trajectories has brought a shift of emphasis to the developmental understanding of violence. Historically, models of aggression have tended to focus on how human aggression is acquired through learning, rehearsal, and reinforcement of aggression-related knowledge structures (Anderson & Bushman, 2002). Yet aggression appears to be there as a problem from early childhood, arguably from toddlerhood and perhaps from birth. It is the failure of normal developmental processes to deal with something that is naturally occurring that violence ultimately signals.

At this juncture we should perhaps acknowledge Freud (1920g, 1930a) and classical psychoanalytic views that have consistently suggested, in line with modern developmental data, that social experience is there to tame a destructiveness that is inherent in humanity. Psychoanalysts expect to find violence in all individuals since it is a fundamental destructive urge, or, in Freud's words, an "independent aggressive instinct" (Freud, 1930a). The word "independent" is crucial, showing aggression to be much more than a secondary phenomenon only coming into being as a result of external pressures: "The element of truth behind all this, which people are so ready to disavow, is that men are not gentle creatures who want to be loved, and who at the most can defend themselves if they are attacked; they are, on the contrary, creatures among whose instinctual endowments is to be reckoned a powerful share of aggressiveness" (p. 111). Biological predisposition and social influence do not create destructiveness, but, rather, compromise the social processes that normally serve to regulate and tame it. Not that aggression always shows the failure of some system. We shall argue that environment can spectacularly fail in providing the infant with the wherewithal to come to regulate, pacify, or tame his destructive potential. Violence may be the individual's attempt to tackle a damaging environment and as such, can be seen as a sign of life, as Winnicott (1958) called it, a sign of our struggles to carry on as living beings under intolerable conditions. The innate aggression theory must take proper account of the existence of positive, survival-oriented aggression and also of aggression that is a genuine protest against very considerable hardships in life.

Thus, it appears that violence ultimately signals the failure of normal developmental processes to deal with something that naturally occurs. Biological predisposition and social influence do not create destructiveness but, rather, compromise the social processes that normally serve to regulate and "tame" it. The key concerns of prevention are the individual, behavioural, family, and wider societal characteristics of the boys who do not desist from aggression during childhood.

The quality of early relationships and violence: the attachment theory framework

Attachment and self-regulation

Conceiving of the development of violence as a failure of the normal developmental process allows us to reconsider what we know about risk. The longitudinal data suggest that the socialization of natural aggression occurs through developing self-control. Self-control requires attentional mechanisms and symbolization (Posner & Rothbart, 2000). Self-control and symbolization depend on the mother–child relationship (Belsky & Fearon, 2002). The attachment relationship is therefore quite likely to be a key component of the socialization of natural aggression. We can therefore expect a poorly functioning attachment system to increase the risk of violence.

Among the important evolutionary purposes of attachment is the socialization of natural aggression through developing self-control through the efficient exercise of attentional mechanisms and symbolization (Fonagy, 2003a). Given that the attachment system is driven by the infant's anxiety (seeking a secure base to obtain safety), a formulation that places attachment processes at the centre of mastering aggression is consistent with fearlessness as a predictor of the failure to tame the aggressiveness of early childhood. Fearlessness compromises the normal functioning of the attachment system. If the infant is "fearless" the attachment system is bound to be dysfunctional. The attachment system is driven by the infant's anxiety (seeking a secure base to obtain safety). Fearless infants will not seek contact with the primary caregiver and therefore will not acquire the control mechanisms there to "tame" the aggressiveness of early childhood. A recent study of 310 low-income boys followed from 1.5 to 6 years examined the relationship of attachment and the child's capacity to self-regulate anger in a frustration task (Gilliom, Shaw, Beck, Schonberg, & Lukon, 2002). The boys classified as secure in their attachment at the age of 1.5 years were more likely to disengage from frustrating stimuli and to ask when and how obstacles would be removed. Positive maternal controls also helped children learn to shift attention to less frustrating aspects of the environment because this strategy had been modelled in dyadic interaction. Rejecting mothers failed to model distraction used to reduce frustration, and in addition they modelled anger as a primary affective response to challenging situations and a means of influencing others.

A similar line of developmental findings has emerged from the exceptionally elegant studies of Grazyna Kochanska (Kochanska, Gross, Lin, & Nichols, 2002). In laboratory testing repeated annually between 1.5 and 4.5 years, she led children to believe that they had damaged a valuable toy. The child's emotional reaction was coded for signs of guilt. Again, fearlessness signalled a likely absence of guilt, but negative mothering—in particular, maternal power assertion—appeared to undermine the development of children's guilt. Importantly, power assertion at 22 months predicted less guilt at 33 months, implying that the mother's use of positive influence—the lesser use of threat, pressure, negative comments, or anger—increased the likelihood of the child manifesting appropriate guilt, which is likely to be another self-limiting influence on aggression.

Mentalization

It has been suggested that our progress from non-human primate to *Homo sapiens* rests in our capacity to presume and understand the subjective experience of our conspecifics (Tomasello, 1999), what my colleagues and I have called mentalization (Fonagy, Gergely, Jurist, & Target, 2002). Mentalization is the capacity to interpret the behaviour of others (and oneself) as explicable in terms of mental states (beliefs, wishes, feelings, desires). Assuming that others have minds means that we can work together collaboratively, or alongside each other. Mentalization is at the core of self-control and self-regulation and has three components: (1) representation of mental states, (2) the attentional control of mental states, and (3) the capacity for reflection on mental states. We are the only species that hope to learn about the world (including ourselves) from our conspecifics and start life with the wish to share our mental experiences with those around us (Liszkowski, Carpenter, Henning, Striano, & Tomasello, 2004; Tomasello & Haberl, 2003).

There must be a price to pay for such increased harmony. The natural urge to control the behaviour of less powerful members of our group through the threat of violence becomes maladaptive (de Waal, 2000). The threat of physical violence directly interferes with mentalization, and thus it is essential to curb it. It remains adaptive, "a sign of life", in harsh social environments, such as Romanian orphanages (Smyke, Dumitrescu, & Zeanah, 2002). But within the primordial "troop", evolution has dictated that the free exploration of the mind of the other ensures survival for the individual within the collaborative social group.

Faced with the conflicting requirements of retaining the potential for violence in environments beyond interpersonal understanding, but inhibiting it in the context of the social group, evolution came up with the device of making violence largely incompatible with a simultaneous representation of the subjective state of the other. The latter capacity (for mentalization) is linked to attachment: we learn about minds, ours and those of others, through experiencing our internal states being understood by another mind (Fonagy et al., 2002).

In summary, faced with the problem of retaining the potential for violence in environments beyond interpersonal understanding while inhibiting it in the context of attachment relationships—biological family, the social or work group—evolution's solution was to make violence largely incompatible with a simultaneous representation of the subjective state of the other (either mentalize or be physical). Physical aggression, the wish to control the other by damaging or disabling them, becomes taboo with those whose subjectivity is known to us (the group to whom we feel attached). This would explain why evolution has dictated that physical aggression should gradually disappear from the behavioural repertoire of boys and girls over the early years of life as mentalization is increasingly firmly established (Wellman, Cross, & Watson, 2001; Wellman & Liu, 2004). Physical aggression, the wish to control the other by damaging or disabling them, becomes taboo within the troop (marked by the activation of attachment), along with incest. It is intriguing that the attachment system is probably also used by evolution to mark intra-familial sexual associations (Erickson, 1993).

Violence and the absence or inhibition of mentalization

The common path to violence is via a momentary inhibition of the capacity for mentalization. This requires one of three conditions: (1) a particular biology where intentional states are not normally responded to by the individual ("I cannot recognize"); (2) a particular personal history where the person cannot recognize intentional states, as his or her intentional states were not normally responded to ("I am not recognized"); (3) a particular social environment where the individual feels merged with other subjectivities and the biological need to see self and others as intentional is temporarily removed, as might happen in a large group or part of military training ("I cannot be recognized"). Each mode of violence demands a different degree of inhibition of mentalization depending on factors such as (1) felt anonymity, (2) the physical proximity of the victim, (3) the time it takes to carry out the act, (4) the amount of eye contact that the violent act entails, as it is through the eyes that intentional states are normally read (Baron-Cohen, Wheelwright, Hill, Raste, & Plumb, 2001). Modes of violence requiring less inhibition of mentalization are likely to be practised by a wider range of people in a wider range of contexts and are therefore more dangerous (thus using one's hands to kill someone takes longer than using a knife, which involves more proximity than the use of a gun, which in turn requires more inhibition of mentalization than the use of a bomb).

There are two groups of individuals for whom this evolutionary design proved ineffective. The first group are likely to be there because of genetic predisposition rather than social experience (Moosajee, 2003; Sluyter et al., 2003). Thus individuals constitutionally poor at recognizing mental states in others through facial expressions or vocal tones may not fully acquire mentalization and thus inhibit their natural violence (Blair, 2001; Blair & Cipolotti, 2000; Blair, Morris, Frith, Perrett, & Dolan, 1999). In line with the terrible threat such individuals represent, we dismiss them as "psychopaths", a term intended to create maximal distance between *them* and *us*.

Individuals in the second group may not acquire the capacity to interpret minds simply because they never had the opportunity to learn about mental states in the context of appropriate attachment relationships. Alternatively, their attachment experiences may have been cruelly or consistently disrupted. For yet others, a nascent capacity for mentalization has been destroyed by an attachment figure who created sufficient anxiety about his or her thoughts and feelings towards the child for the child to wish to avoid thinking about the subjective experience of others. We have claimed, along with others, that the capacity for mentalization is linked to attachment (Fonagy et al., 2002; Meins, Ferryhough, Fradley, & Tuckey, 2001). We learn about minds, our own and those of others, through experiencing our internal states being understood by another mind.

At least three types of dysfunctions of attachment may lead to violence: (1) attachment experiences that have been consistently disrupted by a combination of social circumstance and parental failure; (2) attachment problems associated with a child's temperament (e.g. fearlessness leading the child not to seek out attachment figures, in turn leading to a failure to acquire the capacity robustly to mentalize); (3) later attachment trauma when a nascent capacity for mentalization has been destroyed by a powerful figure, who created sufficient anxiety about his or her thoughts and feelings towards the child for the child to wish to avoid thinking about the subjective experience of others (see Fonagy, Target, Steele, & Steele, 1997; Fonagy, Target, Steele, Steele et al., 1997). It is important to retain an awareness of the possibility that violence may be rooted in the disorganization of the attachment system. A child may manifest an apparent callousness that is actually rooted in anxiety about attachment relationships. Perhaps this is also part of an evolutionarily adaptive scenario, as a harsh early childhood could signal greater future need for interpersonal violence (see Belsky, 1999). In favour of this model are studies that demonstrate that the association between childhood maltreatment and externalizing problems is probably mediated by inadequate interpersonal understanding (social competences) and limited behavioural flexibility in response to environmental demands (ego resiliency) (Jaffee, Caspi, Moffitt, & Taylor, 2004; Shonk & Cicchetti, 2001).

The group whose aggression is high in early childhood and continues into adolescence and early adulthood are, we argue, likely to have had attachment experiences that failed to establish a sense of the other as a psychological entity. We know from other longitudinal work (Rutter, 2000) that environmental influences that divert the child from paths of violence and from behavioural disturbance often imply the establishment of strong attachment relationships with relatively healthy individuals. Here the adolescent can acquire implicit knowledge of minds. To reduce the risk of violence to us, we need to ensure that social institutions supporting development (families, nurseries, schools) are designed to enrich representations of mental states in self and others. For example, teachers should help the class to reflect on incidents of bullying rather than adopt power-assertive strategies of exclusion (Twemlow et al., 2001; Twemlow, Fonagy, Sacco, O'Toole, & Vernberg, 2002).

Neuro-cognitive vulnerability to inadequate mentalization

There is much biological evidence that is consistent with this presupposition. The prefrontal cortex implicated in various forms of antisocial personality problems (Raine, Lencz, Bihrle, LaCasse, & Colletti, 2000) is also implicated in understanding mental states. Such evidence does not preclude the relevance of social environment. Most of it pertains to the localization of the dysfunction that violent individuals and those with specific executive problems share. We have suggested that the primary developmental role of early attachment is neuro-cognitive in character (Fonagy et al., 2002). Differences in language capability between violent and non-violent individuals, for example, might reflect differences in the quality of early relationship experiences rather than merely constitutional determinants restricted to language capacity. Early relationships are there not simply to protect the vulnerable human infant, but to organize the functioning of the brain (Hofer, 2004) and to create the environment in which a capacity for self-mastery can be achieved via creating a representational structure for mental states.

Maltreatment and trauma may undermine the development of cerebral structures crucial to mentalization, but the re-experiencing of trauma (i.e. in post-traumatic flashbacks) is also associated with alterations in cerebral functioning consistent with impaired mentalization. Arnsten (1998; Arnsten, Mathew, Ubriani, Taylor, & Li, 1999) and Mayes (2000, 2002) have linked extreme stress to altered dynamics in arousal regulation in a way that is highly pertinent to trauma. They describe how increasing levels of norepinephrine and dopamine interact with each other and differentially activate receptor subtypes so as to shift the balance between prefrontal executive control and posterior-subcortical automatic control over attention and behaviour. Mild to moderate levels of arousal are associated with optimal prefrontal functioning and thus to employment of flexible mental representations and response strategies conducive to complex problem solving. On the other hand, extreme levels of arousal trigger a neurochemical switch that shifts the individual into posterior cortical–subcortical dominance such that vigilance, the fight-or-flight response, and amygdala-mediated memory encoding predominate. In effect, high levels of excitatory stimulation (at alpha-1 adrenergic and D1 dopaminergic receptors) takes the prefrontal cortex off-line. This switch in attentional and behavioural control is adaptive in the context of danger that requires rapid automatic responding. Yet Mayes (2000) points out that early stressful and traumatic experiences may permanently impair the dynamic balance of arousal regulation, altering the threshold for this switch process. Hence, sensitized individuals may be prone to impaired prefrontal functioning in the face of stress, with automatic posterior-subcortical responding taking control of attention and behaviour, undermining flexible mental representations and coping. In line with this suggestion is the observation that N-acetyl-aspartate, a marker of neural integrity, is lowered in the anterior cingulated region of the medial prefrontal cortex of maltreated children and adolescents (De Bellis, Keshavan, Spencer, & Hall, 2000).

Genetic predisposition and maltreatment experience appear to interact in meaningful ways. Recent evidence has linked the polymorphism of the promoter region of the monoamine oxidase A (MAOA) gene with aggression (Caspi et al., 2002). MAO metabolizes neurotransmitters such as norepinephrine (NE), serotonin (5-HT), and dopamine (DA) polymorphism with differing efficiencies. Genetic deficiencies in MAOA activity were weakly linked with aggression in past studies. Transgenic mice in which the gene encoding MAOA was deleted showed increased aggression and increased brain NE, 5-HT, and DA (Cases et al., 1995). There is evidence for maltreatment predisposing most strongly to adult violence in children whose MAOA is insufficient to constrain maltreatment-induced changes to neurotransmitter systems. The Dunedin multidisciplinary health and development study involved 1,037 children tested at ages 3, 5, 7, 9, 11, 13, 15, 18, 21, and 26 years. They were exceptionally well-characterized with regard to environmental adversity (8% severe maltreatment, 28% probable maltreatment, 64% no maltreatment). They were also rigorously assessed for antisocial outcome at age 26. There was (as has been cited) a powerful main effect of maltreatment on antisocial behaviour. There was no main effect of MAOA polymorphism on antisocial outcome.

However, in the presence of low-activity MAOA and maltreatment, 27% of the sample had antisocial outcomes, whereas high-activity MAOA appeared to protect from maltreatment, with antisocial outcomes only observed in 12% of this group. The attributable risk fraction was 11%. Deficient MAOA may predispose to hyperactivity to threat and prevent habituation to stress and lead to the prefrontal cortex being taken "off-line", as described above.

We propose a synergy between psychological defences, neurobiological development, and shifts in brain activity during post-traumatic states such that mentalizing activity is compromised. The shift in the balance of cortical control locks the person with maltreatment history into a mode of mental functioning associated with an inability to employ alternate representations of the situation (i.e. functioning at the level of primary rather than secondary representations), an inability to explicate the state of mind (meta-representation) of the person they face, and a predisposition to enter a mode of mental functioning associated with states of dissociative detachment where their own actions are experienced as unreal or as having no realistic implications (Bateman & Fonagy, 2004). Threats to self-esteem trigger violence in individuals whose self-appraisal is on shaky ground because they exaggerate their self-worth (narcissism) and are momentarily unable to mentalize, to see behind the threats to what is in the mind of the person threatening them.

Efforts at prevention of early trauma: child abuse

The physical maltreatment of children is known to be associated with adverse consequences and transgresses the child's human rights. Abuse is relatively common: its prevalence is 1%–10% (Browne & Herbert, 1997; Emery & Laumann-Billings, 2002). Child abuse prevention has been a key target of prevention because of a strong association between child abuse of all kinds and the development of personality disorder in adult life (Johnson, Cohen, Brown, Smailes, & Bernstein, 1999). Studies by our group (Stein et al., 2002) and others have demonstrated that maltreatment impacts capacity to envision mental states (see review in Bateman & Fonagy, 2004). A history of being parented poorly is a robust correlate of the development of personality problems, and an association between parental psychiatric disorder and subsequent personality problems in offspring was due to experiences of poor parenting (Quinton, Gulliver, & Rutter, 1995). Continuities in antisocial behaviour across generations are partly mediated by parenting (Smith & Farrington, 2004).

There are at least twenty studies testing the effectiveness of a range of methods of physical abuse prevention. They aim to reduce stress on parents, increase support, enhance parenting knowledge and skills, and promote child health so as to reduce the demands that children place on vulnerable parents. The programmes entail home visiting, behavioural parent training, life-skills training, stress-management training, and the provision of paediatric medical care for children. In some studies these are offered in isolation, whereas in others complex combinations of programmes are offered.

Home visitation studies

The effectiveness of home visitation was evaluated in eight studies (Affleck, Tennen, Rowe, Roscher, & Walker, 1989; Barth, Fetro, Leland, & Volkan, 1992; Barth, Hacking, & Ash, 1988; Gray, Cutler, Dean, & Kempe, 1979; Hardy & Streett, 1989; Infante-Rivard et al., 1989; Larson, 1980; Olds, Henderson, Chamberlin, & Tatelbaum, 1986; Olds et al., 1998). In four studies the home visitation was by a nurse, and in the other four by para-professional women with parenting experience. Visitations occurred from 4 months to 2¼ years. In some of the studies the visit started before the birth of the child, and the visits provided social support, advice, and education about childcare. In some instances, respite care was also offered. In all, a non-judgemental supportive attitude on the part of the visitor and modelling and encouragement of effective parenting were features. Across these studies the results are impressive. The risk of physical child abuse may be reduced by 50%. Poor unmarried teenage mothers are at greatest risk and benefit most. The likelihood of childhood hospitalization is reduced by 50%. The decrease in maltreatment was associated with a reduction of early-onset problem behaviours, which are normally clinically assumed to be a consequence of maltreatment (Eckenrode et al., 2001). The impact (measured by effect size, ES) on parental well-being is small (mean ES = .93). Mothers' reports of their child's health and welfare show only small effects. Programmes where home visiting began prenatally are more effective, but no consistent differences emerge between nurses and para-professionals. Drop-out rates across these studies were surprisingly low (20%), even though some programmes lasted over two years. Drop-out rates are higher in non-experimental studies (circa 40%) particularly in the absence of regular supervision of home visitors and younger, non-Hispanic mothers (McGuigan, Katzev, & Pratt, 2003).

Behavioural parent training

Six studies tested programmes aimed to improve practical parenting skills and to address inaccurate expectations of infants and lack of awareness of age-appropriate capabilities of young children that is common among perpetrators of physical child abuse. Parents are helped to develop practical skills to understand the infant's preverbal and early verbal communications and acquire skills for meeting the infant's physical needs (Barth, Blythe, Schinke, & Schilling, 1983; Burch & Mohr, 1980; Field, Widmayer, Greenberg, & Stoller, 1982; Peterson, Tremblay, Ewigman, & Saldana, 2003; Resnick, 1985; Wolfe, Edwards, Manion, & Koverola, 1988). These parent-training initiatives lead to marked improvements in parental wellbeing that are well-sustained at follow-up (mean ES at follow-up = .7). Marked short-term improvements in parenting skills are reported (mean ES = .6), but these are not maintained on follow-up (mean ES = 0). In the most recent study, parenting efficacy and child anger continue to show some therapeutic benefit. Furthermore, the average drop-out rate is 50%.

Multi-modal community interventions

Three studies, all involving the provision of a range of health-care, social, and educative services, looked at the prevention of child abuse (Lealman, Haigh, Phillips, Stone, & Ord-Smith, 1983; Lutzker & Rice, 1984; Marchenko & Spence, 1994). Across the studies the risk of physical abuse was 6% compared to 17% in families who did not participate. These multi-modal community-based programmes reduced the risk of hospitalization by a factor of four in at least one study (4% vs 19%). Most families completed the programme, and drop-out rates were low (6–27%). The long-term effects of the programme, however, are not known.

Summary

All these programmes, including stress management and inpatient programmes not reviewed in detail, modify risk factors for child abuse or reduce the risk of physical abuse or both. Home-visiting programmes, particularly those beginning before the birth of the child, may be particularly efficacious in this regard, but they do not impact on parents' self-reported well-being. Stress-management training and behavioural parent-training programmes bring about marked improvements in parental well-being, but these appear not to be maintained at follow-up. Multi-modal community-based programmes appear to combine the advantages of home visiting and behavioural parent training. These programmes also have low drop-out rates. Thus programmes conducted on a group basis in community centres show greatest potential in the prevention of physical child abuse.

Efforts at preventing antecedents of violent behaviour in middle childhood

There have been two distinctly different approaches to preventing the emergence of conduct problems in middle childhood. The universal approach has been directed at a total population, typically of a school, to promote the development of social and emotional competence, teacher behaviour, and school atmosphere (Kellam, Ling, Merisca, Brown, & Ialongo, 1998; Reid, Eddy, Fetrow, & Stoolmiller, 1999). (This kind of programme is also described in Twemlow, Fonagy, & Sacco, 2004.)

Parent-training programmes

Parent-training programmes as a preventative intervention have grown out of treatment work with families with oppositionally defiant children. Some parents appear to regulate the child's behaviour through coercion and criticism, fail to praise, and are inconsistent with reinforcements (Patterson, Reid, & Dishion, 1992). Webster-Stratton extended her video-based parent-training programme to explore the value of parent training as part of a Head Start curriculum. A large disadvantaged sample was exposed to eight or nine sessions of group videotape parent training (Webster-Stratton, 1996, 1998; Webster-Stratton, Reid, & Hammond, 2001).

The results were that 69% of mothers in the intervention group and 52% in the control group showed marked changes in behaviour, and 73% versus 55% of the children in the treated and control groups, respectively, showed reduction in externalizing behaviour. The differences were no longer significant at one year. A similar large-scale implementation also failed in the Worcester public school system (Barkley et al., 2000). More successful implementation was reported from Australia (Sanders, Markie-Dadds, Tully, & Bor, 2000). Toddlers were recruited by advertisement stressing maternal concern about child behaviour. Clinician observed ratings confirmed that the parent-training programme was successful in improving the child's behaviour, particularly when supplemented with coping-skills training. In general, parent-training programmes have been of limited effectiveness in the prevention context because of substantial problems of client engagement. This problem is less evident when atypical parents concerned with their child are recruited by advertisement.

Targeted developmental prevention based on early signs of violence

The second approach has been to identify young children at risk on the basis of what is known about the developmental pathway of conduct problems (Tremblay, 2000). Prevention trials have employed both child-focused and parent-training components. The Montreal experiment (Vitaro, Brendgen, Pagani, Tremblay, & McDuff, 1999) was a two-year intervention that, at end of treatment, found no effect of parent training and social skills training, but at three-year follow-up the intervention boys were rated less aggressive by teachers and were less involved in delinquency. The First Steps Program (Walker, Irvin, & Sprague, 1997) provided high-risk kindergarten children with social skills building and their families with in-home consultation on supporting adaptive child behaviour. Immediately post-intervention the effects were large (Brotman et al., 2003), but long-term outcome was only reported in one study.

The most ambitious programme so far, the Fast Track Prevention trial (Conduct Problems Prevention Research Group, 2002a, 2002b), combined universal (the PATHS curriculum) and targeted intervention in a multi-site study planned over ten years. There was a clearly significant intervention effect, but the reduction at clinical level was only 10% (from 37% to 27%). The effect size on teacher rating is small (ES = .27). With an intervention of this magnitude, greater differences might have been expected. Nevertheless, a 37% relative difference was achieved, and the 10% reduction in prevalence is generally considered large (Scott, 2003).

Why targeted prevention can be a problem

Violence-prevention programmes have mainly been concentrated on high-risk groups, based on the knowledge that within most communities the 10% of adolescents who exhibit violence account for as much as 70% of violent acts (Loeber, Farrington, & Waschbusch, 1998). A number of elementary-school-based multi-component studies show that interventions were either increasingly (Farrell, Meyer, Sullivan, & Kung, 2003; Stoolmiller, Eddy, & Reid, 2000) or uniquely (Kellam, Rebok, Mayer, Ialongo, & Kalodner, 1994; Metropolitan Area Child Study Research Group, 2002) effective for high-risk children. Most of these interventions focus on changing the behaviour and social cognition of youth related to violence. However, even if relative risk increases as a function of cumulative risk, the prevalence of a particular level of cumulative risk may be such that the largest cumulative risk is only experienced by a very small proportion of the population (Davis, MacKinnon, Schultz, & Sandler, 2003). Thus, prevention programmes guided by identifying the most high-risk groups may not always have the greatest public health benefit in reducing the problem outcome.

The strategies that have offered strongest evidence of violence prevention have been universal, family-based early interventions (Howell, 1997; Yoshikawa, 1994, 1995). However, as a recent statistical modelling analysis (Cuipers, 2003) shows, in order to demonstrate a reduction in the incidence of new cases within the universal-prevention design, literally tens of thousands of subjects would need to be randomized. Thus, in order to show statistical effects researchers have to focus on high-incidence groups with multiple risk factors. The limitation of this approach in the present context is that we do not know from current studies (August, Realmuto, Hektner, & Bloomquist, 2001; Conduct Problems Prevention Research Group, 2002c; Lochman & Wells, 2002; Metropolitan Area Child Study Research Group, 2002) what is the relative impact of universal violence-prevention interventions on high- and low-risk youths or selective interventions for high-risk youth relative to universal ones for low-risk youth (Tolan & Gorman-Smith, 2002).

Conclusion

Both the glamorization and the demonization of violence help us avoid having to understand the violent mind. We should enter the violent person's subjective world, not just in order to be able to offer treatment, but also to better anticipate the nature of the risks they embody both to themselves and to society. The attempt at explanation does not amount to an exculpation; rather, understanding is the first step in the prevention of violence. The answer to the riddle of how an individual can lose restraint over his or her propensity to injure others must lie in what is ordinary rather than extraordinary: *normal human development.*

Prevention related to the recognition of the role of early developmental influences and their impact are under development and are enjoying relatively high levels of success. Psychosocial models of violence will need to take account of the differential genetic susceptibility of individuals to life experiences. We will have to study longitudinally how individuals with varying genetic susceptibilities cope with different classes of experiences across time. While non-human experience may be measured objectively, the impact of human experience on the unfolding of genetic potential is mediated by the subjective appraisal (conscious and unconscious) of the interpersonal world. We need to understand better the protective mechanisms available to individuals through, for example, the early experience of secure attachments leading to a relatively high capacity to interpret and therefore protect the self from adverse interpersonal experience. Only through careful studies of the objective and subjective environment will we understand how genetic influences create biological risks for the human organism. The future of violence research (and perhaps treatment) is in the thoughtful and targeted integration of developmental, psychosocial, and molecular genetic epidemiological strategies.

CHAPTER TWO

Violence in children

A. H. Brafman

How and why a person comes to be able to inflict pain on another being has been the focus of attention of innumerable thinkers. The multiple ways of interpreting such acts has led to the creation of many different words that aim to convey the speaker's particular interpretation of a specific deed—antisocial, delinquent, violent, sadistic behaviour are some of them. One person's "fight for freedom" is another person's "vicious murder". One couple's exciting sexual practices can be somebody else's idea of cruel exploitation of dependence. One person's view of tattooing as enhancement of beauty can arouse horror in others at the violence against the body's integrity. A toddler's grabbing or pushing can be seen as exploratory or self-assertive, much as it can be interpreted as destructive and sadistic. Clearly, the interpretation of a piece of behaviour depends entirely on who it is that is putting it forward. Each of these interpretations involves an assessment of what feelings, motivations, and intentions underlie the other person's actions. But the complexity of this situation becomes compounded when an observer sets out to assess not only the violent act, but also the unconscious elements that can, supposedly, be inferred from the behaviour under consideration.

World audiences were fascinated and shocked by the 2003 Brazilian film, *City of God*, directed by Fernando Meirelles. This showed the degree of violence that children could inflict on other children and on adults. If this was, apparently, a tale recounted by a transformed ex-member of the gangs, the film still depicted the way in which some children could be seduced or forced into complying with the murderous violence practised by seasoned violent youngsters. But this film is not the first such illustration of this disturbing and puzzling phenomenon. *A Clockwork Orange* (Burgess, 1962) also showed how cruel adolescents could become, and the earlier book *Lord of the Flies* (Golding, 1954) depicted how unusually traumatic circumstances could lead youngsters to extreme violence. Sadly, this artistic depiction of violence is not simply the creation of literary imagination but, rather, an attempt to illustrate events that occur all around us in ordinary, daily life. There is bullying in our neighbourhood-school settings, and we have been exposed to reports and photographs showing children being abducted and groomed to become members of insurgent armies.

As I write, newspapers report how Israeli soldiers refuse to take part in some military operations, claiming that these have created and propagated a cultural posture that offends and perverts what has always been seen as a fundamental element of Jewish life: not to inflict violence on another human being. Throughout my life as a Jew, each time I learnt of Jewish families where physical violence was used as part of their daily life, this was seen as an exception, an indication of abnormality and pathology. With time, I came to discover that some cultures adopt physical techniques as a disciplinary tool, much more often than others will find acceptable. But would people brought up in these communities describe their behaviour as "violent"? "There is nothing wrong in slapping a disobedient child", they might argue. Is there a point where that "slapping" becomes an example of violence that is learnt and adopted by the child? Predictably, the child, the adult, and an observer might give three different interpretations of each particular case.

However, I believe there is a crucial line to be drawn between "violence" as an *act* where pain, damage, suffering, or even death is inflicted on another person and "violence" as a thought, a wish, an urge, and yet no more than a fantasy. Among the papers I consulted when preparing this chapter, I found two quotes worth repeating here. Meloy (1992), at the end of the introduction to his book, quotes Ibsen in *Peer Gynt*:

> The thought perhaps—the wish to kill
> That I can understand, but really
> To do the deed. Ah no, that beats me.

Shengold (1991) quotes Primo Levi:

> I am not an expert on the unconscious and the mind's depths, but I do know that few people are experts in this sphere, and that those few are the most cautious; I do not know, and it does not much interest me to know, whether in my depths there lurks a murderer, but I do know that I was a guiltless victim and I was not a murderer.

These quotes emphasize the importance of self-control, the capacity to become aware of a particular impulse and yet keep oneself from acting on it, transforming a supposedly highly charged urge into a piece of behaviour that can produce damage and pain. We cannot but be baffled by that puzzling expression, "I never knew what I was doing—I seem to have acted on an impulse." Does this phrase imply regret or simply surprise? How much can we trust the explanation given by someone who has been found to have committed a violent act? When are such words a feeble excuse, and when do they imply guilt and remorse? We might declare this as an obvious piece of denial, and yet rare is the person who has not found him/herself having done or said something that is profoundly regretted. But this "regret" is a sentiment that seems to be absent from many of those instances of violent behaviour we try to understand. We have come to consider the capacity to feel guilt and remorse as important steps in the development of the individual psyche. These sentiments are clearly linked to the awareness that one's actions impinge on another being's physical self, and this is the point that has mobilized analytic theorists for decades. We are dealing with the capacity to differentiate between self and other and to experience guilt, as well as with the capacity to recognize an impulse and subject it to the scrutiny that we call self-control. Klein (1940) described it as the "depressive position", and Winnicott called it a "capacity for concern" (1963). The literature on violence takes up these well-recognized developmental steps and tries to fathom out what factors make it possible for these stages to be acquired by each individual. This chapter presents some of the arguments that have been put forward to explain the origin of violent behaviour and the factors that influence how the individual deals with them.

In our psychoanalytic world, it was August Aichhorn (1951) who first described helping troubled adolescents as human beings having emotional needs, rather than deserving punishment or restrictive, disciplinary techniques. From the late 1940s Barbara Dockar-Drysdale (1993) followed this model in her Mulberry Bush school for maladjusted children, and so did A. S. Neil (1968) in Summerhill, a school where adolescents were given the opportunity to discover socially accepted ways of expressing their feelings. During the Second World War, Winnicott was very involved with the care of children who presented severe behaviour and emotional problems as a consequence of being evacuated, and he came to formulate in conceptual terms the rationale that underlies this kind of work. He coined the expression "antisocial tendency" to describe the behaviour of these youngsters. His thesis, as outlined by Jan Abram (1996), was that this problem indicated that, as an infant, the youngster "had experienced a good-enough environment during the time of absolute dependence that was subsequently lost. Therefore, the antisocial act is a sign of hope that the individual will rediscover the good experience of the time before the loss occurred" (p. 37). This implied that instinctual forces were not the causal factor for the delinquent behaviour and gave a rationale for the therapeutic results obtained by giving those adolescents a caring, nurturing experience.

All analytic authors see an experience of conscious or unconscious trauma and/or frustration as the trigger for violent behaviour. However, regarding the origin of the propensity to violent behaviour, the psychoanalytic literature is split into two basic lines: those who believe in the presence of an instinctual force, inborn and perhaps amenable to amelioration, but (by definition) incapable of elimination, as against others who emphasize the importance of the environmental input. Among the latter, we find authors who argue the causal relevance of frustration and trauma experienced at any age, whereas others emphasize the exclusive importance of frustrations experienced in early infancy and childhood. Understandably, different authors have coined various concepts to describe relevant factors in each of these categories, but these only give complex appellations to the same basic ingredients. However, we find some authors who are prepared to admit that many cases cannot be fully explained by a single theory, since they can be shown to present data that would point to both of the above aetiological categories. Nevertheless, even when admitting the influence of later experiences with peers, most analytic texts trace the origin of violent behaviour to the earliest days of a person's life. Even knowing of this universal interpretation, I was still shocked when I found in de Zulueta's (1993) book on violence this quote from Glover (1960):

> The perfectly normal infant is almost completely egocentric, greedy, dirty, violent in temper, destructive in habit, profoundly sexual in purpose, aggrandizing in attitude, devoid of all but the most primitive reality sense, without conscience of moral feeling, whose attitude to society (as represented by the family) is opportunist, inconsiderate, domineering and sadistic. In fact, judged by adult social standards, the normal baby is for all intents and purposes a born criminal. [Glover, 1960, p. 8]

I was quite surprised by this view of an infant, but then I found that Winnicott (1946) had written several years earlier:

> What is the normal child like? Does he just eat and grow and smile sweetly? No, that is not what he is like. A normal child, if he has confidence in father and mother, pulls out all the stops. In the course of time he tries out his power to disrupt, to destroy, to frighten, to wear down, to waste, to wangle, and to appropriate. Everything that takes people to the courts (or to the asylums, for that matter) has its normal equivalent in infancy and early childhood, in the relation of the child to his own home. If the home can stand up to all the child can do to disrupt it, he settles down to play; but business first, the tests must be made, and especially so if there is some doubt as to the stability of the parental set-up and the home (by which I mean more than house). [Winnicott, 1946, p. 115]

Though perhaps only purporting to be descriptive, I cannot but view these portraits as pointing to characteristics seen as intrinsic to the being under consideration—that is, raising the idea that these were inborn traits. If my interpretation is correct, these statements would only represent a different version of what Freud and so many later authors have explained through invoking the presence of negative, hostile instinctual forces. Indeed, this view of the infant being possessed by powerful, destructive instinctual impulses has acquired a remarkable degree of acceptance among psychodynamic practitioners. I was, therefore, not surprised when, in a seminar on infant observation, a student presented a report on the visit to 7-week-old twins:

> "Margaret" became distressed. I lifted her to my shoulder and started to rock her gently. Her crying stopped. I think she's hungry, I said to Mum. Mum said it was possible, as she didn't eat enough. I knew the reality was that she would have to wait till her sister had finished her turn. She was lying with her head against my shoulder. With great strength, she turned her head towards my shoulder and opened her mouth. Then she made sudden movements with her neck to try and locate the nipple. She was desperate. I felt so sorry for her. Then suddenly she stopped, focused straight into my eyes, and looked at me with rage. I just felt the emotion go straight into me with her gaze.

Regarding a previous visit, the same student had reported the other twin "attacking the breast, producing great pain in the mother". I queried these interpretations of the behaviour of 7-week-old babies and invited the students to discuss to what extent they believed these emotions and impulses were actually *in* the babies or were, instead, in the student's perceptions of the babies. The other students tended to see their colleague's view as somewhat exaggerated, and they thought that perhaps the student was being influenced by his favoured theoretical postulates.

I would like to focus on Winnicott's (1946) phrase "if the home can stand up to all the child can do to disrupt it . . ." (Winnicott, 1946, p. 115) in the passage quoted above. To my mind, this depicts the infant driven by inborn instincts, leading him to display his destructive impulses, while the parents act as the decisive influence that can neutralize these instinctual manifestations and lead the infant to more positive, acceptable attitudes to the others in his world. This picture has come to be linked to the concept of the "good-enough mother" who contains the child's hostile impulses, much as in the Kleinian view that the mother does not retaliate to the child's murderous attacks, thereby helping the infant to form a more positive view of his objects. Winnicott's depiction of the mother as providing the infant with measured frustrations that help the development of a healthy child has, somehow (wrongly), come to be seen as the totality of his perception of mothering. The mother is given a more "active" role in the writings of Bowlby (1969) and his followers. In attachment theory, both the child and the mother are active participants in a dynamic mutual interaction that is studied in terms of the kind of attachment it provides to the developing infant/child.

Focusing on the parental side of the equation, what I have seen of early life can indeed confirm that there are parents who interpret a baby's crying or body movements as hostile complaints and demands or attacks, but these parents are in a striking minority. We also find parents who argue that there is no particular communication in a baby's crying, and then the majority of parents who take the crying or particular body movements as indications of a state of physical or emotional need. Predictably, whichever interpretation a parent reaches determines his/her approach to the baby. Of course, this is the fundamental characteristic of any kind of human intercourse: we are guided by our own perception (interpretation) of anybody we are interacting with. But when babies are involved, this is enormously important, since, as all parents know, babies learn very quickly how each parent responds to their behaviour. The mother who describes her baby as very demanding is invariably seen as rushing to her infant at each cry, much as those mothers who complain of the baby "refusing to sleep in his cot" are found to bring the baby into the marital bed as soon as it cries. Each of these babies is continuously behaving in a manner that confirms the mother's assumptions. We have now rich research evidence to show that infants react to the parental response by internalizing it and producing behaviour that shows an adaptation to that input. This should not be surprising, since this is the essence of the learning process of adapting oneself to each person and each environment that persists throughout life. Furthermore, if such adaptation does not occur, this is an important pointer to the possible presence of a disturbance in the child's capacity to relate to the objects around him.

Because of what I have called this "mutually reinforcing vicious circle" (Brafman, 2001), by the time the child and his or her parents are seen by a professional, it can be virtually impossible to determine what is cause and what is effect. The challenge for the professional is to establish how much of a child's behaviour stems from his or her constitutional endowment and how much results from environmental influences on the development of these potential abilities.

My experience with infant observation seminars has shown me that each family has its own techniques of teaching children the parameters of their style of life. In the context of the present discussion, this can be seen at its clearest in their way of dealing with the toddler who attacks the newborn younger sibling. I have not obtained long-term follow-ups on these families, but the observations that cover the period of a full year do give evidence to the possibility of recognizing (prospectively) how a parent's style will set in motion specific behaviour patterns in the child. One toddler hits the baby, and the mother will scream "If you do that again, I'll hit you, good and proper!"; another mother, though, will say "That is not right, really—why don't you kiss the baby better?" My hypothesis is that each of these reactions carries a statement of the mother's image of how a person should be treated, but it also conveys an implicit message of what the mother believes are the toddler's abilities, endowment, and self. The first mother assumes the toddler is likely to hit the baby again, whereas the second one sees the incident as potentially self-limited. More importantly, the first mother states that hitting is a valid means of expressing one's feelings, whereas the second mother urges comforting and reparation as a remedy for causing pain to another being. As the weekly observations unfold through the first year of the baby's life, there is a remarkable persistence of these attitudes. We cannot but assume that both toddler and baby gradually introject these injunctions. The mystery we still have to solve is why one child will identify with the notion of "hitting" being acceptable and adopt it as a habitual way of expressing his or her feelings, while another one will strive not to put this into practice. However, I believe that expressing whatever powerful emotions through hitting or attacking another person can originate from similar apparently ordinary situations where physical punishment is put into practice as an integral part of the language and habits of the family in which the child grows up. In the above examples, I would see the toddler's hitting or grabbing as natural steps, congruous with his developmental abilities, to express his feelings—that is, spontaneous but exploratory gestures—while the parents' reactions are the fundamental factor in teaching different ways of expressing oneself or, conversely, sanctioning this behaviour as compatible with the family ethos.

A different formulation of the last phrase is found in Fonagy (2003b): "Physical aggression peaks at perhaps around the second year of life, and subsequently shows distinct developmental trajectories in different individuals" (p. 190). What I describe as the toddler's exploratory physical expressions of affects and intentions does indeed belong to what we consider "aggressive behaviour", but only subsequent developmental steps will show the fate of these physical acts. In most children, this brand of aggression is gradually modified into other verbal or nonverbal, but not physically hurtful, behaviours. Only in a minority of children will we find physical aggression persisting in what we will eventually call "violent" behaviour. So, what precisely determines that one, rather than the other, course of development comes to occur?

The literature on violence is simply vast. Long before psychoanalysts began to offer hypotheses to explain it, philosophers, sociologists, religious thinkers—ever so many people have offered ideas to make sense of this particularly disturbing type of behaviour. Comparisons have been drawn with other animal species, and perhaps it is not surprising to discover that, even if humans are granted the status of "thinking beings", our behaviour contains more similarities to than differences from that of other animals.

Psychoanalytic literature has repeatedly debated whether "violence" results from the operation of instinctual forces or whether it is due to the child's experiences with his or her environment. I do not propose to offer a comprehensive review of the literature. This can be found in, among other sources, Felicity de Zulueta's book *From Pain to Violence* (1993) and in the work done by the Anna Freud Clinic in its research project on violence (e.g. Fonagy, 1999; Perelberg, 1995, 1999). For an illuminating study of the violent act from a legal point of view that may not be so well known in our analytic world, I recommend a paper ("Episodic Dyscontrol: A Look Back at Anger") written by Philip Lucas (now an analyst) in 1994.

Perelberg (1999) refers to the "confluence between the thinking of Parens, Stoller and Kohut, in that all three (in spite of their divergent theoretical frameworks) see aggression as reactive to the experiences of the individual" (Perelberg, 1999, pp. 31–32). Parens (1987) describes infants and children displaying objectionable, aggressive behaviour, and he feels that all children are bound to feel intense displeasure that can lead them to cry and perhaps experience rage. But he stresses that whenever there is rage, there is also an underlying "excessive pain or distress in one form or another" (Parens, 1987, p. 11). It is important to note that at this point, he adds: "In rare instances in childhood, some children with brain disorders—such as those that cause epileptic seizures—may have rage reactions that may not be triggered by experiences of excessive unpleasure. These we assume to be uncommon" (p. 11).

Parens (1987) formulates a concise summing-up of what is not only his own, but the view of many writers on this subject:

> Thus, hostile destructiveness—like the other types of aggression—is basically an act of asserting oneself over and controlling oneself and one's environment. Under the influence of excessive distress or pain, it becomes a wish to inflict pain and effect the destruction of the thing or person being controlled. We believe this is what hostility, hate and rage are about. [Parens, 1987, p. 14]

Most of our analytic knowledge is derived from seeing children, adolescents, and adults in the consulting room. Some of these come into therapy because of their actual violent behaviour, but quite often the violence referred to is part of the patient's verbal material—that is, neither directed at the analyst nor a real external event. Lynda Miller (1992) described a case where external circumstances made it impossible for the young, violent, and confused patient to engage in a meaningful therapy. Anna Maenchen (1984) describes a case where after being beaten repeatedly by the child, she got the 9-year-old girl patient and her mother together and spelled out the conditions to continue treatment—that is, no more physical violence. The girl responded: "Can I call you stupid?" This question made it quite clear that the child accepted that violence was not an acceptable manner of expressing her feelings. Maenchen, of course, said "Yes", and this became the name that the child would call the analyst for the rest of the therapeutic work. Presumably, if at first this word indicated aggressive feelings, in time it must have become an expression of non-violent feelings. I found this work of Maenchen's (1984) a beautiful example of the analyst teaching a child a more socially acceptable (and ego-syntonic) manner of expressing her feelings. It is also an instance of the enormously subtle balance of what are a patient's abilities and the analyst's definition of his or her therapeutic role. I have known of other cases where the child attacked the therapist repeatedly but, when given an ultimatum, somehow stopped the physical aggression. If I can be allowed a digression, I believe the issue of patient and analyst having physical contact also involves this problem of what constitutes the patient's needs, the manner in which these are expressed—and, correspondingly, what determines the analyst's response and the consequences of this decision.

The two fundamental questions when deciding whether to treat a violent child are: the assessment of the child's ability to overcome his or her violence, and the therapist's preparedness to cope with this challenge. In relation to the assessment, the child's age is a most important factor, but the diagnostic evaluation of the child should be extremely detailed and thorough. It is dangerous to assume, *ab initio*, that the "violence" is a piece of behaviour that can be overcome through insight-directed therapy. If the child displays violence indiscriminately—and particularly if he also presents self-damaging behaviour—it is important to investigate the possible presence of some physical and/or mental disability. Personally, I also place great importance on a careful evaluation of the parents' view of the child's problems. This gives us an opportunity to study the parents' history and what was their experience of disciplining techniques. We aim at an evaluation of their psychopathology and the influences they had on the child's development. But, quite specifically, we should assess their unconscious investment in the child's presenting problems or, in other words, their capacity to support a change in the child's behaviour. A simple example: when a parent sees "violence" as legitimate self-assertion or, conversely, sees conformity as a sign of weakness, this is bound to influence the prognosis of the therapeutic endeavour.

If a child presents not only violent behaviour, but also a complex delay in language acquisition and/or other developmental problems, this need not signify that psychodynamic therapy is contraindicated; however, if it is undertaken, it must be geared to that child's actual abilities. Furthermore, any other disability brought to light in this evaluation should receive appropriate attention. I believe that in such circumstances, parents should be fully informed of the role to be played by the analytic intervention in the wider context of the helping programme.

Perhaps I should clarify my reference to the therapist's "preparedness" to treat violent patients. I believe that each therapist—much as all other, ordinary people—has likes and dislikes that determine his or her enjoying or, otherwise, resenting his or her life experiences. Training and practising as analysts or therapists, we go through situations that allow us no room for choice of patients we become involved with. However, clinical experience must be used to recognize which patients lead us (or allow us) to function at our best. I strongly believe that we owe ourselves the right to utilize our skills to the best of our abilities, and this will only happen if we respect our likes and dislikes. I have found colleagues who would not take on suicidal patients, and others who refuse to treat alcoholics or addicts in general. Conversely, I have seen colleagues who prefer to work with these patients. Some professionals can work with educationally disabled patients, much as others will refuse to take on such cases. Conceivably, some people will consider my words in terms of weakness or strength, open-minded or prejudicial thinking, if not simply judgmental attitudes towards our patients. Personally, I would argue that when we learn to obtain the conditions that bring out the best of our abilities, this is the best we can do to help our patients. In the context of the present discussion, if the therapist has strong negative views about working with violent children (or patients of any age), he or she is fully entitled to pass the patient on to another colleague.

Clinical examples

1. I was asked to see a 7-year-old boy who kept hitting his mother. I saw the boy together with both parents, and they gave a detailed account of the impossibility of controlling the child. I was told that there were times when similar behaviour occurred at school, but on the whole the boy's teachers were happy with his progress. Gradually, the mother told me that occasionally when disobeyed she would hit the boy, but the virtually daily crises involved the boy grabbing her and hitting her mercilessly. She would try to stop him and often run to the bathroom and lock herself in there, but he would carry on trying to break the door open. The father said that he had no such problems with the boy.

At the end of quite a long interview, I put it to the mother that the reason the boy hit her was that he thought that his parents saw this as essentially acceptable behaviour. Both parents were shocked at such a comment, and the mother asked the boy whether he thought I was right. To their surprise, he nodded his head vigorously and promptly stopped himself and said "No!", which made all of us burst out laughing. I could only urge the father that he had to use his presence to make the boy respect his mother.

In the next interview I saw only the parents. This was a very acrimonious meeting. Again, the father depicted himself as a quiet person, but now he described his wife as very volatile, often displaying violent outbursts. She admitted this was true and came to describe a situation where she felt so exasperated by her husband that she attacked him with words and then plates; finally, when he was lying on the floor, she had smashed a suitcase on his head! He packed some things and left the house. He said that the wife had then bombarded him with phone calls, and he eventually returned after four days. This was a dramatically different picture from the initial account of an uncontrollable child!

But there was still another twist to come. The next appointment was cancelled, since the father thought these consultations were pointless, but when speaking to me on the telephone, the mother said that the husband had just packed all his things and informed her that he "had had enough". This time she had obviously decided to be more candid and said that she was also "tired of this marriage! All my husband does it to hit my son mercilessly all the time!"

I urged the parents to allow the boy to have individual psychotherapy, but this was not pursued. I have not seen the family again, but I found it most interesting to have two other families seeking my help for their children's problems, on the advice of this boy's mother!

2. A colleague asked me to see a couple who were friends of his, for help with their 19-year-old son. He kept having fights with a younger brother and had also been involved in serious fights with peers. Some years earlier he had had a furious argument with his father and ended up causing him serious harm by a punch to his face. I first met the parents, and I heard an account of an ordinary middle-class family, where both parents were very successful in their careers and the children had also achieved good academic results. However, the adolescent in question had had considerable behaviour problems throughout his school life. When consulting me, the boy's presence in the home had become untenable (certainly undesirable), and the parents wanted an assessment of the boy's needs and, hopefully, a recommendation for him to live elsewhere.

Seeing the young man was quite a challenge. He voiced thoughts that suggested paranoid ideation and a rather precarious grasp on reality. I thought he was obviously under the influence of drugs and, though he treated me with respect and consideration, he was reluctant to engage in a more revealing dialogue. He refused to see me again, and I saw the parents several times to discuss what to do. For a time, the parents managed to keep him at home, and now we had situations where his younger brother would provoke him into emotional outbursts, though he succeeded in controlling himself not to hit him. After a further domestic crisis, the young man was admitted to a psychiatric hospital, and it proved difficult to decide whether he was presenting a psychotic illness or a drug-induced psychotic crisis.

The reason I mention this patient is the fact that some ten years earlier he had been in analysis with a colleague. For a long period, sessions were enormously difficult, since the boy would kick and punch the analyst. Interestingly enough, when the analyst gave him an ultimatum that the analysis would come to an end if this violence continued—he stopped. However, the meetings with the parents brought to light the fact that the father had been continuously subjected to extreme violence by his own father. Reluctantly, the parents admitted that for quite a few years of the son's childhood, the father would smack him when his behaviour became intolerable.

It is not difficult to agree that where there is violence, we can find an underlying explanatory affect and that when the patient is in analysis, it is likely that the analyst will try to find some unconscious fantasy to give further justification to the violent act. Seeing aggression as "reactive to the experiences of the individual" refers to affects of disappointment, pain, frustration, rage, and so on, but I believe this formulation leaves out my impression that all or, at least, most of these individuals have suffered physical violence in their early years. In other words, I believe physical violence is not an original discovery made by a child at some stage of his development, but, rather, a means of expressing affects that is learnt, much as we learn the language, the customs, and the ethics of those around us. This is not to say that violent children or adolescents are, exclusively, the result of being brought up by equally violent parents. Violence can also be learnt from siblings or peers, but in these cases I believe it operates as something like the language, customs, and other rituals that are shared by the group. Physical violence (or, in some cases, sexual behaviour) comes to constitute the manner in which the pair or wider group express to each other or to others what they feel and want.

Repeating myself: from a theoretical point of view, the central issue of debate over the causality of violence is whether we postulate an innate destructive (death) instinct that leads the infant, child, adult to behave violently or, instead, whether this is an acquired response to environmental influences. Time and again, however, I find myself getting lost when trying to establish the precise differences between the formulations of one author and those of another. "Identification with the aggressor" and "turning passive into active" are clear enough formulations, which seem, implicitly, to suggest that *if* the infant had not suffered frustration and trauma, he might have developed into a peaceful and peace-loving being. But this is never claimed in the literature, since all authors believe that frustration is an integral, unavoidable part of normal development. So, what decides whether frustration is a building block towards effective independence or, instead, a trigger for violence, sadism, and/or sexual perversion? The easy way out of this conundrum is to postulate innate factors, to argue that the child has an inborn powerful destructive instinctual drive that transforms his or her environmental input into negative experiences that foster resentment, anger, hatred against him/herself and/or against figures in the external world. I am putting forward the idea that being on the receiving end of physical violence is an important, if not indispensable, element in the development of the use of violence as a means of expressing certain affects. As we all know, not all children who are hit by their parents or peers turn into thugs, and this is where our theories find the stimulus for endless speculations. We do not know how to explain why this position of victim leads some children to become perpetrators, while other children with the same experiences will turn into non-violent beings. Indeed, we can resort to the idea of a "strong destructive instinct", much as we can postulate the incapacity of "mentalizing" (Fonagy, 1999), not being able to appreciate the pain being suffered by the attacked person. Sadly, however, these theories remain speculative, and we have to wait for further evidence to turn them from explanatory into conclusive constructs.

I believe our central problem (not only on the issue of violence) is that our theories of development are expressed in prospective language, but they are in fact theoretical constructs attempting to explain retrospectively our clinical experiences. Furthermore, for their confirmation we have to rely on retrospective investigations, whether this be the patient's memories or other clinical material. To make matters worse, when we try to use "research" and "observation", we find ourselves inevitably falling into the trap that our pre-existent concepts cannot but influence our interpretation of our findings. We have here a problem similar to what Daniel Stern (1985) tried to solve by emphasizing the difference between a conceptual infant and a clinical one. When we have an individual patient under the microscope, it is not difficult to describe our findings and present our evaluation of individual and family pathology and, accordingly, explain the concepts on which we base our formulations. But when, like all our analytic ancestors, we try to extrapolate from our views on our private caseload, we risk being confronted by no end of objections from colleagues.

I think that our theories will acquire much-needed weight when we succeed in predicting which ones of our babies will become violent. We all know of families where one or both parents used violence as a frequent means of enforcing obedience, but where not every child went on to become violent. So far, we have many studies based on work with individuals, and I would suggest that the very fact that these were patients willing to cooperate with analysts and continue their attendance for interviews already suggests that they had hope and wish for change, which probably distinguishes them from the hardened violent adolescent or adult.

My concern with the theories that postulate deficient or absent parental nurturing as the cause of violence is the implication that given the right treatment these children, adolescent, or adults would develop those stunted psychological abilities required to express feelings in ways other than violence. Indeed, I agree that many violent persons belong to the category of "antisocial behaviour" or "lack of mentalization" or any other similar concepts. Nevertheless, I suspect that we are not born with equal potential. I fear that we do have individuals who are born with a severe incapacity to grasp the individuality of the other—not as a result of deficient mothering or parenting, but because of physical factors that we still have not been able to identify. When someone with such disabilities finds him/herself brought up by violent parents or gets involved with violent peers, we have the development of the violent person who is not likely to respond to our therapeutic endeavours.

CHAPTER THREE

The kick of life

Roderick Macleod

I worked psychotherapeutically with "Sarah" over a 24-month period. We met in the playroom of a clinic in the North of England for once-a-week therapy. It became obvious shortly after starting that many more sessions were needed in a week, and yet unfortunately I was not able to offer this at the time.

Sarah had been referred to therapy as a result of her aggressive behaviour towards her peers. Minimal information came with the referral note, but it was known that there was a history of neglect and abuse in the family. Sarah was one of my first clients in the placement, which was linked to a lengthy training programme. The child and family clinic worked with disturbed children referred by schools and social services. My work with Sarah was a mandatory part of the social workers' intervention on behalf of Sarah. This chapter chronicles most of what happened for the two-year duration of her therapy.

At the start of the therapy my expectations of what I would experience over that time were very limited, and it is possible that if I had been told what I was going to witness, experience, and be part of, I might not have had the courage to start out in the first place. All in all, as a psychotherapist in training, it was a very challenging albeit rewarding experience—both professionally and personally.

Swearing and spitting

"Fuck off", she screamed, her 9-year-old face contorted with rage and anger as she vented her anger towards me. I tried again to interpret her desire for me to "fuck off" with the fact that she was angry that I was leaving, and that we would shortly not be seeing each other any more.

My efforts were met with a well-aimed missile of spittle in the middle of my face that was more shocking in its intensity than anything else that Sarah had shown me over the previous 18 months. As her saliva slipped down my cheek, I again tried to interpret that her behaviour towards me was coming from her feelings of hurt and abandonment, and that I had hurt her by leaving and that my words also hurt her.

A quick, sharp kick followed, which landed solidly on my shin and was accompanied by a torrent of abusive language: "Fuck off, you pussy hole—I'm going to really hurt you!"

With a now-well-honed ability not to show that her kicks were actually quite painful, I again tried to link her rapidly escalating violent behaviour with our imminent ending. This painful interpretation was met with a slap in the face, followed by a whirl of destructive activity that quickly saw the playroom descend into a scene of chaos and destruction. More swearing followed, ending with "I don't care about you, fuck off!"

I once again intervened verbally by saying that hurting me was not allowed but we could talk about her violent feelings, and that we could talk about how angry and hurt she was about my leaving. I added: "I can see that you want to destroy things between us, and maybe you feel I have destroyed what we had by leaving. Maybe you are worried that the reason I'm leaving is because you can get so angry and violent." Her behaviour continued, however, along the same lines, up to the point where I had to end the session, as had been the case in previous sessions where her behaviour had become uncontainable. My actions were met with more violence, abusive language, and spitting. I told her that if the violence continued, we would have to stop. This injunction was made alongside psychodynamic interpretations as to the meaning of her violence.

Although this behaviour in itself was not out of the ordinary for Sarah, the spitting action was a new arrow in her quiver of emotional expression and had not been seen before. But more importantly the session showed a dramatic change in her recent behaviour, which was compounded by the fact that I only had two more sessions to go with her before our therapeutic relationship was going to end.

Over the last twenty-four months I had been witness to extremes of behaviour that were indicative of a borderline mental state with blurred boundaries of body and mind. This failure to regulate her behaviour, and her expression of it through acting out with violence, can be connected to Sarah's fundamental difficulty in thinking. As Perelberg (1999) states "There is a tendency for body and mind to become confused, so that violent acts on one's own or another's body are used to get rid of intolerable states of mind" (p. 6).

What I was asking myself at this point was whether or not Sarah was able to distinguish between me as the target for those intolerable thoughts, and me as the "good-enough" therapist, and, if so, would those aspects of our relationship have a lasting effect on Sarah, without being destroyed in spite of her best efforts.

Because the abusive language, spitting, destruction of the room, and kicking was not simply the attempt to destruct all the good and to keep at bay feelings and experiences that Sarah was probably deprived of as a young child, but also an expression of Sarah's will to fight, to be heard, and not be forgotten—it was her expression of the will to live. This "will to live" as expressed through violence has been documented in other cases, such as Boston and Szur (1983), who in their work with violent children wrote: "It might be speculated that, in some cases, the fighting spirit indicated less emotional deadness than seemed to be present in the more superficial personalities" (Boston & Szur, 1983, p. 35). That "fighting spirit" was something that I had seen in abundance over the last 24 months.

The therapy

Sarah presented as a very outgoing and energetic 9-year-old child. Through casual observation of her interaction with her peers, she seemed popular and obviously had the ability to form friendships. Her interaction with adults was also very positive, and any efforts to help her on their part were warmly received by her. Sarah lived with her mother and two brothers. Her father was in prison; the reason for this was unknown.

The course of the therapy can be condensed into four separate phases; an opening phase that was banal in comparison with what came later; a second phase that was extreme in its expression of anger and violence; a third phase that oscillated between good and bad as glimpses of hope emerged in our relationship; and a final phase where we both came to terms with the ending of the therapy.

Phase I: The calm before the storm

For the first phase (a non-violent stage), the pattern in the room was dictated by some passive play on the part of Sarah, with growing signs of attachment to me through the use of items such as glue and Sellotape. As recorded by Boston and Szur (1983), the use of these sticking objects could be analysed on several levels, where "sticky techniques functioned not only to express [her] sense of 'sticking' to the object of her attachment, but also to control and possess, to mess up at times, and to cover up or obscure dangerous and frightening feelings at other times" (p. 94). In the context of what followed, Sarah was evidently using the glue and Sellotape to obscure the dangerous feelings that were being aroused in her, but which were yet to surface.

Sarah's dangerous and painful feelings did start to surface towards the end of the first phase, when she began to display severe sibling rivalry—she became increasingly agitated about the fact that I saw other children in the therapy room. When she asked me directly if I did see other children, in my novice state I denied it—I replied with an emphatic "No", which was the opposite of what I had intended to say. Transference and countertransference feelings were becoming intensified in many ways. It was as if, through my actions, I was getting to see how a little of her internal world operated—that in the same way that I had "split" the reality of seeing other children from the fantasy that I was not, Sarah's thoughts could be one thing, and her actions and words another.

This unthought-through, quick response to her question made me later confront the question: Was I becoming like other people in her life who lied to her?

My non-truth, if you will, was received by Sarah with the disdain that it deserved, and she left that session 10 minutes early. She then missed the next session completely, and it took the intervention of a carer to get her to come back to the room. It only became possible for her to let go of this point when I acknowledged to her about a year later that I had indeed made a mistake, and that it was wrong of me to tell her that I did not see other children when I actually did. Meanwhile, the quality of these early sessions began to radically change, with Sarah becoming increasingly more difficult and the sessions taking on a rather chaotic and frightening tenor.

Phase II: Chaos and destruction— the emergence of hurt and desperation

The relatively sudden descent of the sessions into the chaos and destruction that was to be the norm for the next year was not obviously down to any one thing. My denial of the reality that I saw other children was certainly precipitous, but other factors were at play. It became increasingly difficult to get her to leave the therapy room at the end of sessions, and she was often openly rude to me if she saw me in the corridors of the clinic outside our session times. The actual content of the sessions also started to become more agitated.

A session taken from the second phase of the therapy demonstrates the establishment of the more disorganized and threatening behaviour:

> Sarah starts the session off in a relatively good mood. She then begins to mark things in the room, writing her name in books, as if to "mark" her territory, and then she states that she is not leaving the session that day. I interpret that it is very difficult to leave the session and that she would actually like to spend all her time in the room with me. My comments start to make her more agitated and manic, which culminates in her using the scissors to cut up some clothes from the dressing-up box and then to cover herself with a blanket and "pretend" to stab herself in the hand. Sarah tells me that she is going to report me for hurting her. While removing the scissors from her, I interpret that maybe she feels that nobody would care if she did hurt herself, which results in her telling me that I have hurt her

> and she is going to "tell on me". She then goes to the sink and spends a long time washing her hands. I interpret that perhaps she is trying to "wash her feelings down the sink", to which she shouts at me, "Shut up, you fucking idiot!" I interpret that it must be hard to be in the room with a "fucking idiot" who gets things wrong sometimes. She then climbs onto the windowsill and tells me she is going to jump out of the window. I interpret that it is easier to leave the room than be in it with her feelings (the windows are secured shut, so there was no risk of her actually managing to jump out of the window), which results in her beginning to tip up boxes of toys and throwing books around the room.

Although she has as yet to introduce physical violence towards me into our sessions, the beginning of a mixture of a sadistic and masochistic behaviour pattern is beginning to emerge. My interpretations appeared to accentuate her feelings, with the result that her rage became directed onto herself or onto me via language or actions such as trashing the room. These actions proved to be the beginning of very powerful emotional expressions by Sarah, which can be partly understood through the Kleinian concept of projective identification, which Klein related to the paranoid–schizoid position of infant development (Klein, 1946). Elizabeth Bott Spillius (1992) talks of Klein's concept of projective identification as follows: "The most basic and primitive anxiety of the paranoid–schizoid position is a fear of annihilation from within the personality, and that in order to survive the individual projects this fear into the external object as a defensive mechanism" (p. 60). Sarah had begun to project her unbearable anxieties and feelings onto me as well as items in the room, as if her feelings would destroy her from the inside if they were not ejected. Sarah may have also been expressing some of the instability, madness, and violence that she had experienced in her own real family setting, as well as her frustration with me as a therapist who hurt her by ending sessions and perhaps making correct—and also incorrect—interpretations.

A couple of sessions later, the projections became more threatening:

> She swears at me, and I interpret that she wants me to know what its like to be talked to like that. She swears again and says, "Shut up, you sly little slut!" I ask her what is going on today,

> and she threatens to hurt me unless I shut up. She goes into the toilet, and I interpret that it is easier to be out of the room rather than in it with all the nasty feelings. She comes out brandishing her fist, saying, "If you go on I'm going to give you some of this!" I ask her if she wants me to know what it feels like to be threatened like this—is somebody threatening her like that? Sarah climbs on to the windowsill, puts the pull-chord of the window blind around her neck, and says that she is going to hurt herself. I tell her that I will not let her hurt herself, and I remove the chord from her neck. She throws a couple of pulled punches at me. I flinch, she flinches, and we both end up shaking.

My reaction to these sessions and others like them was very physical. I would be exhausted by the time I left the clinic, and writing up the notes from the session was quite difficult as I tried to recall the events. The ferocity of the behaviour was such that in some ways I could not actually meet it head on—it was easier, in part, to remain an onlooker and observe from some sort of detached clinical perspective. This split between my mind and body was again a possible manifestation of what it might have been like for Sarah: the solution to unbearable thoughts was to shut down the body and mind and make it difficult to think.

I was fortunate enough to be in individual supervision on a weekly basis, so each session I had with Sarah was matched by a session with my supervisor. This was important in order to work through some of the powerful projections that Sarah was putting into me, and also to be able to start to listen to my own countertransference that underlay the understandable anxiety I was feeling in the room. My own therapy was also very crucial at this stage, combining with the supervision to create my own personal space from which to engage in the clinical work that forms the bedrock of psychodynamic training.

My reaction to Sarah was probably how others—such as teachers—towards whom she demonstrated this behaviour were receiving her: that her aggressiveness and frustration were almost too much to handle at times. It seemed that she used this behaviour to push people away from her. Although I do not know the details, there was probably an abusive relationship of some sort with one or both parents, and possibly that was what she was showing me in the room. Social services had been involved for years, and yet they were never able to get definite evidence. Given her early experiences, her treatment of me was consistent with her distrust of adults based on her reality—she had been let down tremendously and could probably see no reason why I should not be the same as all the others. Indeed, to be shown any other reality was potentially very difficult for Sarah to accept.

So the sessions continued in this strange bidirectional way that was deeply ambivalent and yet deeply interlinked. Our time together was creating a stronger relationship, which Sarah also became aware of, and this in turn created behaviour in her that tried to destroy that relationship and the goodness that was inherent in it. Sarah still continued to come to the sessions, despite her attacks, and I continued to stay, despite those attacks. Surviving, containing, and thinking through these experiences, along with creating safe and secure boundaries, and not retaliating, formulated the key components of working with this violent young child.

As the sessions progressed onto the next level of actual physical violence, Sarah also became increasingly more attached to the room, and the endings of sessions started to dominate the entire 50 minutes. It was as if she could not bear to be in the room, so she attacked it—but she also could not bear *not* to be in the room, so she attacked it. It is possible that these states could be explained in terms of the defence mechanism of reaction formation. The violent attacks on the room and me were a defence against the desire to stay in the room with me all day long—something she knew we could not do.

Over time she did find it easier to leave the room, which from an attachment perspective could be explained by suggesting that she was finding it easier to internalize aspects of me, and also to have some trust in herself that both she and I would return the following week. As Holmes (2001) says: "The aim of psychotherapy is to help create a secure base, both in reality and as an internal representation within the patient" (p. 139). At this stage in the therapy, Sarah did not have that level of internalization, but the aim was certainly to attempt to create a secure base that she could build from, through the process of understanding the therapeutic work and all that she brought (emotionally, behaviourally, physically, and socially) to the sessions.

In the matter of the ending of sessions, a pattern emerged in this phase of the therapy whereby she would say early on that she was not leaving the room that day. Although I would make my best efforts to interpret this by saying that it was very difficult to only come once a week, and I would forewarn her of a holiday break if necessary, my emotional reaction was not so clinically proficient. Even though I could see that she wanted to stay all day long and that it was painful for her that she could not, instead of waiting for the ending I would pre-empt by saying that she would have to leave on time. This ensured that from the moment she told me of her intention not to leave, the session deteriorated as my anxiety combined with hers to create a very unsafe and volatile environment, which might have reflected in some way the world in which Sarah grew up. Again, Sarah was projecting into me her own anxieties, and at this stage I was not holding them for her and making them more acceptable to her. From Bion's (1962) perspective I was failing to act as a reliable container for the projections of her unbearable thoughts and separation anxieties (Bion, 1962). I, too, like other adults before, was failing her.

Towards the end of the second phase of the therapy, the threat of physical violence turned into a reality, and the introduction of paint as a weapon took the therapy into its most chaotic state.

The following session conveys some of that chaos:

> Sarah gets some paints and starts pouring them into pots. She is being a bit abusive, but we are trying to play. She then shouts orders at me to get her paper and paint. I say that she is very angry today and maybe that is because she did not see me the week before. I notice that as I make this interpretation she is getting more agitated, mixing the paints with water and slopping it over paper, table, and floor. She has paint all over her hands, and she speedily approaches me shouting—"I'm going to rub the paint into your face!" She then starts flicking paint at me, and I try to stop her by holding her off me. She is kicking and screaming. I say that if she continues like this we are going to have to end the session. She finally calms down a bit. I start to talk out loud: "I wonder why Sarah is behaving like this—I wonder if she is worried that I will forget her unless she behaves like this." Sarah says "You will forget me!" and then tells me to stop talking to myself. She then tries to remove the dolls from the room, and I ask her not to. She again starts to kick and punch. I interpret that she wants me to know what it feels like to be hurt like this. Sarah then hits me again and gets

> very physical—there is a sad look in her eyes as she throws her punches. It is the end of the session but she refuses to leave, and she tries to get me engaged in a game. She eventually leaves with a bag from the dressing-up box.

The taking of objects from the room presented a challenge to my holding the therapeutic frame. Should I stick to the rule, discussed in supervision, of taking nothing out of the room, or should I accept that she needed some representation of me and the room through the retention of a transitional object that might help her keep the room and me in mind until the following week? In talking about transitional objects and deprived children, Winnicott (1965b) spoke of the need to allow them to create objects for themselves that give them some sense of a "shared reality that can be objectively perceived" and that "the condition of these children cannot be cured simply by giving them a new object" (pp. 143–144). In the case of Sarah, she needed a concrete representation of the room and her experience of it with me. This need was further recognized at the time of her birthday, when I gave her a small gift. The issue of giving Sarah a present had been discussed with my supervisor, and by her with her supervisor. Although no physical gifts would normally be given, it was considered an allowable transgression from the norm because of Sarah's particular history with the room and with me. I gave another gift to Sarah in our last session together, as described later.

At this point in the therapy there were several things in play. First, the reaction to the ending of the sessions was creating a space of highly charged anticipation that was never far from the surface. Second, the violence was always constantly in the room, and it continued to shock both of us. The third was her use of paint to attack me. The above three factors created a very challenging therapeutic space in which to work.

It was interesting to note, however, that reports from outside the therapy room suggested that her behaviour both in class and in the school had in general improved considerably. This positive feedback suggested that the therapy was working, by allowing her to bring all the disturbance and fear into the room, to be worked through.

Nevertheless, the day of our sessions became something that loomed like a threat in the near future, but then entered the past with a rush of relief as it meant I had survived another week. At this stage it would have been easy enough to "throw in the towel" and move on to less trying placements—indeed, I could have taken the view that if this was what psychotherapy was about, then maybe it wasn't for me. Yet there was something that was alive in that room that was impossible to turn away from—something that was raw in its intensity, but also desperate in its message. There was also a sense of concern about the fact that only individual once-a-week psychotherapy was being used, and that the parents and other family members would not attend for family therapy. Attempts to encourage them to attend had been made, but with no success.

In trying to listen to where Sarah's feelings were coming from, and to actually hear what she was trying to tell me before the dynamics inside the room destroyed it, I had to try to sort out what feelings were coming from her, as well as what feelings were coming from me. Certainly the room was an anxious and, at times, dangerous place to be. But why did a fully grown man, at least a foot-and-a-half taller than Sarah, and four times as heavy, find part of himself almost overtaken by anxiety, anticipation, and threat as soon as the sessions started? This state of accentuated countertransference was, for me, partly described by Christopher Bollas (1987), who said: "The most ordinary counter-transference state is a not-knowing-yet-experiencing one. I know that I am in the process of experiencing something, but I do not as yet know what it is, and I may have to sustain this not knowing for a long time" (p. 203). From a clinical perspective, this was what I was trying to do: sustain the not-knowing, while at the same time having a real sense of "knowing"—that is, knowing what could happen in terms of the violence, failure of the setting, and so forth.

From a practical perspective it was not that easy, and sometimes I failed. At those times I found myself in a state of "projective countertransference" (Grinberg, 1962). Grinberg describes this as something that happens as a result of excessive projective identification, which in turn links back to the patient's own infantile experiences. It was perhaps at these times that I was like Sarah's early carers: I was failing to reduce her own anxiety.

Phase III

By the end of the second phase, the sessions had entered a stage that was characterized by an extremely ambivalent and disorganized attachment pattern, with features of uncontrollable violence and rage, followed by some remorse and guilt. While a lot of the focus was on the violent elements of the therapy, there were other aspects that may have been offering Sarah some experience of "good-enough" things between the two of us.

I began to simply "survive" the sessions and pulled right back from interpreting her actions too much, as it was evident that whatever I said was intensifying her feelings and was bringing no relief. Therefore, in one session when, five minutes into the session, Sarah said that she was not leaving at the end, I did not interpret or say anything. I just listened.

It seemed that my previous interpretations were simply increasing the tension she was already feeling. It was perhaps also true that my feelings, too, were contributing to the cycle of distress, as I would also be anxious about the process of ending the session due to the chaos that usually ensued.

Reducing the number of interpretations and recognizing the cycle of anxiety that was caused by some of my comments, specifically around the issue of ending, created a significant change in the therapy.

When it came to the violence and extreme physical behaviour, which saw her crossing the normal body boundaries as if she was almost trying to fuse herself to me, I again stopped interpreting that she wanted me to know what it felt like to be hurt, and I simply made sure that she did not do any harm to herself or to me.

I also introduced one interpretation into the sessions that I was to repeat hundreds of times up until the end of the therapy. In response to Sarah's reaction to leaving the room, I began to say words to the effect of: "Maybe you are afraid that I do not have space in my mind for you and that I don't remember you when we are not in the room together." At certain times I would say: "Sarah, I *do* have a special place in my mind for you. You are in there even when we are not in the room together. When we are not together I can think of you in this special place in my mind." While saying this I pointed to a place at the front of my head. I remained aware that reassurance does not reassure, but I kept the focus of the interpretation on her fear that she would be forgotten and her fear that I didn't have a place in my mind for her when we were not together in the room.

The first time I introduced this, in the last session before a long summer break, Sarah began to accept the idea that I did actually have this physical/psychic space in my head. She would actually point to a specific place in my head when we discussed being remembered.

Prior to this, I had on many occasions wanted to simply reassure Sarah that I did think of her, remember her, and care for her by simply using words. It seemed that my own feelings of protection, and perhaps denial, made me want to make everything better for her, which obviously I could not do in a practical, external sense. Of all the things I was learning, this holding back from the natural urge to soothe a troubled child was the most difficult to control. Although Anna Freud did see reassurance as part of "subsidiary therapeutic elements" (A. Freud, 1965) to be used in non-neurotic cases, it would have been a complete failure of containment had I used it with Sarah.

Towards the end of the third phase of therapy, a particularly disruptive period developed in which Sarah literally destroyed the physical space of the room, and she also made many attacks on the therapeutic relationship. The paint was leaving an excessive mess, and furniture had to be replaced as a result of it. Walls also had to be extensively cleaned.

Sarah was fascinated by the process of rectification and remained curious that she was not punished for her behaviour. She seemed relieved that things could be fixed and that nothing remained completely destroyed. Sarah also began to show more remorse and guilt.

I had introduced a rule that if the room was in an extreme mess, we would have to start to clear up the room early. After particularly chaotic episodes, Sarah would quickly become full of guilt and try to tidy up with me. This never lasted more than a couple of minutes, but it was significant in that she did understand the consequence of her actions and was always very worried that I would tell someone else in the clinic what she had done. This element of reparation in Sarah was indicative of her movement from one state to another within a short period of time, and it can be looked at in the context of an infant's movement between the paranoid–schizoid and depressive positions posited by Klein. In Klein's words, "Depressive feelings and guilt give rise to the urge to preserve or revive the loved object, and thus to make reparation for destructive impulses and phantasies" (Klein, 1932, pp. xiii–xiv).

Less talking, more feeling

After a particularly paint-spattered session in the third phase, I had to introduce some strong management into the room, which proved to be of help in creating more containment. I removed the paints from the room completely, as well as any objects that might be used as weapons—scissors, spray water-bottles, and the like, but most importantly the paints. I explained to her what I was doing and why I was doing it.

The above-mentioned changes, alongside the interpretative changes, created in me a greater capacity to think and to contain Sarah and all her destructiveness. By creating a more therapeutically inclined space, I was able to contain her powerful projections and her fears of abandonment and loss. I felt that I was better able to help her with her anxieties by not giving it straight back to her in the form of an interpretation.

Time to play

At the same time, as the room became a relatively easier place for both of us to be in, we actually started to play. Although there had been elements of play in the room up until this point, her state of mind and my overly active urge to interpret her feelings back to her meant that we never got very far. Our play involved role-playing games, hide-and-seek, and some active running games that involved Sarah beating me in "races" around the room.

Of these games, hide-and-seek was therapeutically the most revealing, and developmentally necessary. In our role-playing Sarah liked to "surprise" me. She would make me pretend she wasn't there so that she could rush up to me, and then I had to extend my "surprise" that she had suddenly appeared.

Extending this surprise play into a hide-and-seek game, I was able to incorporate her need to be found with the idea that although I could not always see Sarah, she could be seen/found in my mind. We played this nearly every session for the second half of the therapy, and it nearly always solicited an ecstatic response from Sarah at being "found".

The game developed further as she denoted some parts of the room out of bounds, and others where I was allowed to go. Sarah's sense of boundaries was developing. She would hide in places that were very small and seemingly difficult to get into—such as under a table, inside the now empty paint cupboard, or under a pile of dressing-up clothes. I would make a big thing of trying to find her and would talk about her as I did so. A session from the third phase of therapy illustrates this-

> Sarah hides in the empty paint cupboard. This symbolic use of the space that used to house the paints is perhaps a signifier to me that where there used to be messy paints, there was now Sarah. I uncover my eyes, having counted to 30, and start looking for her. I say "I wonder where Sarah is—she loves it so much when I find her—she gets really excited, and I know that it means a lot to her when I do find her. I wonder where she is." I make a few attempts to find her and say "I wonder if Sarah worries that I cannot find her in my mind when she is not here—that is why things sometimes get a bit difficult here in the room for Sarah." I then find her, and Sarah's face lights up with joy and she runs around the room, telling me it's my turn. I stand with something on my head and pretend to be a lamp (it is difficult for a fully grown man to hide in a therapy room). Once found, Sarah quickly sends me to the washroom to count while she hides. I come out and start looking for her; "Maybe Sarah wants others to find her in their minds; but when they don't it is very painful." I then say "Sarah is in my mind, even when we are not together, and when I am not here with her I can think of her because she is in my mind, but I know that sometimes Sarah is really very afraid that I don't find her or don't remember her."

This game, along with the previously mentioned technique of showing Sarah a physical space in my mind where I could "find" her, marked the beginning of some signs that Sarah was able to internalize me as a "good-enough" object, and believe that I would re-appear if I was hiding, or find her if she was hiding. This was also symbolic of trusting that I would return after a break. As Willock (1990) writes: "The steps in this series of games (i.e. hide & seek) connote increasing levels of confidence that despite separation, the primary object is still there and reunion will occur. Each new step on this developmental line thus expresses and contributes to the growth of basic trust" (p. 322).

The hide-and-seek game would be played at various points in the session and would often be preceded by episodes of violence and abuse, as if testing this new-found trust. New tactics of destruction were invented, albeit more playful than before, such as soaking the books in water, filling my shoes with water, using a mixture of glue and water to create a lethally, sticky fluid, to name a few. However, there were patches of togetherness in the room that were beginning to remain.

Phase IV

In the fourth phase, Sarah began to actually leave the room at the end of the session without removing anything or creating a confrontational situation that would require me to physically remove her. It was evident that Sarah was finding other ways, more playful and less destructive, to make sure that I kept her in my mind when she was not there.

The room gradually became an easier place in which to work, and with that my own ability as a therapist began to develop. Containing her anxiety allowed me to reflect on what my feelings were, and where they might be coming from.

I started to work with this more considered and positive countertransference from the beginning of this phase of therapy to some effect. One of the most revealing areas was the sudden change in mood that Sarah was capable of, whereby in a matter of seconds we would go from an almost tranquil setting to a "violent meltdown", for no noticeable reason. Before, I would be preoccupied with managing the outcome of the mood swing and managing the threatening situation that came with it. Now I was able to do that but also *think* about what had happened before, during, and after the point of her mood changing.

Once I was able to see the suddenness of the mood swing as a pattern, I began to interpret, gently, that there was a very sudden change in the room and that it must be quite frightening for Sarah to have these feelings that change so suddenly. I also asked her if there was somebody in her life who had sudden changes of mood, like those that happened in the room sometimes, and I was given a simple "Yes". However, she never expanded on this simple one-word response. This interpretation was used with good effect on several occasions and seemed to give Sarah some respite from the turmoil she experienced in the room, and no doubt inside herself.

The fact that Sarah's family did not engage in any sort of therapy themselves was always an impediment to Sarah's own progression in individual psychotherapy. Ideally in situations such as this, the family would be in family therapy together while the child continues his or her individual psychotherapy. This enables the family to understand what the child is going through and to think about the impact that the child's behaviour has on the family unit as a whole and vice versa. It is also a way of looking at the dynamics of the family and of offering further support where necessary.

However, where a family does not follow up on referrals, as in Sarah's case, there is no law to make them attend. In those cases the only thing left to rely on is the family's capacity for concern for the child's mental well-being—which in this case was not evident.

Partway through this phase, I introduced the fact that I would be leaving the clinic in six months. Up to this stage things had improved to a great extent in that there was less violence and disruption in the room as well as outside it. I had also started to re-introduce some interpretations, which Sarah would receive and not immediately reject or attack. Outside the clinic she was doing better in her class-work, and her disposition seemed generally better than when the therapy started. She was still rude to me in public and was prone to almost nostalgic fits of violence and destruction, perhaps to check that I could still survive her attacks and not leave her.

Up to this point in the therapy, which amounted to approximately forty sessions with her, there had been only minimal exchanges between us concerning Sarah's life outside the therapy room. Although this was very present and real in her actions and the feelings she projected into me, there was a dearth of actual biographical information. Indeed when I would broach any issues to do with her parents or siblings, Sarah would get very angry and upset. However, I did not feel at any time that this lack of information was detrimental to the course of the therapy, because Sarah was very able to work in the "here-and-now" of the room and our relationship.

We can assume, however, that things were extremely desperate in the family setting, and that they were perhaps characterized by neglect, abuse, and physical punishment. This was not manifested in any physical way (i.e. cuts, bruises, etc.); rather, it was shown in abundance through her emotional, psychological, and social behaviour. Her lack of offered narrative about her family situation could also be interpreted as her efforts to keep the two spaces apart—the room and her life outside it—thereby unconsciously creating a "refuge" in the room from the pain and anxiety of her life. These attempts often failed, as was manifested in her violent behaviour in the room.

As I reflected on how little I knew about her outside the room, I also realized how much I had learned about her inside the room.

Endings

> Sarah comes to find me prior to the session to tell me she will be in the computer room when it's time for her session. I go there and collect her on time. I tell her I want to talk to her about something: that I am going to be leaving at the end of the next term. She shouts "hooray!" I say that there are another 17 sessions together and give her a calendar showing when the sessions will be.
>
> "I'm really happy", she says. I tell her I am sad because I have liked being with her and that although she will always be in my mind, I will miss not seeing her. She says it doesn't upset her and proceeds to give me a certificate with a gold star on it for "being a good boy for 2½ years". She then writes a note to my mother telling her what a good boy I am. Later on she says, "You are lucky I am in a good mood today."
>
> We go through our routine of games, but there is a sad, almost empty feeling in the room. Sarah finds it difficult to leave the room at the end of the session. She asks if I will come back and check if she is OK. I say "You want to know that I will come back and see you and check that you will be OK", adding how hard and painful it is that we are going to be saying goodbye in 6 months. Sarah replies, "I'll do all right."

In this early stage of the final phase of therapy, Sarah was clearly very emotionally dissociated. At a time when an element of calm had entered the room and we were beginning to operate in a relatively violence-free space, the introduced ending was clearly a big disappointment—for both of us. I was very apprehensive about what would happen next, but I tried to focus on the need for her to internalize the good experience of the therapy room and our time in it together, and to help her with the loss.

I had some expectation, from supervision, that she might revert to previous modes of behaviour as she worked through the necessary grief work. In the session following the introduction of the ending, Sarah refused to come into the room. My feelings as I sat in the empty room were of desolation and emptiness—a very powerful projection from the not-present Sarah of how she perhaps felt about being left by me. Although my reasons for leaving were brought on by the need to change placements and other requirements of my training, I was very conflicted in myself about ending the therapy with Sarah, and it was hard to let go.

This pattern of non-attendance was to continue over the next few sessions, where Sarah would often threaten not to come into the room but would eventually turn up. I continued to interpret that it was very difficult for her that I was leaving and that she wanted me to know how it felt, but that there would always be a place in my mind for her even when I was not coming to the clinic any more. What was evident with Sarah was that this was not enough for her—my physical presence was the only way that she could remember me.

The final few weeks of therapy were influenced not only by my impending departure, but also by changes in Sarah's circumstances that I was aware of through the clinic and her social worker. Sarah's father was going to be released from prison and would move back into the family home.

Once this had occurred, there was a noticeable change in Sarah's normally neat appearance. She began to attend sessions in dirty clothes, with fleas in her hair and excessively bitten fingernails. She was also not doing as well as before in class, and on one occasion she came to the clinic with a bruise. As a sign of some internalization in progress, Sarah told her social worker, when asked if she had told me about her bruise, "He is for my insides, not my outsides." Perhaps if the therapy had continued Sarah would have been able to talk about the real abuse she had suffered, thereby connecting her external experiences with her internal feelings.

I made several written statements to social services and the clinic expressing concern about her appearance, and these became more urgent as we approached the end of the therapy.

With this as a backdrop, we moved towards the end of our time together. As predicted, and not helped by her new home situation, her behaviour did regress quite powerfully, culminating in the session involving spitting that was related at the beginning of this chapter. Prior to that session, there were several episodes of the room being trashed and of very strong verbal and physical abuse. It was as if she were testing me at all times as to how much I could bear, but also as if she were showing me the behaviour that she, at some level perhaps, believed was driving me away from her. She started to refer to the "bad man" as if she could project her own bad feelings into me, again showing signs of blurring the boundaries between the two of us. Also, I was a "bad man" for leaving, which aroused in her the terrible fear of being forgotten and abandoned. These feelings were made more powerful for her in that they were a real part of her life at home and something that she had experienced in reality before.

On several occasions in the middle part of therapy I had to physically force Sarah to leave the room. The level of physical intervention was sometimes felt to be almost created by Sarah as a way of getting me to physically reach out to her and hold her. Sarah's refusal to leave the sessions became difficult to manage, and I had to start introducing the idea of getting a staff member to come to the room to help me get her back to the waiting room.

In order to make things easier for Sarah as we drew nearer to the ending, I once again began to let her take small things out of the room if she attempted to do so. I would also interpret that it was easier to leave the room with something to remind her of me and the space. It seemed that if she could take a pencil, a rubber, or a piece of drawing she had done, she was able to leave without the anxiety that was beginning to reappear. This may have also had something to do with my own anxiety reappearing and not wanting to return to the chaos of previous sessions so near the end of the therapy.

I continued with my interpretations about the place in my heart for Sarah, and I tried to get her to visualize that through drawings. She started to come to the room with food and ate crisps, chocolates, and sandwiches in front of me. I interpreted that maybe I was not giving her enough food, especially as I was leaving, and she was showing me that she could feed herself, albeit with "junk" food. Sarah was perhaps saying that the "food" I was giving her was not substantial enough or sustaining enough any more, and that feeding herself in front of me was a way of covering her anxiety about what would happen when the sessions finished.

The final goodbye

I arrive at the clinic for the last session, only to find that Sarah has not come in that day. I ask the clinic to telephone her mother and tell her that it is very important that Sarah comes in for her final session. We hear nothing back from the mother. I pace the room waiting to see if she is going to turn up. An hour later, as I am looking out of the window, a car screeches to a halt and Sarah gets out of it. She comes up to the room and tells me she didn't want to come. I thank her for coming and say that it might be difficult for her to come considering it is the last session. She tells me she doesn't care and starts to draw. I ask her about her trip the previous week. She is a bit sullen and depressed. I tell her I have a present for her (it is her birthday). She says she doesn't care. We talk about people who do care for her and that after I am gone there will be other adults who can help her. She is playing with a small set of keys. I ask her what they are, and she says they are a toy. I ask her what she will remember about the room and she says nothing.

I try to cajole her a bit and tell her what I will remember—"I'll remember the paints—do you remember them?" I get a little smile from her. I tell her that I have a special pair of trousers at home that are covered with paint and I call them "Sarah Trousers". She starts to grin and begins to cheer up considerably. She then starts to open the card I have left on the table. She says nothing and goes back to the drawing. She draws two people on a swing and says it is me and her. I draw a see-saw with her and me on it. We draw a bit more, after which she starts moving anxiously around the room. She tells me that she is staying until 2 pm.

We play hide and seek, and I go into the other room. I hear her open the present—it is a small heart-shaped locket attached to a bracelet. I come out of the room, and she asks me how much it cost me. I tell her that the price is not important. She gets more insistent, and I get avoidant. I eventually say: "Between £1 and £100." Sarah asks me whether it didn't cost me £200.

I tell her I wanted her to have something to remember our time by, and that she would remain in my heart and be remembered. She puts the bracelet on and tells me she likes it more than the present I gave her the year before. She opens the locket and says: "I could put a picture of you in here."

We talk about the locket, and then she gives me the keys and says "these are for you". I tell her how special that is and that I will keep them "forever", and that I will always have a place in my heart for her. We play our final games with joy.

I ask her where she is in me, and she says: "I'm in your heart," I then ask her "And where am I in you?" and she touches her heart and says "In here."

She starts colouring the drawing we were doing together. She finishes by colouring in the heart and says "this is for you". I tell her how special that is. I ask if she wants to go through her box and decide what she wants to take. She says she is going to take all of it. She tells me that her Dad is going to come to pick her up and tells me to follow her downstairs. I do so, carrying the box. The clinic is empty, and there is no sign of Sarah's Mum or Dad. We wait in awkward silence. She scowls at me. Another child turns up, and she starts to be rude to me—"What are you doing here? Bog off!" The clinic coordinator arrives, and I say goodbye and leave.

Concluding remarks

In writing this chapter, I reviewed and thought through many of the session transcripts.

It appears to me that they do not fully convey the feelings at that time of apprehension, confusion, and fear that I felt in and around the room when things were at their most chaotic. Yet even when I read the excerpts of the most extreme episodes, I find it hard to connect to the real feeling that was going on at that time. I believe that an even more significant dissociation was there for Sarah. I do not think that there was a connection for her in her mind between the Sarah that played hide-and-seek and gave me the parting gift of the keys, with the Sarah who propelled herself across the room at me with the intent to harm.

As is the nature of working in this clinical context, I have not had contact with Sarah since the therapy ended and have had no information about her life after our therapeutic relationship ended. I do know, however, as she knew, that she had another psychotherapist organized to work with her for the following term. The impact of having worked with Sarah is one that has had, and will continue to have, a significant impact on my professional development. When I think about Sarah and the work I did with her, I find myself often wondering if she was able to hold on to and internalize any of the "good" that she experienced there. Her answer in response to my question of what she wanted to take with her in relation to her box and its contents may have been a positive indicator of the good she hoped to keep inside her once the therapy was over—"I want to take all of it!"

But, of course, my taking notice and holding on to those words could also just be about my need for reassurance and an attempt to deal with the anxiety of "not-knowing" and my concerns about her well-being.

CHAPTER FOUR

Violence and babies

Stella M. Acquarone

In this chapter I attempt to explore the issues of violence *towards* babies and of violence *from* babies, including how violence may develop, may manifest itself, and, finally, how it may be understood. There are three main types of violence that are of relevance during the early stage of development:

1. Active projection of hate *towards* babies from parents due to the parents' own trauma or deprivation.
2. Environmental violence exercised in active acts *towards* babies through neglect or maltreatment by parents or institutions, or occurring during wars.
3. Violence *from* babies who may be endowed constitutionally with unusual aggressive tendencies *or* babies who may have a short reactivity span (usually seen within the context of the absence of a secure attachment relationship) that makes them vulnerable.

Exploring the theme of babies not only as victims of violence, but also as those who subject parents, siblings, and others to their violence, is a complex matter. The concept of innate violence in some babies has often been either discarded as "evil" or viewed as something that is not possible. Perhaps the inability to accept the idea of this innateness and the need to help these vulnerable babies is a defence against this painful awareness. Thinking about these issues may feel too unbearable, and due to impotence or guilt it therefore becomes difficult to help babies with violent tendencies.

To explore this hypothesis further, I shall consider in detail the events and experiences that occur between parents and babies. Briefly, when experiences in early infant life are mainly positive, they get integrated into a coherent, functional mind, and there is probably little thought about how this process occurs. In other words, when what the baby experiences is "good enough", we tend to "expect" that all will be well. Conversely, when babies experience devastating circumstances or difficulties, or when experience becomes traumatic either for the baby or for the parents and the baby, the effects of this seem difficult to predict or understand.

Parents and professionals often do not, or cannot, see the early signs of disturbance in infants, and therefore valuable signals from the baby are missed. Professionals may wait to refer on to other professionals, *or* they may wait to see if the nastiness, and all other demons, whether internal or external to the baby, will "by magic" just go away or if the baby will just "grow out of it". Even then, when they do refer the child and/or parents, concerns about the baby's tendency towards violence may not be fully acknowledged or understood.

Field observations

Distinct individualities in babies have been observed from birth; however, there are particular behaviours and characteristics that might be seen as important signals indicating struggles towards survival and attempts at adaptation. These signals may manifest in simple ordinary mechanisms that may themselves become exacerbated; for example, the quantity, quality, and use of sleep; crying; avoidance behaviours; gestures; and muscle tone.

Disturbed babies usually have difficulties from birth, which may be expressed in many different ways, such as in high levels of irritability; excessive crying; abnormal reactivity levels; body rigidity or flaccidity; fixed gaze or gaze aversion; no success in comforting themselves (e.g. some babies suck thumbs, others do not) or in being comforted; lack of expressions in hands, body, and face; and stereotypical expressions or hand movements.

Inner characteristics that may be expressed in their behaviour include being too greedy, too jealous, too envious, no imagination, no capacity to negotiate, difficulty in communicating individual needs, global emotional reactions (hate, rage, love), unknown sensibilities (related to their different senses), special needs, fragility, fussiness, and features related to premature births.

Theories on the origin of violence

The theme of violence and its origins is one that has been explored for millennia. In particular, questions pertaining to genes (innate) and the environment (external) have been raised and examined in many different ways.

After extensive research into the various theories around human nature within the nature-versus-nurture debate, Ridley (1993) proposes a resolution to this dilemma by viewing the process as one of "nature *via* nurture" and claims that "nature *versus* nurture is dead" (p. 280).

After long hesitancies and vacillations, Freud (1940a [1938]) continued to propose and explore the death and the life instinct in his theory of instincts: "We have decided to assume the existence of only two basic instincts, Eros and the destructive instinct. This concurrent and mutually opposing action of the two basic instincts gives rise to the whole variation of the phenomena of life" (p. 149).

Freud believed that variations in the quality and quantity of the energy of these instincts were responsible for powerful effects, and he thus suggested that "Modifications in the proportion of the fusion between the instincts have the most tangible results. A surplus of sexual aggressiveness will turn a lover into a sex murderer . . . while a sharp diminution in the aggressive factor will make him bashful or impotent" (Freud, 1940a [1938], p. 149).

Freud proposed that within the process of emotional development, destructive tendencies could be expressed in different ways. Freud continued: "When the superego is established, considerable amounts of the aggressive instinct are fixated in the interior of the ego and operate there self-destructively. This is one of the dangers to health by which human beings are faced on their path to cultural development. Holding back aggressiveness is in general unhealthy and leads to illness" (Freud, 1940a [1938], p. 150).

Klein (1952), in line with Freud's instinct theory, suggests that "in periods of freedom from hunger and tension there is an optimal balance between libidinal and aggressive impulses. This equilibrium is disturbed, whenever, owing to privations from external or internal sources, aggressive impulses are reinforced "(p. 62). Klein continues by raising the point that "In addition to the experiences of gratification and frustration derived from *external factors*, a variety of *endopsychic processes*, primarily introjection and projection, contributes to the twofold relation to the first object" (p. 63).

Alvarez (1992) highlights the important point that some children have difficulties in these processes (of introjection of good experiences and projection of bad experiences), which could lead them to being at risk of not being able to introject good aspects of their first relationship.

Again, in line with an instinct theory, Lorenz (1966) maintains that aggression is an instinct to be found in human beings and that it holds important functions in relation to its service in individual and group survival. Lorenz further proposes that this same instinct may become destructive because of the technological development of modern society and thus maintains that the future will depend on how well we manage our dangerous and aggressive drives.

The contribution of de Zulueta (1993) to the field of attempting to understand violence lies in the linking of violence to trauma and attachment. She proposes that in order "for violence to take place, there must be a cognitive process of dehumanization of the 'other' backed up by a narcissistic rage of the traumatized self, in addition to the neuropsychological manifestations of a disrupted attachment system" (p. 294). She considers that this disrupted attachment system can be brought about through deprivation, loss, rejection, or trauma.

I came to understand the different kinds of processes of attachments, and their consequences in parent–infant relationships by integrating research from three different spheres: neuroscience, psychoanalysis, and clinical practice.

Relationships and connections: models of attachments in the parent–infant space

The caregiving provided by parents influences the baby's development, and vice versa—that is, the personality or make-up of the baby also influences the caregiving. It is believed that what the baby experiences early on in life leads to what the child becomes, and it is this belief that is at the heart of the nature–nurture dialogues. There are four models of attachment related to caregiving:

1. *Caregiving (normal development).* The baby grows up in a secure attachment relationship with parents who are predictable, protective, and loving and is then able to internalize this process and become a child who is curious, secure, loving, and able to use his/her intelligence according to his/her possibilities. The child is also able to confront challenge. (See Figure 5.1.)
2. *Scare-giving (hypervigilant development).* There may be a situation where a parent (or both the parents) drinks too much, or takes drugs, or is violent to the other, day after day. The child's needs for growing up safely and being able to trust a person are not formed; instead, the child behaves in an erratic and frightened way and experiences the parents as "scare-givers" (Acquarone, 2004). (See Figure 5.2.)
3. *Little or no caregiving (delayed development).* The third type of attachment behaviour is a subset of the second, but I have chosen to make it a separate category because there are issues of neglect and absence which can be traumatic to a developing child who is eager to relate interpersonally with an active, caring, and loving caregiver. In this category the caregiver might, for example, be extremely depressed and not taking medication and might also be without a partner. Under these circumstances, delayed development can occur, along with failure to thrive. (See Figure 5.3.)

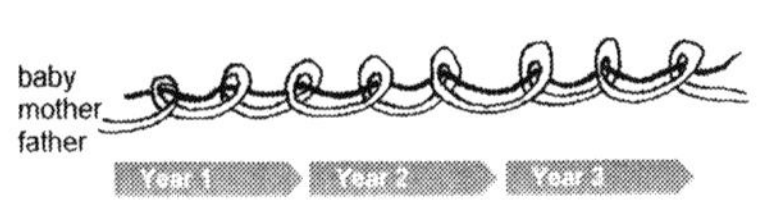

FIGURE 5.1. Caregiving (normal development)

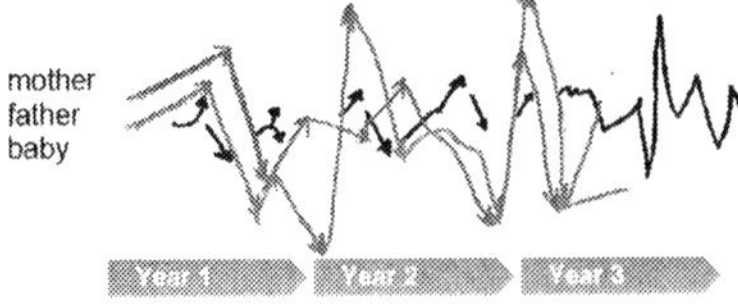

FIGURE 5.2. Scare-giving (hypervigilant development)

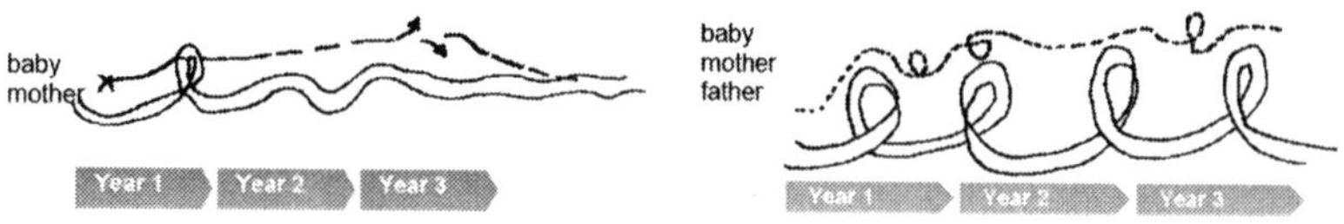

FIGURE 5.3. Little or no caregiving (delayed development)

FIGURE 5.4. Vulnerable infant (deficient development)

4. *Vulnerable infant (deficient development).* In the fourth attachment relationship we find parenting that is caregiving and good enough and yet the parents feel that they are mostly disconnected from and misattuned to their child and are unable to attach to the baby. The child seems not interested or not willing and sometimes is rejecting of the parents, who in turn start feeling not wanted or not good enough for the baby. These babies may be excessive criers, lethargic, easily frustrated, and self-harming. Parents might feel horrified by their impotence or their denial of the problems. (See Figure 5.4.)

There is a strong correlation between the attachment model and brain activity (neural connections), with corresponding effects on the development of emotions and cognition.

Model 1: Caregiving

In the first model we encounter good-enough parents who are responsible, caring about needs, loving, and protective of their newborn, with relatively few mistakes or misunderstandings of their child. There is usually a fairly good capacity to learn from their mistakes, and the parents are intuitively attuned to the baby and to the other members of the family. The parents and other caregivers together form a net of support. The parents are aware of their baby and their baby's feelings. If troubles do arise, they seek to know the cause of the distress and then address their concerns and anxieties. A secure attachment takes place.

Problems may, nevertheless, arise, and these may lead to the establishment of an insecure attachment, especially if the parents do not immediately become aware of these difficulties. If parents ask a health visitor, GP, or other professionals for help, it is a sign of remediation. Early psychodynamic intervention in the form of infant–parent psychotherapy would be timely as it would facili-

Table 5.1: Parenting: Caregiving

RELATIONSHIP	CONSEQUENCE	HELP
Secure attachment: Main feelings: security, joy.	*Normal development:* Promotes brain growth by connecting.	*Insightful type:* Could benefit from early infant–parent psychotherapy.
INSECURE ATTACHMENT: Main feeling: distress in the relationship. Seeks help.	There is brain growth by connecting with upsets.	

tate parenting by providing insight into these circumstances and therefore be advantageous since it will help parents to understand the cause of their difficulty. If the parents search for help early, it is possible that in three to five sessions the new understanding between them will allow for the relationship to become secure again. (See Table 5.1.)

Model 2: Scare-giving

We move now to the *second model* of parent–infant interaction. With unpredictable parenting where domestic violence is involved, the child grows up insecure and frightened of his/her parents or caregivers. Erratic behaviour in the adults does not allow the child to know where, when, and why he/she is going to be assaulted. The child's brain learns to behave in a "flight–fight–freeze" manner. Bruises, burns, and cuts might heal, but the child's emotional and cognitive development is impaired, and later in life his/her

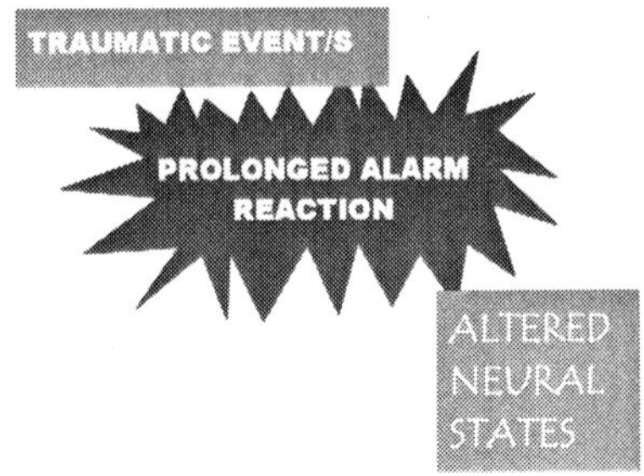

FIGURE 5.5. Maltreatment–neglect. The impact of the deprivation of critical positive experiences during development varies based on onset and duration.

Table 5.2. Parenting: Scare-giving

RELATIONSHIP	CONSEQUENCE	HELP
Traumatized attachment: Main feelings: anger or panic and stress in the relationship. More resilient babies learn to dissociate. *Disorganized/disoriented*	*Hypervigilant development:* Promotes inhibition of positive connections, brain growth of negative connections, hyper-arousal, constriction, and addiction in more resilient babies who learn to dissociate	*Paediatric support & infant-focused therapy:* Could benefit from infant–parent psychotherapy

behaviour becomes centred around escaping, avoiding, ignoring, and dissociating if pain becomes too overwhelming. These children behave in an aggressive, erratic way due to the disruptive aspect of violence and as a consequence of identifying with the aggressor. Main and Cassidy (1988) propose that by the age of 6 years, these infants from homes with domestic violence have developed a control form of reunion behaviour, which is either punitive in nature or caretaking in nature.

Balbernie (2001) maintains that a child who has had traumatic early experiences (such as domestic violence) may display reactions linked to fear, anger, and dissociation, and they may in turn exhibit hyperactivity, aggressiveness (identification with the aggressor), and have difficulties in thinking. Thus, these early experiences will profoundly affect all aspects of their later life.

In these circumstances the kind of attachment that might develop between both the child and the parent would be of an anxious–avoidant nature. In these instances, both the child and the parent would benefit from infant–parent psychotherapeutic intervention. (See Table 5.2.) The parents themselves may have been subjected to so much early trauma that it is a difficult task to make them aware of their own and their child's needs. At the Parent Infant Clinic we have devised specific interventions for this model.

The following vignette highlights the above-mentioned points.

Case example: "Rona"

Background: 6 months old; referred as failure to thrive; low weight (birth weight still held at 6 months old); mother diagnosed with chronic depression; father violent towards mother, baby, social workers, health visitors, and other neighbours and had been in prison because of this. The baby had been hospitalized for a week twice as a precaution against maltreatment from the father.

After multiple referrals from different agencies, our meeting took place at the health centre with two other colleagues (their health visitor and a trainee). The caretaker of the building waited outside the door, since the father had previously assaulted other professionals who had tried to help.

In the first meeting, the father attended with the mother. He was domineering and did not allow the mother of his child to speak, and he issued all kinds of threats to her. He also displayed bizarre behaviour towards the baby—at one stage he hooked the baby from the mouth like a fish and made her walk. The baby was very floppy but reacted in a stiff, startled way to the father's manoeuvres. The baby maintained a grin on her face and had a startled look in her eyes.

I was trying not to feel provoked into acting, judging, advising, or being sick and vomiting. The level of anxiety in me was expressed by the tone of my voice, and by my doubting the extent of the dangerous behaviour I was witnessing. It was as if I was colluding with the father's murderous behaviour, and I felt very frightened as a result of it.

I later observed how the father would hold the baby on the top of his head with one hand, hardly balancing her, and not even looking at what he was doing. He told me that the mother was telling him what to do, when she was a useless nut who every now and then needed a good hiding to shut her up. He said that to be under the cold shower in the summer with the baby for two hours was cool. He laughed in a provocative way. He said he enjoyed having a little soft girl just for himself; however, he would know when and how to punish her if necessary. He said that she needed to learn early that she should not cry with him.

His threatening monologue indicated the insecurity in his relationships and showed how internally he had very threatening internal objects that would not allow vulnerability, and jealousy to be worked out nor reverie to be experienced with his baby. I had not been able to help. His lack of empathy and of attunement to his baby showed dissociation from his own traumatized background and a tremendous fear of losing power. I felt that the priority was the baby, and yet the father needed to feel contained in all his nastiness, without me losing track of the infant.

The mother did not have a chance of emerging next to him. I followed his argument, reflecting and making comments so as not to agree, but creating instead a *third space* for thinking and being firm. I really felt quite nauseous, and I found myself wishing I wasn't there. I felt tormented by the open cruelty and the delicate boundary I needed not to trespass. I was filled with guilt at the end of the consultation, thinking somehow that I had had an opportunity to help the baby but had lost it. Even though we made an appointment for a fortnight's time, I had no hope.

I showed the videotape of the consultation to relevant colleagues in order to help me to understand the anguish produced, and to assist in digesting the experience. By not having been able to deal efficiently with the disturbing situation, I had felt threatened by the father and frightened of being attacked. As a consequence of these strong feelings and the ensuing helplessness, I felt that I had reacted like a coward.

To my surprise, the mother came alone to the second meeting. All the thinking and advice I had about the case just left my conscious mind, and I created a niche for the mother to talk, feel, and just be. I had such a relief that she had come against her partner's wishes, and I realized that she suddenly felt attached to me. I was then able to adopt an analytic stance and once again began able to start thinking. I allowed the mother to set the scene from her side, and she started tentatively to speak about her concerns regarding the effect of the violence on her, and how depressed she had become by her sense of impotence. I felt sympathetic, since I had lived through a bit of the family drama in the previous session. She then expressed intense feelings of despair and fear when she talked about hearing in her fifth month of pregnancy that the baby had a chromosomal defect: chromosome 7 was too short. She told me that this chromosomal abnormality was also present in her first child (now 5 years old), and it had created some mild physical abnormalities and also delayed cognitive development. The father also had this chromosomal abnormality.

The mother was overwhelmed by anxiety, and yet she managed to answer a few questions in relation to her family, her background, and her support system. Although she had parents who lived in the countryside, she was distant emotionally from them as a result of all the conflict with her partner. On the two occasions when her mother tried to help her, around the time of her babies' births, she had found it unhelpful, as her mother was also traumatized by the Caesarean birth, and having to deal with the genetic deformation (extra toe and thumb) and by her violent and unpredictable partner.

I wondered how she had got involved and had stayed with this violent partner, but I did not ask her this. I wanted to start her thinking and tried to validate her feelings as a mother in a way that was not too frightening or intrusive. The baby then started screaming and screeching. It was an awful noise, making it difficult for us to talk. I realized that the mother had learned to ignore, deny, or not attend to the awful requests, and she had also learnt not to show any signs of distress, terror, or abandonment herself.

I started talking softly to the baby: "You would like to be included in our conversation, be part of our nice dance of words, our soft encounter with trying to understand what is happening. You would like to be holding hands and to be with somebody." The baby stopped screaming and looked delighted, and then slowly she began to smile—both at the mother and me.

I said aloud: "We will sit you in your pushchair looking at your mother and me, and we will talk, the three of us. You can tell me how terribly frightened you feel at times, when you don't feel protected and feel horrible because of the shouts, screams, thumps, anger, and sorrow when Mummy is battered, and you are hanging in Daddy's or Mummy's arms not knowing about safety and comfort."

The mother started sobbing and saying that she knew it was bad for the baby, but she had always been hoping that her partner would change as he always promised. I said that she was crying for herself because she becomes so frightened that she freezes, becomes numb, and puts it out of her mind. But it does not go away, it happens again and again. I told her that I thought we should also talk about her ideas about the chromosomal problem and about how much she feels that her children are alien to her and her family, and her feelings about the "monster father", who also had physical signs of the chromosomal abnormality.

The session continued with an extraordinary openness from the mother as to her healthy parts and a curiosity about identifying the personality of the baby for the first time. By addressing the baby's personality and identity, she realized that she did not have a clue about her son's identity.

There seemed to have been an insecure–disordered attachment pattern established, in which the parents had a heightened fear of and/or anger towards the child's attachment behaviour. This leads to a disorganization or abandonment of the caregiving role, and thus caregiving is transformed into scare-giving. This role appears to be related to an ongoing, unresolved trauma in the caregivers. Within this particular case there appeared to be an unresolved oedipal conflict in the mother that made her choose a violent partner and to become stuck in a vicious circle of dissociation, neglect, and guilt.

In her narrative the mother was explicit about her difficulties in having a relationship with both her mother and father. She could only have relationships when only two people were involved—that is, either with the mother or with the father. Attunement and reciprocity needed to be developed, alongside the process of facing her pain in order to restart a circle of security, first with the therapist and then with her own children. It was a challenge to think about how the chaos that prevailed at home could be changed.

We decided to make a therapeutic alliance where we understood that the baby, in her pathetic nonverbal communication, was talking about the story of them: mother and child. We talked about how I was standing for the new development in both of them, thus creating a new relationship that was different from the parental one and yet reflective enough so as to include them as first good objects that somehow had become transformed into persecutory figures by the birth of her children. It seemed that she suffered from jealousy, which had never surfaced or been dealt with before.

After our hour-long meeting, in which mother and baby started playing and cooing on the floor, the child suddenly screamed and needed to be fed. The mother then almost choked the baby with a bottle, as it was given in an uncaring, automatic way. This allowed for further elaboration on her capacity to engage in emotionally cut-off actions, as if there were a deep sense of jealousy in her that had never been looked at. I had the impression that the totalitarian/dictatorial father system at home, which was ingrained with terror and anger, had unconsciously colluded with an immature development of emotions in the mother. This had not been tested much because she was an only child, and both parents had held a unilateral relationship with her and were frightened of her reactions if they provoked her by expression of emotions in front of her.

Shortly after the session, the mother took her two children by herself to her mother's house for a month. During this time away she had begun to discover the individuality of her two children. When she came back her baby had put on weight, and she wanted to explore further the reasons why she was in such an unhappy, violent relationship.

The sessions appeared to have mobilized the mother's emotions alongside many other capacities—especially the capacity to think and to play. These capabilities became entwined in her developing and maturing, newly felt mothering capacity.

A subsequent session involved a family meeting, in which the father was not allowed by the mother to handle the baby and was asked to sit on the side, where he was allowed to speak. The 5-year-old started playing in a cruel way with the baby, and the father began justifying the boy's behaviour. The father said that if the baby fell the boy could not do it again, but if the baby did not fall he could carry on doing it.

The mother got confused. The baby, who had come in looking gorgeous, with a nice age-appropriate expression on her face, crumpled up into a helpless baby. I looked at the mother, who had become frozen again. I mentioned that individual needs were clashing and how the baby could be damaged and that she was not to be a toy for the boy.

Taking into consideration that the father seemed to be handled so well by the mother's newly gained strength and determination, I expected the mother to react well. A short discussion took place with the father, who defended the boy's need to learn to play, but the mother then started doubting herself. The mother picked up the baby, and toys were then brought into the situation (by the therapist) to be used as mediators for the different needs.

The work in the remaining five meetings concentrated on exploring the origin of the mother's masochistic attitude. Consequently, important personal information appeared: she had recently found out while she was with her parents and still in infant–parent psychotherapy with me that they had adopted her immediately after the cot death of their own baby. A whole new unknown story was unfolding, and the only reference was that she must have been overwhelmed as a baby having to change mothers while her adoptive mother was also still grieving. However, the adoptive mother had told her that she had never suffered because she had just replaced one child with another child. I understood how difficult it must have been for this so-called chronically depressed mother to achieve an identity and rights of her own under the circumstance of being a replacement child.

Discussion

I was terrified in the first meeting with this family as I had heard all about the father's physical assaults of professionals involved, his imprisonment for this, and the maltreatment and hospitalization of the baby.

The family was brought in a car by a social worker and their health visitor as the last resource before removing the child from the home. Following the initial consultation, I think that it was my naive (and shocked) open attitude, with my body suffering the suffocation of my anxiety in the face of the abused baby, and holding it all in my mind, that allowed the mother to come back against her husband's wishes not to come back. This was, however, her first step towards becoming independent again and recovering her capacity for thinking and reacting. Only then could the mother begin discovering and reflecting on her own individual experiences.

It was important to hold the intensity of emotions with flexibility and firmness and to keep thinking, and to lean on the psychoanalytic community to help me to hold the deep anxiety I was left with for two weeks. Brazelton and Greenspan (2000) suggest that a parent and child who are at risk should ideally, even before birth, be part of a "village network". I think that the same principle applies to work that psychotherapists undertake with extremely disturbed patients—they need help and support from their colleagues in the psychoanalytic community.

Under this class of violence to babies, with "scare-giving" parenting, I have just described a case of domestic violence that came to receive help because the baby was referred as a "failure to thrive" baby. There are other cases of violence to babies done in other ways: neglect, sexual, verbal, or physical abuse coming from the use of alcohol, drugs, and/or the repetition of trauma by sexually abused parents, victims of incest, perverse parenting which could include rituals of abuse, and, finally, gender mistreatment. All these are also related to what parents may have had to endure themselves and could only pass on in the same way or in even more violent ways in an attempt to resolve the conflicts, pain, and trauma to which they themselves had been exposed.

Domestic violence, for whatever reason, is one of the principal causes of infant death in pregnancy and in the first year of life. The link between spouse abuse and child abuse has always been around 40% to 50%. Browne and Hamilton (1999) confirmed from police records an overlap of 46%. A complex problem seems to exist in care proceedings when the mother, who is the abuser, remains in care of the child. One question is how to measure the protective capacities of the mother or the caregiver who is in a violent relationship, as in the case just presented. The fortnight wait until the next meeting was a torment for me due to my concerns, but the attitude of the mother on her return without the father reassured me that she had been able to develop a protective capacity towards her baby. However, other mothers/carers might not show such a speedy recovery, and in those cases the mother and baby would have to be in a monitored environment if they wanted to be together, and this is especially important if there are no clear signs of mother (or caregiver) being able to exercise protection.

Help then takes the form of helping mother to attach to her child in the midst of her numbness created by the violent partner. The metaphor is that the mother needs to have a new development with the therapist that would then become a model for her to be used with her child (if she had an abusive childhood) or to sew back on her model of attachment if it has become detached by trauma. In the case discussed above, the trauma could be seen as being married to such a violent partner.

There is a subgroup in this model—
that is, war, rape, and babies.

Under this topic, I remember chronicles about civil and other wars where babies, children, and teenagers are not spared from all kinds of atrocities. I shall consider here the after-effects of rape, including rape by several soldiers, and the state of mind that the woman is left in—not just by the fact of becoming pregnant and not knowing who the father is, but that the face of the child might be of the father if the baby doesn't look like her or her family.

Bonnet (1992), in a study about mothers who abandon their children in the streets or public places or who kill their babies, discovered a history of neglect or abuse in their childhood which became reactivated by the presence of the foetus in pregnancy. This abuse was often connected to sexuality and sexual pleasures. This past would intrude in their mind, producing uncontrollable anguish and panic, and thus they were not able to distinguish well between their past and the foetus present in their womb. As a result of this, they often decided to eliminate the baby as a concrete act in order to attempt to eliminate the past.

In my experience there is another way of understanding the hate and wishes to kill a baby, and this is related to a traumatic event or events in the present or immediate past—not necessarily the childhood experiences as is usually emphasized.

The following vignette is from my work with refugees.

Case example: "Maria"

Maria, who was 20 years old and single, was the mother of a 4-year-old girl, "Carmen". Maria was pregnant with a second child. Carmen didn't speak. Maria did not speak any English. The adult psychiatric department at the hospital referred her to me, as they were worried about the quality of her mothering. She seemed not to have any memory of her past. The department assumed she was of South American origin as she had been met at the airport by a Peruvian person and brought to the hospital requesting asylum. I am South American and was thus approached to try to help.

I did three home visits with the mother, child, and social worker until I established a relationship, and then the mother came ten more times to the hospital. Each time she was brought by a taxi and a social worker.

I didn't know what to say or ask, so I spoke in Spanish softly about the horrors that she must have lived through and that perhaps she wasn't sure whether she was in a safe place, and whether I was going to keep information to myself or tell others.

She cried, while Carmen played well in the room. Suddenly Carmen played out a tragic scene of a woman being battered, with screams from everybody, and a child crying over a dead body. There were big, nasty men all around. Maria, the mother suddenly starting talking clearly in Spanish, saying that her daughter was helping her to remember what she couldn't.

Maria started sobbing and said she remembered a horrible bit of her past. She was kidnapped for ransom and raped. The kidnappers did not want to give her up and she was held clandestinely for four years, where she found herself always running in panic and blindfolded. She thought she lived in hell with her beautiful daughter, who was the daughter of one of her captors, probably the chief. One day, after a police raid, when shots were fired, mother and daughter were found and sent to England. She could not remember details. In the shooting, she herself was also shot. Maria had no idea what had happened to her family. She also did not know who sent her to England, and this still remains a mystery.

Both mother and daughter were suffering from severe posttraumatic-stress disorder, and they clearly needed more help than I could offer. There were several stages to fulfil. I had to unfold her story, and she needed to work through it. Both Carmen and her pregnant mother needed care and an inner working-through of their trauma. Afterwards, there would be a need to find her family and heal the breaks in family relationships as a consequence of time and war. They went to a protected sheltered accommodation for women and babies, which offered supportive therapy. I remained available and did follow-ups.

The early silence in the sessions was real, and not self-imposed. It came from the aberration of shame, hurt, trauma, pain, and the many horrors suffered. The many professional services available to her were also paralysed, as they identified with the numbness of the suffering. Empathy probably was the first rudimentary bridge that needed to be built, with humility towards what to do being the second, coupled with being patiently available for the actual walking over the bridges. We still have a lot to learn about how to approach pain in a realm that we know so little about and where the horror produces—both in the client and in the therapist—a physical and mental paralysis or a wish to run away.

Model 3: Little or no caregiving

In the third model the situation may be one of an extremely depressed mother on her own, and the initiatives of the infant to seek adult responses are not met. It is also common that the infant's physiological needs are not met either. These infants may feel the pain of hunger, cold, dirty nappies, and not having their cries attended to. The baby is growing without emotional, cognitive, sensory, motor, and other stimulation, and the brain cells do not get connected as they should; consequently there is a loss of neural growth at a vital stage of development. Usually failure to thrive sets in, and this is then picked up by health visitors or GPs. Also, as Murray, Cooper, Wilson, and Romaniuk (2003) have shown, development is delayed. (See Table 5.3.) In extreme cases, babies might die if health visitors or other professionals do not discover them in time. The fact that the mother or family does not care creates a child who, if he/she survives, may never be equipped for the challenges of life unless he/she is removed from the home and helped.

Case example: "Stacey"

Stacey, 6 months old, whose mother was chronically depressed and agoraphobic, was referred because she was at a seriously low weight and weighed less than she had at birth. My early

Table 5.3. Parenting: Little or no caregiving

RELATIONSHIP	CONSEQUENCE	HELP
Little or no attachment: Little or no relationship. *Ambivalently attached:* Some children develop ADHD.	*Delayed development:* Little brain growth (unless very resilient). (Hospitalization or the like) Emotional and cognitive delay.	*Paediatric support & infant-focused psychotherapy to the mother and infant:* Could benefit from infant–parent psychotherapy.

intervention had to be in the mother's flat because she did not want to leave her home. I had only six sessions in which to generate an interest in the mother's emotional and mental state and that of her baby. In the first session the baby was lying flat in a pushchair with a grin on her face, with a rag doll lying on top of her. Slowly, the baby started moving her weak limbs and eagerly paid attention to my words, actions, and expressions. I asked the mother to pick Stacey up, and it became evident that she really didn't know how to pick up or hold her baby. The mother continued to hold her baby like a sack of potatoes. I commented about the baby's individual features.

Over the six-week period I related to the baby with warmth and love, feeling the huge deprivation, neglect, and abused self in the baby that was deprived of any substantial caring. I continued to work consistently and empathically with the mother as well.

The success in this treatment was due to an attachment that the mother was able to make to me, which revived the long-hidden despair in which she was deeply immersed. This put the mother in touch with the source of her pain and longing, and this then allowed her to give and to receive love in the relationship with her little, live baby. I felt the urgent need to address the almost dying baby in her hands and link this to the inner baby in herself that felt like dying due to the abuse she had experienced.

I understand paediatric support to be a kind of infant–parent psychotherapy, which is focused on picking up on the individual needs of the infant and explaining them to the mother. This is done while mothering the mother, in order that she begins to feel the love and care she never had (Acquarone, 2004). In this model of attachment, it is also possible to include children who could develop attention deficit hyperactive disorder as a consequence of not having felt a container for their anxieties in an active caregiver and who, instead, create a body boundary in the development of movement.

Model 4: Vulnerable infant

In the fourth model of parent–infant relationships, I explore babies who are at risk of developing autistic tendencies or Asperger's, or who are withdrawn or psychotic. In this instance the parents or caregivers are good-enough but the infant is difficult to understand or it is difficult to meet his/her needs because of a number of the following features: a complicated mind, strong aggressive tendencies or very subtle tendencies, unknown sensibilities (e.g. relating to touch, hearing, bad sense of balance, low tolerance of frustration, being too jealous, too possessive, too greedy, etc.), auditory or visual impairments, lack of good balance, very sensitive skin, or difficulties in introjecting goodness that would help with the necessary integration of experiences. The actual experiences the babies may be having might be completely different from the ones that we think they are having, and instead they then might feel tortured (by pain and confusion) by the loving parents. (See Table 5.4.)

The parents, though they may be good enough, cannot attach to the baby because they feel the baby's rejection or pain when connected, and thus they start to distance themselves and lose interest. These parents fear not understanding their child and often try to have another child in the hope that the new child will be more rewarding. The difficult child then gets lost in the parent's own emotional and sometimes cognitive development. Here we find that good-enough parenting is somehow not able to match the child's needs. The parents often feel strange, and sometimes anxious, about not knowing their child. This anxiety is increased by all the different opinions they hear about what to do, the labels that are attached, and the indifference they may at times encounter from professionals and family alike. An early psychoanalytic intervention established at this stage would aim to discover and understand these personal traits and ways of functioning with the mother or caregiver in order to avoid any delays in development due to uncontrolled violence against themselves or others. Early intervention

Table 5.4. Parenting: Vulnerable infant

RELATIONSHIP	CONSEQUENCE	HELP
No attachment: Distraught relationship	*Deficient development:* Little brain growth of positive experiences. Brain growth of self-comforting and stereotypic behaviours Apparent delay, becoming deficiency	*Immediate infant focused therapy with parents & siblings:* Could benefit from infant–parent psychotherapy Important to intervene early & skilfully

would also prevent these infants from being included in the autistic spectrum of disorders and therefore not being interested in relating to their parents or others. In these cases, emotional experience within the infant is not digested, elaborated, or integrated, and thus a deficient development takes place.

Violence from babies

The hypothesis that I have formed as a result of many baby observations is that some babies are born more aggressive, more irritable, more greedy, or more needy and possessive than others. Often the negative characteristics in a baby are attributed to conflicting projections coming from the parents, rather than from the individual babies themselves. It is a complex and difficult hypothesis to pursue as it seems difficult to accept that some babies are made more vulnerable by their innate tendencies. It is possible that if these innate tendencies are not contained they could lead to self-destruction; however, through specialized work they might be contained and thus the baby helped.

If a baby is irritable, acts uncaringly, and transmits anger, frustration, and rage most of the time, the mother or caregiver will need extra support from the partner, family, and friends in order to cope. The baby is likely to feel more fear than usual, due to the uneasiness that is provoked, and he/she might enter into a state of panic if left alone. In a panic state, the baby's level of adrenaline would be very high, and a vicious cycle of behaviours and emotions may start to develop. It is possible that anger and rage that is not contained might go into bodily movements for discharge, as a result of too much negative energy accumulating in the little body.

Observations show that there are babies who from birth can suck their thumb or hand if hungry and who are thus able to comfort themselves as they wait for a feed or to be held, whereas there are others (classified by Chess & Thomas, 1984) who have short quick tempers, are irritable or hypersensitive, and may have a tendency to react strongly for longer than expected. They usually express anger and overwhelming anxiety. Some good-enough parents find parenting this kind of baby very difficult and frustrating, and if they can afford it emotionally, they usually find themselves secretly hating the baby.

Some babies awake in their parents more despair and negative feelings than is "normal", and there is then an important role to be played by the extended family, groups, or friends by supporting the parents and thus allowing them to re-energize and recharge themselves emotionally. Psychoanalysis understands the process of parenting as creating new attachments and a relationship with the newborn, which also creates a reactivation of past experiences in the parents that colours the quality of their new experience.

When the bond between parent and child is mainly positive and creative, the past positive experiences become reinforced and development occurs in the line of a happy life with an inherent richness of feelings. Conversely, when the experience becomes frustrating, tiring, or over-exhausting from the supremacy of negative experiences, this reactivates negatives experiences from the parent's past. Continuous anger, misunderstanding, and misattunement, in addition to other demands, may trigger negative relatedness with the child.

There is another hypothesis that suggests that the difficulties never actually start in the child but, rather, within the parents, who may project their traumatic past, hidden feelings, and unresolved conflicts into the child. I would like, however, to continue trying to understand how to be able to accept and think about behaviours that are present in some babies from birth, and how these behaviours seem to be overwhelming for both them and their parents. This is a very important area to understand, as it is these various behaviours and interactions that mould the quality of the attachment relationship. It may then even be possible to understand the complexity of anorexia, extreme anger, continuous despair, and self-harming behaviours in babies.

Information from neuroscience

Neuroscientific evidence presented by Schore (1994, 2000) and Panksepp (1998) shows that anger is located in the amygdala, which itself belongs to the primitive, reptilian brain, and observations show that a newborn baby will tend to react in a massive, unregulated way if not emotionally attended to. The cortex and neocortex perform the function of containing emotion, and the regulation and the stimulation of these in a baby needs the presence a constant, attuned caregiver. This ensures that the emotions can be felt and eventually named, recognized, and managed.

It could well be that a traumatic experience for the immature newborn may result in the baby being overwhelmed by rage or frustration at the beginning of external life, which becomes all too much to deal with. We can therefore imagine how overwhelmed and traumatized an infant may be who doesn't feel contained firmly by his parents but feels left to the destructive tendencies all by him/herself. Bick (1968) talks about the need that some infants have in creating through their continuous movement a second skin that would serve as a container for the psyche, when the mother's emotional or psychological holding is not enough. Bick explains how a mother suffering from depression may not be able to offer optimal care to her baby. I would also include here situations in which parents are not able to contain their infant because they feel overpowered by their babies, or because they become frightened by what they feel towards their infant.

In this way, it is possible to think about how exacerbated anger could initiate a vicious cycle through the experience of lack of containment and not enough holding or love. The void can then become internally persecutory for the baby, and sometimes even externally persecutory if the infant feels that the mother has become damaged or affected by the baby's own rage. Thus in the absence of containment from a carer, the baby may feel at the mercy of his/her own uncontained, primitive anger, and fury.

Studies from the field of genetics and temperament show that different traits are associated with individual differences. Calkins and Fox (1994) identified a relationship between attachment classifications and later behaviour towards novel events. They found that a relationship existed between early irritability and insecure attachment with behavioural inhibition in toddlerhood. Kagan and Snidman (1991) found that infants who displayed high amounts of negative affects and of motor activity in response to novel stimuli tended to be fearful at 9 and 14 months of age. Furthermore, Zuckerman (1994) studied a specific trait called impulsive unsocialized sensation seeking (ImpUSS). Chronic criminality is often an expression of an antisocial personality disorder and thus may represent the extreme manifestation of the ImpUSS trait. Zuckerman maintains that the ImpUSS trait has strong heritability links and that it appears at the upper range of what is usually considered typical for personality traits.

Last but not least, Badcock (2000), an evolutionary psychologist, talks about genetic conflict occurring intrapsychically in the brain of the infant from its early formations. Badcock proposes that the cortex is created exclusively by maternal genes, while the limbic system (which has a capacity to motivate behaviours) is produced by paternal genes.

Studies from my own clinical research on excessive crying in infants identified a kind of infant who did not smile, even by the age of 6 months (Acquarone, 1994). These infants had no means of expressing their distress other than through crying. They seemed to remain stuck in the most primitive expression of disconnection, and thus it made it difficult for them to attach to a maternal figure that would be able to facilitate development and growth. These children demonstrated a disturbed pattern of behaviour after the age of 1 year, and they tended to use dissociation or transformation of experience into various self-harming behavioural patterns.

After extensive work with infants (4,120 cases of infant–parent work, 20 years of infant observation, and work with 600 two-year-olds and their mothers) I hypothesize that a baby may feel traumatized not only by what has been inflicted on her/him from the environment, but also by the *perception* of hurt, which forms an internal representation in his or her mental apparatus.

The value of research into experiences of trauma, whether from an external or an internal source, will help us to better understand the importance that *individuality* plays in the recovery from or treatment of violence. Once a persecutory phantasy has formed and is linked to guilt towards the harmful object, then overwhelming anger, rage, or anxiety that is not contained becomes split off. The vicious cycle that ensues between the baby and the mother needs to be addressed and explored alongside the equally eroding effects of the unknown sensibilities and vulnerabilities.

The birth of siblings, or disturbed siblings, accidents, and surgery may also promote early stressful overstimulation for an infant. The experience of strong negative feelings will block the capacity to form a healthy relationship with the mother. Here the infant may not find the mother to be helpful or caring, and he/she may then experience persecution and abandonment to the frightening inner, raw expressions of sensations/feelings.

If an infant has not been able to attach to his mother or caregiver, the infant could develop antisocial behavioural patterns later on, since lack of attachment does not allow the child to feel loved nor to love themselves. That might still be the case if the difficulty *is in the child* and not just in the mother or father. It is then possible to think of the subtle causes that might not allow certain babies to form a relationship with their caregivers that would make them feel safe and protected.

I wonder whether in this category there are children who have loving parents and yet their sense of merging with their parents at the beginning of life is with such catastrophic, negative feelings of hate, destructiveness, and fear that it is possible that they "fear" destroying the parents with their destruction and their fear, and they therefore keep a safe distance or distort the communication in order to protect what they feel are vulnerable or not strong-enough parents. Here I am referring to some children in the spectrum of communication disorders and psychotic disorders. These proposals result from clinical work that I have been doing with two psychotic 4 years olds who have been in treatment with me for several years.

Case example: "Baptiste"

Background: 2½ years old; baby brother, 1 month old; sister, 7 years old; professional married parents in their late twenties; Caucasian; British.

Baptiste was brought to the consultation because he was wildly hitting his baby brother. He was very expressive verbally, and he said he wanted to kill his brother like an ant. Baptiste had only one milk tooth because he had lost all the others in accidents or falls. He had no neurological problems and had been seen by various specialists with regards to probable physical problems, but nothing organic had been found. He had been expelled from five nurseries by the age of 2 years because of his hyperactivity and nastiness towards other children.

The parents, and in particular the mother, had had a good experience with the first-born, five years previously. They recalled that this child had been a very alert, calm girl who seemed to know what she wanted, and the mother could satisfy her needs easily and also enjoyed her.

Baptiste was born two years after he had been planned, and the family was overjoyed with the birth of a beautiful baby boy. Baptiste, however, showed different traits from the beginning—he was inconsolable, would scratch his face, would making grunting noises, was very uneasy, and didn't form rhythms for sleeping and eating. His caregivers and others felt irritated and annoyed by these features that created a very demanding and difficult baby.

The formerly joyful parents were pretty soon overcome by frustration, by lack of sleep, and by being unable to console an excessively crying infant who could not be satisfied for very long and wanted or needed constant attention. He liked to be breastfed on demand and for a long time; his mother felt that, at least then, he was quiet and seemingly happy. The mother felt that breastfeeding was an enjoyable activity for both her and her son. She noticed that he tended to be at the breast for very long times. After 6 months, it started to be extremely difficult for the mother, and she thus introduced bottles at night so that she would be able to rest on alternate nights.

Her own mother had remarried, to a retired man, and she had decided to go to live in Bali and did not come to either of her grandchildren's births. When I asked the mother how she felt about this, she replied that she did not mind as she felt more comfortable with the presence of her husband at the births rather than her mother.

The mother explained that her father's second wife lived around the corner from them, and she was very helpful and was a keen substitute for the missing real grandmother. The maternal grandfather was also around, with or without his wife. He was helpful to the mother. The father also had parents in England who were willing to help. The whole family was helpful in the first months following the birth of Baptiste. They all agreed that he was difficult and angry and that he cried continuously and would scratch himself. As a result of the dangerous scratching, he started to wear mittens.

At the time of being weaned he began spitting, and he seemed to enjoy upsetting everyone with this behaviour. Everyone was warned of his scratching, biting, and other nasty behaviours. They tried to ignore his difficult behaviour and reward his calmness and smiles, but everybody was irritated and worried about him. As soon as he walked he was gone wherever possible, so they thought of a taking him to toddler groups. In these groups, he was aggressive with adults and children, and he was expelled from two groups. At 2 years of age he had a place in a nursery, but he could not stay with other children or with teachers.

With his older sister he was as aggressive as with other people, and very soon the sister learnt to avoid him and she started asking mother for another sibling.

At the family consultation, Baptiste would knock himself and throw blows at his baby sister and made the big sister cry. By then the parents were exhausted and worried. They felt as if they had a little criminal and a crazy little person with them; the last incident was with the grandfather at a fairground, where he threw himself from the roundabout when it was going and broke the rest of his teeth! At the meeting he had fierce, angry feelings about the baby, and he behaved like a wild, fierce little child.

Family history revealed that mother and father had met at university at the age of 18 and started a relationship that ended in a happy marriage. Both families were similar in background and composition, and there had been four siblings in each family. However, mother felt very rebellious in her adolescence because she was the eldest and had to fight for her rights to be trusted and to go out late with boys, and so on. Her parents divorced when she was 16, and both remarried five and six years later. There were no acrimonious fights or reproaches, but just an end to the love and interest in each other. The father's family had stayed together and was average in their family disagreements.

The mother felt that the constant care, and the rare and aggressive personality of the baby, had changed her considerably. She had to be on guard as to how she treated her son, and she said she found that all her attention was focused either on his behaviour or on the consequences of his behaviour. She was becoming mistrustful and at times tired and depressed. She was learning to make compromises, and she started not going out unless she had a babysitter. She felt that she was attending less to her daughter and that she did not have any activity or time of her own. She had been told that that was usual at the beginning with a demanding baby, but she felt that it had all continued for too long and he was still not normal.

The plan of action was for individual psychotherapy three times a week and weekly meetings between the parents and another psychotherapist to examine, discuss, and create the parenting style that would suit this particular child.

The treatment of Baptiste took five and a half years. The main themes that emerged in the therapy were his tremendous jealousy of others, his symbiotic attachment to his mother, his fear of separation, and his strong reactive system, which was embedded in panic and dread. He seemed unable to use his memory of past good experiences when he had to wait, and thus he would become excessively upset.

Other elements important to note with Baptiste was his way of relating to everyone—this was at a very primitive, newborn level, rather than in any mature or age-appropriate way. It seemed as if he was stuck at a continuous early developmental level that I would refer to as newborn.

Whenever there was an obvious change of space and place with stimulation of all senses and a need to adapt, Baptiste found it impossible to adapt. He started with regulatory problems that everybody in the family had tried to help with.

These were good-enough parents within a relatively healthy family, and there were no apparent traumatic experiences. The depressive, exhausted mood in the mother seemed to be a consequence of dealing day after day with a child who seemed to find it impossible to internalize any goodness of experiences and who always wanted more. The greed was manifested in the breastfeeding and keeping mother for himself for as long as he could. The climate of peace was reminding him of the complete unity of the womb, and he could not mourn its loss and move on with "meeting the mother and the others". He could only be in the mother or nothing. Baptiste's pain or impossibility of separation was shown in the hatred displayed towards himself and others.

In the sessions for the first six months, he would cry inconsolably, like he did in the first year of his life. To be with him for just an hour was difficult and it left me with all the sorrow of his initial loss. Session after session he would just cry and eventually cuddle in my lap, sobbing. His aggression towards himself and me were restricted by actively stopping him and talking or singing. Puppets and teddy bears became important elements of softness to his hardened self. His only toy or favourite one (his parents bought many) was a fire engine, about 30 cm long, which was hard, red, and had wheels. He brought this toy, and we kept it on a shelf. He wanted fire engines of any size and material. Storybooks had to have fire engines to interest him. I accepted his constant alarm, and his need to calm deadly anxieties or anxieties about being burnt in his own feelings of rage and uncontainable (possessive) love.

In the following year, when he was 3 to 4 years old, he would express his pleasure in hurting himself by picking on scabs and blackmailing me about letting him go, so that he could do as he pleased. He acted wildly on walls and furniture. The sessions were torturous times for him and me, but I knew he needed to show me the full extent of his inner fury.

We had talked with him until the end of his treatment about a kind of disability he had. I told him that I could understand that everybody was asking him to control himself and yet he had no capacity for doing this.

During many sessions, he learnt to describe what was happening when he "lost it". It was decided with the parents to allow him to attend a school with a nursery that I knew accepted and liked some special-needs, intelligent children. There were four children in a class and two teachers. Working with the school became part of our network, and once a term we had a meeting mainly to hear about him socially and to help in thinking about his needs and behaviours.

The parents brought Baptiste for treatment regularly, and the system worked smoothly. Baptiste started to be able to change and to have fewer incidents, and he was able to move to a level of verbalization, and thus, finally, a reflective self was able to start to develop.

The next period was characterized by his identification with his father and finding sexuality unbearable. The quality of his attachment had changed, however, to a more secure one, but he was still overwhelmed by his sexuality. He wanted to be the sexual partner of his mother and get rid of father. He became extremely aggressive with his father and hurt him as much as he could. He would shout and scream at him in a threatening way and would often hit himself. Terror evolved again, in a form somewhat similar to the beginning, but it was now on verbal terms and was part of the same drama that had not been acknowledged before. Father had been the first third between mother and him. The symbiotic attachment to his mother might have been a consequence of his not being able to accept the third, and the excessive continuous crying an impossible mourning of his deepest desires. It was also as if the hate he felt towards himself and others had become a self-soothing mechanism.

Treatment finished after five and a half years, and he then presented as a shy or "careful" boy, who went to a state school with thirty children in a class. He has two or three friends that come to his house and he goes to theirs. His teachers love him because he is bright and helpful towards other less able children in the class. I did follow-ups every three months during the first year after the ending of the therapy, and then every six months in the second and third year. These follow-ups took place following a request that came from Baptiste himself. He is now 25 years old, has finished university, and is a caring professional who is on the shy side and insightful of his feelings.

Discussion

I came to the conclusion that I had to accept and explore with Baptiste what was not working, and where and how I was to help.

I realized that he had an almost ideal situation with regards to his family background and that the horrors of his emotions were so overwhelming that it was as if we were discovering an innate deficit. To acknowledge this had meant we had to enter into a difficult situation where his emotions had to be transferred to me. His internal objects were as persecutory and terrifying as if he had been sexually or physically abused from birth, because he did not have the capacity to internalize any goodness that could help him to integrate experiences. He didn't see a loving mother with breasts to satisfy his needs; all he was seeing was a depriving mother that had made him leave her womb and put him in a world full of light, temperatures, sounds, and other distracting loves and occupations. He had a nasty mother in his mind that produced hunger, pain, and discomfort. The remedy of being held in her arms, resting and loving the peace, and feeling satisfied when fed or consoled seemed not to count, nor to stay for long in his memory. Instead, what seemed to stay was the irritation at his mother for her causing unease in the separation, or in the awakening of needs that stayed and filled him with bad internal objects that could not be integrated and thus had to be projected onto other people. He felt there was no value inside himself, and he felt full of bad things that in a repetitive way created a vicious circle of explosive anger and deadly persecution. These unintegrated strong affects and anxieties hindered all aspects of his development.

What helps the integration of affects is the primacy of the positive emotions in healthy development. If we can hypothesize that the baby perceives the mother in the moments of anger as depriving, and in the moments of feeling hunger or cold or being anxious as hurting himself, his/her brain becomes accustomed to the stimulation of negative circuits, and consequently the amygdala remains continually reactivated by the internal repetition of the perception of the violence felt inside.

Another hypothesis could be that some babies are born with needs that are very strong, or that go on despite satisfaction—it is as if having their needs met is not enough and this is felt to be unbearable.

(As an aside, when one realizes how the visual apparatus functions at birth and for the first three months, it is possible to wonder whether this could be the origin of monster-like figures. People or objects that are not at a 30 cm distance from babies who are 0 to 3 months old remain blurred in their vision. It is interesting to speculate whether this blurred vision and an experience of dread of the unknown, external world is what produces the bizarre images that appear in delusions or nightmares.)

Conclusion

In this chapter I have tried to explore how violence may appear in infancy, from the parents, from the environment, or from the innate tendencies of some babies. The hypothesis that I hold is related to becoming aware that individual, early assessment of babies could be of enormous benefit to parents so that they may begin to understand their newborn better, particularly if the newborn is struggling with their loving care. I have presented four ways in which parents and infants may relate and develop an attachment that can be helpful. The associated case examples given will hopefully generate further discussion and thinking.

The unmanageable behaviour of some infants from early on may have internal causes, one of them being related to the expression of genes from the different parents, and another being related to different parts of the brain that need to be integrated. Until the neuro-psychological integration takes place, there is a constant generation of unease and conflict.

Another internal factor is the expression of a trait in the genes related to impulsivity and sensation seeking. A high level of this trait might have been involved in the past with hunting, exploration of new territory, and enhancing acquisition of resources essential for survival and reproductive purposes and associated with an evolutionary advantage (Zuckerman, 1994). However, having too high levels of this trait would have been maladaptive. Calkins and Fox (1994), in discussing the complexity of biological predisposition and its link in predicting early behavioural tendencies, suggests that "the biology–environment relationship is characterized by the dynamic interaction of the two, as opposed to one forced or subjugated to the other" (p. 210).

Recovery from the numbness created by an excess of violence in the home, either from domestic violence or having a baby with innate, excessive tendencies that need to be regulated and sometimes modified, lies in the creation of a meaningful relationship with mother and baby; from this, it is possible to understand the cause of the violent behaviour in the child or baby and help him/her to regulate his/her reactions in a manner that is not harmful to him/herself or to others.

I have created a method of supporting couple relationships that have a history of domestic violence by interrupting the cycle of abuse by the integration of the traumatizing event or the individual characteristics of the baby and by providing psychological support whereby personal needs are acknowledged. Containing the mother's anxieties can thus in turn help the mother to contain her baby's anxieties. Integral to this process is helping the mother to develop self-esteem and confidence alongside helping her accept her baby's individuality. The mother is encouraged to notice her infant's positive aspects and is helped to understand and contain the excessive feelings of her infant and thus prevent the development of violent behaviour.

CHAPTER FIVE

Non-retaliation: surviving a violent 5-year-old

Camilla Sim

The impulsive and destructive behaviour of 5-year-old "Dan" was bringing him close to permanent exclusion from school. This chapter describes my therapeutic work with him that took place within a behavioural unit attached to his school. Dan was prone to violent behaviour both within the therapy room and outside it in the unit and the school. In the room he would hit and stab me with a plastic sword, pour water over me, and test every boundary there was. His violence is thought about within the context of having an abusive, neglectful mother and a violent and sporadically absent father. Issues around gender, omnipotence, control, fear, and helplessness were important themes in our work together.

Throughout his therapy Dan "acted out" rather than "thought about" the intolerably painful feelings in his mind, and it was only in the very last few sessions that he felt contained enough to begin to allow space for reflection. According to Winnicott (1962), if a child cannot think, he tends to react. The child that cannot think is at the mercy of "unthinkable anxiety" (Winnicott, 1962, p. 57) and experiences the smallest frustration as a threat—a "threat of annihilation" (Winnicott, 1956, p. 303). My aim was to keep thinking about his violent outbursts and to try not to react or retaliate.

Dan seemed to lack a consistent, reliable, and containing parent that could be internalized. Winnicott (1971a) writes about the importance of the mother's capacity for mirroring her baby. When the baby looks in his mother's face he sees a reflection of himself. A receptive mother responds to the baby using touch, sounds, and gestures. She synchronizes her behaviour with her baby, and this in turn matches the infant's inner states. The baby feels thought about and thus "psychologically held", and the repeated experience of being thought about in turn develops the baby's ability to think.

Dan did not have the experience of a thoughtful mind to help him to process strong feelings. If a mother cannot bear to see or think about her child, the child then cannot also bear to think. Instead, in an attempt to get rid of his anxiety he may retreat to behavioural measures such as kicking, screaming, and biting. Dan was still using his body to express his internal world. He had a behavioural solution to his psychological difficulties. Without someone to receive his communications the child does not get a sense of himself, and this poses developmental problems. Fonagy and Target (1999) propose that the inability to "mentalize" contributes to the violent tendency. By "mentalize" they mean perceiving or interpreting the actions of others as intentional (Fonagy et al., 2002) or thought about. In discussing a violent patient Fonagy and Target write: "Where in his mother's mind there should have been a child with thoughts and feelings, there was too often emptiness, a space, nothing on which he could build a viable sense of himself as thinking, believing or desiring" (Fonagy & Target, 1999, p. 62).

Panksepp's (1998) work on the biochemistry of the brain (further elucidated by Sunderland, 2002) is particularly helpful in thinking about Dan. I needed to use my own frontal lobe to find words so that he could begin to process experiences using his frontal lobe rather than acting out from the more primitive part of the brain. This primitive part of the brain is linked to the fight-or-flight response when the brain is in a high state of arousal. Brain scans have shown that with violent men the primitive part of the brain is constantly aroused (Raine, Stoddard, Bihrle, & Buchsbaum, 1998).

It is possible that most of the time the primitive part of Dan's brain was aroused, which meant he had less ability to think or use symbols (which is linked to frontal-lobe activity). He responded through action rather than thought, and his capacity to use his own intelligent processes declined. I tried to use short, simple sentences in order to begin the work of modulating his physiological and psychological highly aroused states.

Dan's father was known to be violent, and Dan had witnessed his father hitting his mother. I imagined that he had also been a victim of his father's aggression, and perhaps of his mother's too. Such experiences of terror and helplessness can lead a child to "identify with the aggressor" (Fraiberg, Adelson, & Shapiro, 1975), where the child starts acting like the aggressor, in order to feel less scared. If a child does not have a role model for the healthy expression of conflict and aggression, normal anger then becomes terrifying; as a result, anger can build up inside, and this can eventually erupt in a violent outburst.

Dan's experience of having an absent father further contributed to Dan's problems. He had no experience of having someone who provided a positive, ongoing relationship with his mother, and I wondered whether this made it difficult to think of himself in relation to his mother, as he had not developed a sense of separateness from her. In turn, he was not provided with a "good-enough experience" of being cared for.

During our work together I also wondered about his prenatal experiences. Statistics show that domestic violence increases in pregnancy (Brown, 2002). Brown considers whether the mother's preoccupation with her unborn baby may trigger in the father primitive feelings of rivalry, which unleash overwhelming feelings of abandonment and betrayal. He also shows that the battered foetus has a greater risk of infection and ruptured membranes and that the stress of the mother is transmitted to the baby. Of course, one can only speculate that this may have been Dan's experience. However these thoughts were particularly poignant in my mind, as in the third month of our work together I became pregnant.

In terms of attachment, Dan's unpredictable behaviour could be classified as disorganized (Main & Solomon, 1990), which is linked to a high risk of psychopathology. Children with such classifications show an intense need to control their environment, and in our sessions this was a constant theme. If a child has no pattern of safety, which involves another person, they try to control their environment instead. If the adult whom they go to for security abuses them, they are then left in a state of helpless dependency and confusion. In Dan's case, if his mother was physically abusing him, then the person he loved the most would also be the person who hit him the most. This would then leave him in a world where for him it would be acceptable to hit others.

The children's classic *Where the Wild Things Are* (Sendak, 1963) has often been used to think therapeutically about children (Daws, 1985; Phillips, 1999; Raphael-Leff, 2003). In this story a little boy called Max is naughty and gets sent to bed without his supper. His room turns into a wild forest and he goes to the land of the wild things. He joins these wild things and becomes their king. He roars and stomps and gnashes his teeth and then roars and stomps some more. Finally he has had enough, and he sends the wild things off to their beds. He then feels lonely and wants to "be where someone loved him best of all" (Sendak, 1963 p. 29). Then from far away "he smelled good things to eat", and so he goes home and finds his supper waiting for him. Max is lucky because he has a Mummy who loves him despite his wildness. It seems to me, however, that Dan was stuck in the "land of the wild things" because his Mummy could not tolerate this "wildness". There was no one to contain his rage and process these overwhelming emotions.

Winnicott's (1956a) understanding of delinquency as a sign of hope is extremely helpful in understanding some of the complex processes that are involved in working with and trying to understand violent children. The delinquent child is looking outwards to society to replace that which they have lost inside. They still have some hope of rediscovering a "good-enough mother". Some children cry out for what should be their right, and too often the response is punishment and exclusion. Acting out in this way stops learning (Decker, Kirby, Greenwood, & Moore, 1999; Salzberger-Wittenberg, Williams, & Osborne, 1983) and has a huge impact on all the other children in terms of bullying in the playground and teachers being monopolized by the few who are being disruptive.

In this chapter I also think about a child's violence as a way of trying to enter into the mind of the other. Perhaps Dan thought that violence was the only way he could be held in mind. Despite writing about this case several years later, I still vividly remember my work with him.

Referral, setting, and contract

The work took place in a specialist behaviour unit that was attached to a primary school. Within this setting a small group of children spent mornings in the unit and afternoons in the school. Research carried out by Target and Fonagy (1994) has shown the efficacy of working with children aged 8 years and under. Pre-latency children are old enough to express themselves verbally but are young enough to be still orientated towards home life rather than towards peer relationships. The benefit of school-based treatment is that children do not need to depend on their parents to bring them to sessions, which is often a major issue. Furthermore, there is usually no stigma attached to seeing a therapist in school. Often the therapy room is seen as a fun and "cool" place to be spending time.

Dan was referred to me because of his extremely disruptive behaviour in class. School staff reported that Dan was aggressive and manipulative towards other children. On several occasions he had attacked other children, without any apparent provocation. He regularly stole other children's snacks and ate leftover food from the bin or floor. Sometimes he shouted so loudly that the blood vessels in his neck stood out.

Dan was the third of five children, all of whom lived with their mother. The mother failed to turn up to several meetings with me to discuss the referral, so I left it to the special educational needs coordinator (SENCO) to arrange for her to sign a consent form. The SENCO told me that the mother had confided in her that she had "kicked Dad out for being heavy with his hands". The mother showed little affection or interest in Dan and had been overheard saying to him "Come here, you little cunt!" There was a general anxiety at school about what might happen behind closed doors at home if that was the way she addressed him in public. I agreed to see Dan for fifty minutes every week for the academic year.

The room where I worked was in the behavioural unit. In order to get into the unit from the school you passed through a large hall and then through a locked door. The room was used exclusively for therapy. The atmosphere of the school and unit was at times chaotic, and interruptions were regular features of our work. Dan's session was scheduled in the afternoon, so I was responsible for picking him up and returning him to his classroom.

With each child I made the "therapeutic frame" clear to him or her, which included confirming a regular time and length of meeting, explaining about confidentiality and when I would need to talk to another adult, and making a general statement about safety in the room. As work with Dan proceeded, I became more explicit about him not hurting me or breaking things in the room. These rules had to be constantly revisited, as he tested the boundaries continuously.

This was one of my first jobs after qualifying as a psychotherapist, and Dan tested me to the limit. In retrospect there are many things I would do differently, certainly in terms of technique. At times I made mistakes and failed to contain him. However, I am presenting this case study as a way of thinking about what works—and what does not—when faced with a challenging child.

Swords, earrings, and manic flights

On the day of our first session, I collected Dan from his classroom and he immediately took my hand and came to the therapy room. He was a small, skinny little boy with shaved, fair hair and a friendly grin. His clothes looked clean, but his trainers were old and falling apart. On arriving in the therapy room he picked up the plastic sword and sheath. These two objects were to be constant companions to him throughout the therapeutic process. If he was not holding them, he would push them down his trouser leg.

In the room I explained to him that his teacher was worried about his behaviour in class and thought that perhaps I could help. I talked about the therapeutic frame, and as I was talking, Dan moved around the room, checking everything out and brandishing the sword. He proceeded to kill batman and wanted to stab some monsters. He looked through the jewellery box and put on earrings and said he was a girl. He then took them off and said he was a boy. At this point in the session a member of staff came into the room and, on seeing us, backed out again. Dan picked up the sword and said he wanted to kill somebody. I reflected that he hadn't liked being interrupted by that man and that making himself big and powerful with the sword made him feel better.

The sword made him feel big and male, and when he had it he felt safe to express his anger. However, I wonder whether underneath this pseudo-strength he felt extremely small and scared. An important part of our work would be for me to tolerate and recognize these strong and vulnerable feelings and anxieties and try to understand them.

On the way back to the classroom after the session, he found a long piece of wood with a screw sticking out. He picked this up and set off at high speed along the corridor. There were children everywhere, and it was hard to keep up without breaking into a run. Just before we got to the classroom, I caught up with him and firmly suggested that he give the piece of wood to me, which he did.

At our second meeting, as soon as we got to the room he asked for the sword. He then noticed the shield, which he had not seen the week before. He asked me to help him put the shield on, and as I did I accidentally pinched his arm with the strap. I apologized, and he looked at the red mark and rubbed it. A little later he rubbed the spot again. I wondered aloud what it might be like to be in this room with a strange woman who hurt him. He stabbed, chopped, and killed batman and then chopped the head and tail off the dinosaur. He tried to wrench the dinosaur's arms and legs off, but they wouldn't come off, so he flung it onto the floor and very aggressively stamped on it. He then asked me to put the tail back on.

Dan then turned to an aeroplane and asked me where it had come from. He thought that the lights on it were bullets. He kept on asking me "How does this work?" I think he was wondering about the room and my role there. Where did I come from? Will therapy work? How does therapy work? I also think that in asking for my help with putting the shield on and putting the dinosaur's tail back on, he was symbolically asking for my protection and for me to fix broken parts of him.

At one point a child was pounding on the door to the unit, which was outside the therapy room, and Dan quickly rushed to turn the light off. I commented that he seemed to not want anyone to know we were in here. He asked me if I was going to answer the door, and I said no and explained that it was his time. He asked me to get the jewellery down, and he then looked through the earrings. Then he pushed it away and said he didn't want to be a girl today.

He got a man out of the castle and said he liked him because he had a big sword. He pulled out a "little" horse and repeatedly knocked him down with his sword. I commented that he didn't want to be the little one who felt small and helpless. He said he'd been to the room twice now, and I said he would be coming for the next three weeks and then it would be half term. He seemed to be listening very carefully and asked if he could come back after half term. I said he could, and he then turned to batman and thanked him for looking after the sword. I wondered whether these were perhaps the fragile beginnings of feeling looked after by me. I think he was also communicating his fear of abandonment and his difficulty in trusting that something could continue in a reliable, consistent way.

At the end of the session he said that he didn't want to go, and he refused to leave the room. I said that I could see how hard it was for him to leave and say goodbye to me but that our session had finished for today. When he still refused to leave, I interpreted that he was telling me that he needed me to help him leave. In retrospect, I think he needed help with his sad and angry feelings about having to say goodbye. He still would not move, so I took his hand firmly and we walked out of the room. Once outside he clung to the door and then threw himself on the floor and started putting dirt in his mouth. He then heard some children coming along the corridor and insisted on waiting for them. I wondered whether he wanted to show them that he had been in the special room. He then ran off, and I followed him into the hall, where he climbed up the gym bars on the walls and refused to come down. Like the week before, he was testing to see what I would do. Would I chase him down corridors or climb up monkey bars to bring him down? I was aware I needed to get him back to class quickly as I had another therapeutic appointment to keep. With a very firm but calm voice I asked him to come down, and after a few minutes he did and we went quietly back to his classroom.

My difficulty in getting him back to his classroom aroused a complex array of feelings in me. I was anxious that he would hurt himself or someone else, particularly when armed with a long stick with a screw sticking out. I also felt embarrassed that people might think I couldn't get a 5-year-old back to class. Dan, of course, picked up on these feelings and then insisted on waiting for children to come along in order to witness my helplessness. It was important for me to monitor these feelings and examine any countertransference and projective-identification processes. His separation anxiety manifested itself in clinging to me and a terror of leaving me.

The manic flight at the end of the first two sessions was a way of perhaps blanking me out and defending against separation anxiety and loss. My setting limits/boundaries for him provoked his anger and rage, and I hoped to help him to find more acceptable ways of expressing it. Saying no was a painful affront to his sense of omnipotence and aroused anger and frustration in him. I tried to be firm but flexible and preserve a space for thinking. I explored in supervision how easy it was to be overwhelmed by Dan and also how important it was to use interpretations, the tone of my voice, and physical posture to help impose boundaries. I wanted to avoid getting drawn into battles, which clouded my thinking. I also decided that I needed to insist on holding his hand the whole way back to his classroom as a way of containing him and keeping him safe. This strategy proved to be a helpful one.

When I arrived for the third session, I found Dan being shouted at by his teacher for thumping another child so violently that he had been winded. The teacher turned to me in front of the whole class and said he was vile. Dan said the other child had started it by punching him in the face, but the other children said the attack was completely unprovoked. The teacher seemed glad to send Dan off with me. We walked past an older boy, whom Dan called a bitch. The boy ran up and punched Dan on his head and said "That was for calling me a bitch." Dan shouted "bitch" and "fuck" and then ran away.

As soon as we got to the room, he went for the sword and shield. He then got out a jar of soldiers and went through them, identifying their swords and guns as he unpacked them. The more heavily armed ones then destroyed the less protected ones. I thought with him about how he was perhaps showing me how angry he was with his teacher and the boy who hit him. I also wondered whether he was angry with me for not protecting him in the classroom from the teacher and from the boy who hit him.

He then started to boss me around. "Sit down here, stand batman up, get that down, undo this." I interpreted that he enjoyed telling me what to do, but I wondered whether it made it even harder when at the end of the session I told him what to do. He kept on picking things up and asking where they had come from and how did they work. This curiosity was a constant theme, and I thought that it was a healthy sign linked to his interest in me as a new person in his world. He got the jewellery out and clipped on an earring. He said he was Hercules, not a girl.

As we left the session I insisted on holding his hand. I said that I thought he had been showing me how frightened he was about leaving the room and that I would help him to get back to the classroom without getting hurt. He struggled and said he wouldn't play with me any more. He flung himself on the floor and said I was holding him too tight. I said that I could see he felt angry and hurt by me for ending the session and repeated that I wanted to help him get back to the classroom. I waited quietly beside him, and he eventually stood up, took my hand, and we returned to his class.

I thought about his teacher's comment about him being vile. Her sadistic humiliation of Dan in front of me and the other children was inappropriate and un-containing, and it complicated the boundaries between inside and outside the therapy room. She was obviously struggling to contain and teach Dan, and it seemed important to me that Dan felt that all the grown-ups were working together around him. So after school I went to find her. I said I could see what a handful he was, but that there was a part of him that was willing to engage with therapy, and that this needed to be encouraged. I hoped that my observations might ignite some interest in her and that rather than reacting immediately to him, she might become more reflective. I think she was glad to have an opportunity to offload onto me about how awful he was, and I hoped that I had planted a seed of interest in her mind about different aspects of Dan.

Gender issues and boundary disturbances

Greenson (1968) proposes that "The male child, in order to attain a healthy sense of maleness, must replace the primary object of his identification, the mother, and must identify instead with the father" (Greenson, 1968, p. 370). I think Dan was struggling with this process of dis-identification with the mother and showed a possible gender dysphoria in the way that he wanted to be a girl and then aggressively pushed away girlish things and brandished his sword. He both loved, hated, and feared woman.

Greenson (1968) goes on to say that the child must give up the pleasure and closeness that comes from identification with the mother and must form an identification with the less accessible father. Ideally, this process needs to be encouraged by the mother. In Dan's case the father may have been too absent, or perhaps Dan was identifying with a violent, sadistic father. The mother may have had little motive for encouraging a positive identification. By calling him a cunt perhaps his mother was also expressing confusion over gender, besides expressing her capacity to abuse and use sadistic comments to hurt her own child.

My thoughts around this time tended to coalesce around questions like: Do I represent an engulfing mother who takes him to a private room? Does the jewellery box stand for a woman's genitals (Freud, 1905e)? The preoccupation about where things come from and how they work may also have been a link to confusion about how babies are made (Freud, 1905d, 1907c). This preoccupation is easily understood within his maternal social context, the mother having had so many babies—five in total.

The boundaries of therapy were regularly disturbed and intruded upon—for example, people trying to come into the room, children shouting outside or pounding on the doors, teachers talking about children in front of them, and so forth. Throughout our work I regularly questioned how much of Dan's acting out was also a reflection of these boundary disturbances.

I also thought about the encounters with other children in the corridors as reflections of the very disturbed dynamics of the school. I wondered how much Dan's disturbed behaviour mirrored the dynamics of the school, particularly his eating dirt. I wondered whether he identified with the bad dirt. He used dirty words and put dirt into his dirty inside. I also wondered whether I was the "dirty" one for Dan. Perhaps he thought my ending the session was "dirty" or that I was giving him "dirty food".

These first sessions contained the major themes of our work together. Dan appeared to move between two developmental positions: between all-powerful omnipotence and feeling very small. His confusion over his gender identity added to his already confused and disorganized emotional state and chaotic inner world.

The unprotected child

Session 4 started with him climbing on to the table and grabbing his sword. He flung a soldier at me and told me to put its boots on. He then hit him over and over again. He then told me to take the soldier's clothes off, and he chopped his legs off and stamped on him. He started playing with the ambulance and fire engine. He put a child in the ambulance and then said the child was dead because it had been knocked over in the road. He ordered me to stay sitting in my chair and turned his back on me so that I couldn't see what he was doing. I wondered about part of him identifying with this dead child and that he was not sure whether it was safe to show me this part of himself. I thought that this dead child had been neglected by a mother figure that had not managed to protect him. I thought about the attacks on Dan in the school, and I wondered how I was fitting in to the neglectful mother-therapist role.

Dan then proceeded to get the jewellery out and said he wanted to be a girl. He asked me to open the jewellery box, and then after having carefully studied the insides of the box he insisted on shutting it and opening it himself. He then carefully put his sword in the sheath. He repeated this several times and then wanted me to hold the sheath as he put the sword in. When, at the end of the session, I said it was time to finish, he slipped a soldier into his pocket. I said he was showing me how hard it was to leave me, and this special room, and that he wanted to take something of it away with him. We walked calmly back to class, but outside the classroom a larger boy came and lifted him up by the scruff of his neck. Before I could say a word the boy had sauntered off, leaving Dan clinging to my hand, perhaps wondering whether I would neglect or protect him.

As Winnicott (1956a) so clearly demonstrated, stealing can be viewed as a sign of hope. By putting the soldier in his pocket, Dan was clearly showing he had found something that he believed was rightfully his. He wanted more time with me, and the soldier represented something of me, a transitional object to bridge the separation from me. This also appeared to be a development from his refusal to leave the room.

The next few sessions continued in the same way. In one session after having stabbed and garrotted the toys, he turned on me and poked me quite forcefully with the sword, saying that he was killing me. I commented that it was not enough to attack the toys, and that he needed to attack me to show me how he was feeling. In other sessions he ordered me to sit on a chair out of the way of his games, or he would look at me silently and point at things for me to pick up. I felt exhausted being with him and wondered whether this was also part of his exhaustion and his exhausted attempts at trying to get what he needed. My countertransference left me feeling helpless and at the mercy of his violent behaviour.

Dan also discovered the tea set and spent ages carefully pouring tea into all the cups. Once they were all filled, he would then keep going until the water poured over the edge of the tray and onto the floor. Sometimes he would make tea for me and carefully present me with brimming cupfuls. He would often gulp down cupfuls of water. On several occasions he poured water all over me or on my sleeve and into my lap. Each time I would firmly tell him to stop.

I tried to prevent this by interpreting his wish to do this before he acted it out. Gradually this began to work, and the outpourings of water subsided.

In retrospect I realize that I was enacting the part of the victim in him, who was ordered around and abused. This sadomasochistic behaviour usually means that the child has experienced overwhelming impotence and is now set on controlling every aspect of his environment. Using projective identification he was expelling his unmanageable anxiety into me. I then became identified with the submissive victim, and perhaps in my helplessness stayed in this position for too long, rather than feeding back this experience to him in the form of an interpretation.

A hungry baby

On the way to the thirteenth session he scraped up some squashed and muddy sweets from the floor and put them in his mouth. He did this before I was able to stop him, thus again externalizing a neglectful maternal internalized experience and a ravenously hungry child who felt he was not getting enough of anything.

He came into the therapy room and asked "Where's the sword?" Arming himself with the sword, he then picked up a baby's bottle. "How does this work?" He unscrewed the top, filled the bottle with water, screwed the top and teat back on, and tried to suck from it. He could not get anything out so he tried to make the hole bigger with the scissors. I said that by making the hole bigger he got more and that this reminded me that he always wanted more time and that last time he had got very angry with me at the end of the session and had hit me with the sword and had knocked all the toys on the floor. He ignored me and continued pouring water from the bottle to the teapot. He carefully mopped up the water he spilled, and I wondered whether he was trying to please me and make some form of reparation to make up for hitting me in the last session.

He then wanted to go to the toilet. I wondered with him whether he was so full of anxious feelings that he needed to get away from the room and me. We walked to the toilet and I waited outside. Another child came out and said to a group of older boys that "Dan had done a shit". They laughed and went into the toilet and blocked the door. I heard Dan shouting quite frantically to let him out. I knocked forcefully on the door and urgently told them to let Dan out. He evoked the need for a strong protective parent/ therapist who would not allow children to eat dirt or be bullied by other boys.

Dan appeared, and we returned to the room. When we got back to the room he walked around brandishing the sword. I said that perhaps he would have liked his sword when those big boys wouldn't let him out of the toilet. He started twisting it. He asked, " What happens if I break this sword? Will you tell me off?" I thought that part of him liked having the sword but maybe he also thought it was dangerous and that it would be better if it was broken. Also I wondered whether he was afraid that his anger might destroy the very thing he needed: play with the toy sword and therapy with me?

He then looked at the baby things and picked up a dummy and sucked it. I said that he was showing me his baby side and that maybe I was like a Mummy who had rescued him from the big boys. He nodded his head and then threw the dummy away and said that he wasn't a baby any more. "Where's my sword? Get me my sword!" I said that sometimes he liked to be a baby and sometimes he liked to show me he was big and powerful because maybe it felt a bit frightening in here when he felt like a helpless, hungry baby and he needed to protect himself with his sword.

Dan seemed to find being with me very arousing, and he showed me symbolically how big his penis was to make sure I did not lose interest in him. He thrust the sword down his trousers and strutted around the room. I also wondered about the symbolism of the sword and whether he wanted to cut loose from his dependency on a violent mother and father. He experienced me as both exciting and scary. This pouring of water exhibited his attempt to gain mastery over his penis and urinary stream. He filled up all the vessels—the cups, pots, and bottles—and presented them to me as a gift, which was a new form of play and an indication of some progress. Both the sword and the water are very strong penetrating images. At this time I wondered whether he identified with the missing father and filled the gap with stereotypical phallic intrusions.

I became concerned about him drinking from dirty containers and scraping food off the floor. I tried to reflect with him how sad it was that he needed to put dirty food in his mouth; I also tried to explore what it felt like to be so desperate for extra food. I linked this to his need for more time with me, but I also wondered whether he was in reality getting enough food. One of the lunchtime supervisors told me that he always devoured leftover food. She described him as a bottomless hole. It seemed that however much food he had, he was still never satisfied. I wondered whether his mother found it difficult to nourish her children because she was so needy herself. It seemed that his hunger was both symbolic *and* based in reality. I decided that because he was regularly drinking in the sessions, I would provide him with a proper drinking cup. This was to become an important symbol in our work together.

I also wondered whether his mother had turned to her children as substitutes for a partner, to elicit comfort from them. Welldon (1988) writes about the perversion of the maternal instinct where the child is used to satisfy the mother's own desire for control and fusion. I wondered whether Dan was emasculated by these intrusions and whether there was not enough nurturing for the development of a sense of potency and of identity as a boy. Dan's use of the sword in his play was perhaps a compensation for this sense of lack, helplessness, and impotency.

It is possible that Dan's feelings of being overwhelmed by his mother (and by me in the therapeutic transference relationship) led him to resort to using violent attacks on other people's bodies or minds in an attempt to resolve the intense psychological distress. Therapeutically, it was very important that I did not retaliate when he attacked me and, instead, try to explore his anxious and confusing states of mind. Also, I wondered whether Dan feared that his mother was more interested in one of her other children and that I, too, may be like his mother and have more time for other children, either later in the therapy room or when I went home. I also wondered whether his gender confusion might have something to do with him wondering whether he would be preferred or liked more if he had been a girl.

Testing boundaries

Dan projected his experiences into the present by unconsciously moulding situations to communicate what had gone on in his life. Dan was also acting out outside the room, and I needed to bring these episodes into the room and show that I was willing to engage with the most violent and frightening areas of his life. He seemed to be acting out being beaten up with other people watching. On our journeys to and from the therapy room he goaded and taunted other children to react and re-create a scenario that he was trying to show me. It felt as graphic as if he had brought in a home video of what went on in his house. The question "where and when does his violence emerge and in relation to what?" was a useful one to hold in mind to help me think.

Dan began Session 14 by sweeping the soldiers off the table. I linked this to what was happening outside the room by saying that I had been thinking about the times older boys had come and hurt him in front of me. I said I thought he was showing me how dangerous things were for him. I said it worried me, and I thought it worried him too because he was showing me so often how he got hurt. He brought some paint over to the table. He started squeezing paint into the palette and asked me to tell him when to stop. When I said "Stop!" he said "No, I'm going to say stop!" and he continued to pour paint until the dish was overflowing. Once he had filled a dish, he said he didn't want it and ordered me to clear it up. He then started filling the next tray up with paint. He then took another bottle of paint and started shaking the bottle hard, which resulted in the paint splattering all over the table. He then deliberately squeezed paint all over the table and into the containers with all the paintbrushes. I said "I can see you are very angry, but you have to stop doing that now." He continued to squeeze the bottle until I took it from him.

Dan responded by saying "I'm going to tape up your mouth." He found the end of the Sellotape and cut off a length of it. As he did so the cut-off bit became tangled up. He then proceeded to put this over my mouth. Because it was tangled up, he then pulled it off and tried to get another bit of tape. However, the tape had run out, and when I said that there wasn't any more he picked up the sword and hit the table over and over again. The sword bent, and he stopped to check it hadn't broken. Again I reflected on how angry he was and how painful it was for him to hear my thoughts about him.

I am aware that there are differences in technique here as to whether I should have allowed him to tape my mouth. I could have stopped him from doing it and told him that I could see what he wanted to do (i.e. silence me) but he was not allowed to put tape over my mouth—he was crossing a boundary and invading my body, and I could have said no. However, in this session and in subsequent sessions I allowed him to do this. Removing the tape from my mouth could have been painful had he put it on properly, but it was always tangled up.

Taping my mouth made me think of several possible interpretations. The first is described by Fonagy and Target (1999), who wrote about a violent patient who said, "If I kill you, I won't have to think about what you think" (p. 55). I think it is possible that Dan felt this when he taped up my mouth. Thinking was too anxiety-provoking for him—and for me—at this stage! I think he was beginning to become aware of my mind, and this was arousing more anxiety than he could bear.

The second way of thinking about Dan taping my mouth is to wonder whether he was protecting himself from what might come out of my mouth. He was frightened of my mouth and what my mouth could do. Perhaps it was reminiscent of what other mouths had done to him, and this may have been linked with him putting dirty food in his mouth. Being unable to see words as symbols demonstrates a very primitive way of thinking where there is a confusion of physical and mental states. It is evocatively displayed by the abusive and hopefully outdated practice of washing a child's mouth out with soap for saying bad words. I think Dan was projecting his own oral aggression on to my mouth. Discussing this in supervision, I decided to encourage him to be more verbally disgusting and explore with him his fear of what I might do if he said nasty things. I wanted to encourage and further explore the negative transference.

Third, I also wondered whether he was showing me what happened to him in real life, and whether his body had been invaded in the same way. He was making me feel a helpless victim and getting me to experience what it was like to be abused. Was he showing me what it was like when he was "shut up"? Perhaps it would have been useful to wonder with him whether he was showing me how he was treated, but instead I focused on the transference and the here-and-now.

The session continued in a way that made me think my words had had some impact. Dan started to look after things by watering the flowers, and he also started to become curious. He went over to look at a round plastic box. "What's in this? Oh its clay—did you make this? Ugh it smells—I don't want this!" He then took the teapot back to the other table and poured himself a drink. He said "Umm, this is nice coffee" and, pointedly, didn't offer me any. He then said he was going to water the plants. He took the teapot and went over to a vase of plastic daffodils and poured water in saying,

"I'm going to water some more plants." He then went out into the corridor. When I said that it was important that he come back in, he tipped all the water on the floor. I said, "Usually you tell me what to do and that makes you feel in control, but today I have been telling you what you can't do and you don't like it. It makes you feel small and out of control and so you pour water on the floor and paint on the table to show me how you feel."

He came back into the room and ordered me to get the dumper truck down. He then said "Take all those things out! No, leave them in! I'm going to tip them out." He tipped the contents of the dumper truck out and hurled them round the room. At the end of the session he ran out of the room and flung himself on the floor. A woman was sweeping the floor, and she said he would get swept up if he didn't move. He said he would like to be swept up.

The image of him lying on the floor and saying he would like to be swept up by the cleaner is particularly poignant. It is possible Dan saw himself as a bit of rubbish and would rather be swept up than left alone. I wondered whether he was identifying with his mother's view of him or perhaps the view he thought I had of him.

Looking back I realize that he was showing me how uncontained he felt. I should perhaps have had firmer boundaries and said "No!" earlier. My allowing him to hit me, hurl toys around, and splatter paint everywhere resulted in a confusion of mixed messages. What was said and done were different at home, in school, and in this room. Therefore it was difficult for him to internalize any sense of a healthy boundary system. Although I had intended to provide a different setting and therapeutic space for Dan, in fact it seemed that I, too, was acting out the same thing as at home—a lack of boundaries. At this stage of the therapy I knew I was pregnant, and I think the guilt I felt about having to finish work with Dan interfered with my capacity to think, which resulted in me overcompensating. Saying "no" too much felt too punitive. I think it would have been far more helpful to make many more interpretations followed by an injunction before he acted out. For example, "I can see that you want to pour paint all over me and that you are angry with me, but you are not allowed to." This intervention could therefore link the content of his play to the process and to his internal world. Instead I took a more passive stance, which left him feeling uncontained. I always tried to think about these attacks with him and put something into words but I think firmer boundaries and more reflection with him afterwards would have been more productive.

Escalating violence and glimmers of reparation

In Session 16, some unexpectedly warm weather provided another opportunity for Dan to test boundaries. A window had been opened, and by climbing up on the table he could pull himself up to the window and stick his head out. There was a definite possibility of him wriggling out and falling. Yet again I had to firmly take a stand and say that I would not allow him to put himself in danger. Dan stabbed the beanbag with the sword and thrust the sword in and out of the sheath. He then told me to sit down on the beanbag and to hold the sheath while he pulled the sword out. He said I was naughty and whacked my fingers with the sword. I said to him that however cross he was, I would not allow him to hurt me. I said I could see he was showing me rather than telling me how cross he was. His response was to grab the tape, laboriously pick at the end, pull a bit off, and then cover my mouth with it. The tape kept on getting tangled, so he would then start all over again, telling me to be quiet and to keep my mouth shut. This went on for some time, and then he told me to get him some water. He had a long drink and then, taking his sword, attacked a cardboard box by splitting it in two. He then began to mend the box by winding tape round and round it. As he did this he kept checking to see that his sword was nearby.

Looking back on this episode I wonder about the strong countertransference it evoked. I was struggling to make a space for his highly disturbed acting out and, at the same time, struggling to try to keep thinking. As I got him some water, I talked again about how he really needed to shut me up and how maybe he was both angry and frightened at what came out of my mouth. This seemed to allow his play to move on, and he turned from my mouth to the box. The subsequent mending of the box was another sign of reparation.

He then heard voices outside and ran to the window. I caught up with him just in time and leant across to close the window. As I did this, I knocked a tin of crayons over. He was furious and jumped down and said that I had to clear them up. He then stood on the table and tried to hit the light bulb with the sword. I said "no" in a raised voice, and he told me to "fuck off". He then flung down the sword and started kicking the beanbag repeatedly. He then turned to the table, picked up the sword, and swept all of the toys on to the floor. He then ran out into the corridor. I said we had a few minutes left, and he seemed relieved and came back in. He flicked the lights on and off.

At the end of the session I told him it was time and then took his hand and we went out. He told me to let go, and he threw himself on to the floor. He saw a bit of old chewing gum flattened on the ground. He scratched it up with his fingers and put it in his mouth. An older boy walking by grabbed his shirt and twisted it round under his chin and said "Don't fuck with me!" I told the boy in my strongest voice to "Let go!", which he did with a punch into Dan's stomach and then a sideways kick. Dan then clung on to my hand, and we went back to class. Once we got there he walked in without a backwards glance and said "Hello Miss" to his teacher. Later on I saw him wandering the corridors with an 11-year-old boy who was known to be disruptive. He ignored me. I was struck by how helpless I had been when a child in my care had been attacked and had put dirty chewing gum from the floor into his mouth. I reported the incident of Dan being attacked to a stressed head teacher who promised to find out who the older boy was and do something about it.

During this chaotic session Dan reached a peak of acting out. I think the mess in the room was a reflection of Dan's internal world spilling out everywhere and of my difficulty in containing and helping him. I found Winnicott's (1947) paper "Hate in the Countertransference" helpful because I was aware I needed to tolerate the strong feelings aroused in me by Dan, without retaliating. I was aware of my own ambivalent feelings towards him. There was a part of me that was furious and exasperated with him for making such a mess and for his abusive attitude, and it was important for me to monitor my own potential violence as it felt that this child was pushing me to the limit. Besides these feelings, I was also extremely fond of Dan and very protective of him. As I have discussed earlier, these feelings were interwoven with feelings of guilt at being pregnant and leaving him.

In supervision I thought about whether Dan had to escalate his aggressive behaviour in order to keep me thinking about him.

It was hard to think about his manic defences and his rage at the repeated denial of his needs. I had to survive and not reject him. Dan had destroyed and hurt so much, and his fear of retaliation must have been overwhelming. I think the helplessness and hopelessness I felt at times were reflections of his inner world. I reacted differently from how he expected. I kept thinking about him, and he began to realize I had a separate mind of my own, which was distinct from his. I invited him to see that I was thinking about him. I did not end sessions early or retaliate by hitting him back. I also did not ignore him or collapse as a result of the chaos.

I was also aware of my feelings of helplessness when Dan was hurt in the corridors when he was under my care. The staff at the school seemed indifferent or resigned to the children roaming around the school. Again these feelings of impotence were useful to consider in terms of projective identification.

Over the next few sessions we had many battles about the window. Dan would try to trick me into letting him hang out of the window. He tied batman up, stabbed me, and called me a "fucking bitch". Several times on our journeys to and from the room he stopped to scrape some remnant of food off the floor. He discovered a small hole in the beanbag and started emptying out the polystyrene balls. He would beg to be allowed to take his sword to the toilets.

Despite these resistances Dan began to show glimmers of interest in me and in the things that I had to say. Dan was also delighted by his "special" cup and spent a long time pouring, emptying, spilling, and drinking from it. One week he came with cut fingers and a black eye and never fully explained what had happened. In another session, when I talked about the Easter break, he bashed my ankles with the sword and said "Does that hurt? I don't like you!" thus clearly showing me how much I hurt him by not seeing him over the holidays.

After the holidays, when Dan and I were walking to the room, his brother appeared and said he wanted to come too. Dan said, "No! She's my special lady!" He proudly showed me his new shoes and then immediately went for his sword and special cup. He went to one of the dolls and kissed her and then scratched her face. He "accidentally" hit me and shouted at me for getting in the way. He then offered me some breakfast to make up for the shouting. "Sorry Miss", he said apologetically. I suggested to him that by kissing the doll he was showing me how pleased he was to see me but then the scratching was telling me that he was also cross that I had been away. He climbed up onto the shelves and jumped down. He then climbed up again and asked me to lift him down. His asking me to help him was a good sign of his emotional progress. His guilt at hitting me elicited reparation for the damage he thought he had done or had actually done.

Dan began to verbalize more. Dan's calling me a "fucking bitch" and saying that he didn't like me when we had the break was a sign of achievement—words were beginning to replace actions. Dan started to symbolize and show signs of remorse and reparation. I sensed the development of a healthier part of Dan, where his violent rages lessened; when his rage did appear, it was less destructive. The room (with me and him in it) became a safer place for both of us.

Pregnancy and the process of therapy

At the beginning of Session 23 I told him I was pregnant and introduced the fact that our work would be ending at the end of term. He said "Where's the baby? Is it crying? Let's see. Are you going after today?" He grabbed his sword and special cup and started making me pancakes. He said that he was cross with me last time because I wouldn't let him stay in the room. I suggested that he was making up for being cross by making me pancakes and then perhaps I might not leave. At the end of the session he said, "Fuck! I want to come home with you."

The following week another child came up and asked Dan if I was his Mum. He smiled and took my hand. Once in the room he squirted glue all over some paper and then poured glitter and paint on it. He then folded it over and then opened it out to make a butterfly. He seemed pleased with the result, but then threw it in the bin. "How many weeks will you be away for? Who will bring me here?" I repeated that I would be leaving and not coming back and that I could see how painful it was for him and how he perhaps felt I was throwing him away like he had just thrown away his butterfly. Batman then had a fight with a doll, and then they kissed. I wondered with him whether they were kissing to make up after the fight and he said, "No, because they want to have sex." He pushed their hips together. I thought that he was wondering about me having sex and getting pregnant and subsequently leaving him.

Making a picture was an important developmental step for him, despite the fact that he ended up throwing it away. He was showing me in play how he felt. Something, however, that he and I had created in therapy was under attack and was at risk of being destroyed/thrown away.

The next week I showed Dan a chart I had made that showed how many sessions we had left. He counted out the weeks and asked "How many?" He asked lots of questions and then said, "Shall I rip it up?" This seemed like an attempt to blank out the ending, and not think about it, and my comment about this stopped him ripping it up. We played with the puppets, and he did some more painting. He spilt paint over me and then insisted on wiping it up. Batman and the doll kissed. For the first time he talked about Mr X who ran the unit and how it was he who put these toys in the room. I wondered with him whether he thought that Mr X was the father of the baby in my tummy.

My pregnancy was a huge issue in the therapy (Browning, 1974; Fenster, Phillips, & Rapoport, 1986; Lax, 1969; Nadelson, Notman, Arons, & Feldman, 1974). Lax (1969) writes: "It is obvious and understandable that the pregnant analyst might be more vulnerable than she would be otherwise to the different transference reactions of her patients and that these will evoke a variety of responses, conscious and unconscious. Thus the possibility of an increase in countertransference reactions during pregnancy has to be recognized, since only then can it be guarded against" (p. 363).

Both Browning (1974) and Nadelson et al. (1974) discuss the impact of the therapist's pregnancy on children. Recurrent themes that arise are fears of abandonment, sibling rivalry, curiosity about sex, aggression arising from jealousy of the baby, and intensified ambivalence about the mother–child relationship.

When I told Dan that I was pregnant he made me pancakes, as if by looking after me, I might change my mind about replacing him with another baby. This, of course, linked in with my feelings of guilt about leaving him. Dan had been my "surrogate" baby (Fenster, Phillips, & Rapoport, 1986), and I was now going to leave him for another baby. He already had four siblings who he believed took up too much space, and now there was another rival to deal with—my baby. My pregnancy was yet another challenge to his omnipotence and ignited his infantile rage. He swung in an emotionally volatile way between omnipotence, impotence, and humiliation. Bringing a third "intruder" into the room intensified the already ambivalent relationship between us. This became the focus for his aggression and curiosity. It was interesting and a sign of achievement that he was curious as to who had put the baby "in there" and that, in his mind, the answer to that question was Mr X. Dan was thus able to create a couple in his mind, which was a healthy sign.

At the beginning of Session 26 he danced with joy to see me. He rushed into the room to find the sword and sheath. He looked at the chart and asked for his cup. He poured himself a drink and then poured one for me. He asked whether the baby had come out yet. He knocked down the soldiers and horses with the sword. He then tried to get a box off the shelf, but it fell on the floor and batman fell out. He said it was my fault. He said batman was his mate and then proceeded to kill him. I linked this to me being his friend and his wish to kill me because I was going away. Dan then lay down on the beanbag and stared at me for quite a while. He then asked me to sit on the beanbag, and he played with the dumper truck and crane and wound my hair around the teeth of the crane. I said it was hard for him to put things in words when he was sad or angry—especially when sad and angry that we had to say goodbye, and he nodded his head.

The next session was the week before half-term. He got his sword and sat down to study the chart. I explained that we had five sessions left after half-term. "And then you have your baby? Show me your baby—is it still in there? Has it come out yet? Show me. How did it get in there? If I push it, will it pop? Can I stab it with my sword?" I said that he would like to hurt this baby because it was going to stop me coming here. "Get me my shield! Pass me the sword!" He put on the nurse's uniform and then the fireman's outfit and asked whether they had swords. He then gave me his sword and told me to stab his shield. I said, "You've made yourself strong against me so that I can't hurt you." He picked up a ball and said he wanted some scissors because he wanted to pop it. Then he said he was going to have a birthday party but I couldn't come because I was disgusting and pregnant and didn't eat food. He smiled as he said this. He did not want to share anything at his birthday party, and he did not want me to eat. Perhaps if I did not eat, the baby would go away? Or perhaps he thought that when my baby was born I would celebrate my baby's birthday and he would be the one not eating because I would have left. When he told me I was disgusting, he had a sadistic smile on his face, which I think connected with his infanticidal wishes towards his siblings and was a way of defending against his murderous impulses towards my baby.

After the party, Dan went on to say, "Where's my magic cup? Get me some water!" He lay on the beanbag and had a sip and then poured most of it down his front and the rest onto the floor. "Shall I smash this? Can't you go and buy me a glass one? Can I throw this out of the window?" He hurled a pen out of the window and then ran out of the room. He then darted back in and went for the jewellery box and asked me to attach the earrings and put the bracelet on. He then grabbed a car and asked, "Why do you run out of petrol? Why? What happens? Do you get more petrol?" He then lay on the beanbag peacefully asking questions about the car. "Would it go slow or fast? How was it connected? How does this work?" When it was time to leave, he grabbed the doll and threw it in the bin. I responded to his barrage of questions with a mixture of reflections about what he was doing and comments about his curiosity and tried to put into words some of his actions.

Throwing the doll in the bin can be thought about on different levels. There is his desire to throw away my baby but also his feeling of being "dumped" by me. There is a re-emergence of abandonment issues as a result of me leaving. These strong feelings of abandonment appeared to be associated in Dan's mind with things that are not needed and that are thrown away—dirt and rubbish. He feels that he is no longer needed and can be thrown in the bin. I also think that when he asked "What happens when you run out of petrol?" he was wondering about what would happen to him when his therapy ended.

Once I had introduced the pain of termination, it seemed to usher in a distinct qualitative change—a new phase of therapy, despite the painfulness inherent in it. An interesting development occurred, which was that in the last two sessions, after having acted out quite energetically, he sat quietly on the beanbag. He was beginning to feel safe enough to stop and think, which was replacing the acting out. A healthy child begins to realize both that another person can be aware of what he is aware of inside himself and also that the intentions of others can be different from his own. This complex process can be seen as the precursor to the development of empathy.

When we were talking about ending, I told Dan that I was going to arrange for help to continue. I strongly recommended to the unit and the school that Dan needed further psychotherapeutic help as a matter of urgency.

Has the baby gone?

Session 28 began with Dan being very subdued. He had been excluded from school for the previous three days for more violent behaviour towards his peers. He had been involved in a playground fight despite having already been given a final warning for an unprovoked attack on a child in the classroom. "Where is the sword? When is the baby coming out?" He found a box of pencils and asked, "Would it hurt if I stuck these in", as he pointed at my stomach. He then tried to break them.

Dan started the following session by asking if the baby had gone. He filled up all the paint pots with water and drank from them and then poured water down my front. He put tiny pieces of cardboard in a glass and pretended they were painkillers. He threatened to go back to class early, which I suggested was a way of punishing me for leaving. When it was time to leave, he had hidden two trucks in his pockets, which I asked him to give back. I said that I thought he was showing me that part of him still needed this room. He hurled the Lego that we had made together around the room, and we left. The painkillers perhaps represented his wish either to kill himself with an overdose or to kill my baby. Or perhaps he needed some respite from the pain of my leaving. Perhaps therapy was not helping him with his pain so he needed a painkiller, which would obliterate the pain without him having to think about it.

Dan began the next four sessions in exactly the same way. He said, "Has the baby gone?" I explored with him how much he would like the baby to go away. I also wondered whether he was trying to come to terms with the fact of me being gone and going away. In Session 30 he played behind the table and would not let me come near him. I said that I thought he might be showing me that he could play without me and that he did not need me. He said he was not going to come next week but was very preoccupied with how many minutes we had left to the session. A broom had been left in the corner of the room, and when he picked it up the brush came off the pole. His immediate response was, "Will I be excluded?" He then went on to say, "Will Mr X get another one? Can I see the baby? Who will bring me here? Will it be Mr X?"

As I leant down to pick up the broom, he also leant down and we hit heads. My head hurt, but he dismissed any pain he felt and proceeded to cut some tape and stick it on his forehead. He then started winding tape around a car, which he said was broken. He then tried to feed the baby doll with a bottle of milk. He asked me where the mouth was and then asked, "Why do I come here?" At the end he slipped the car into his pocket. I felt he was really trying to process and make sense of everything—the baby, me, him, Mr X, as well as who was going to help him.

Asking about why he came to therapy was a positive sign. He was beginning to reflect on what he was doing, and he was putting things into words. He showed me how terribly afraid he was about coping without me, and he identified that he still needed to come to the room for help. I think his actual exclusion from school was an acting out of his thoughts of feeling excluded by me and my baby. However, he was in control of this exclusion. He did something and was excluded. This felt better for him than being helpless in his experience of exclusion by me. Clearly, my leaving was hurting him enormously. I think he had the fantasy of creating something during the process of therapy. He had created a baby, and each session he came to check whether it was still there or whether it had gone. This reflected his ambivalence between love and hate for me—creativeness versus destructiveness. He wondered whether his potency had worked and whether he had destroyed the baby. And then he showed a mixture of rage and relief that he hadn't killed the baby and that I had managed to protect all three of us—the baby, Dan, and me—from his destructiveness. We had all survived.

When I collected him for our penultimate session, he was crying because he had hit his head. This seemed an interesting link to our previous session, where we had hit heads and he had shown no conscious feelings of pain. I think it also reflected how painful our ending felt. As soon as we reached the room, he played a game where batman started fighting with a doll. Batman started kicking and stamping on the doll's "boobies", and he then looked at me and asked me where my boobies were. Dan proceeded to ask me where I went when I was not at the school. He was perhaps wondering how he could find me when I had gone. He demonstrated both curiosity and need. He then put the doll in the rubbish truck and stamped on her over and over again. He told me he had got two certificates. He insisted on having a drink from his special cup before he left, and as we left the room he again tried to put a car in his pocket.

In our last session he played with the sword and "accidentally" stabbed me in the eye. My eyes watered, and it took me some minutes to recover. I linked this to him being very angry and sad about me leaving. Again he asked if the baby had come out. He then wound tape all around the sword until he had finished the whole roll of tape. He went systematically through all the boxes looking for batman, but when he'd found him he didn't want to play with him. He put his shield and hat on and pointed the sword at me and told me to "Beg for mercy!" He put the sheath down his trousers, and it pointed forward like a giant penis for one last time. He bashed at the paints, made a big mess, and said I couldn't clear anything up. When it was time to end, he walked calmly back to his classroom and went in without a backwards glance or goodbye.

He was showing his anger and pain but also perhaps his fear that I was leaving or having a baby because he was messy and violent. In the second session I had accidentally pinched his arm, and in the third-to-last session we had bumped heads, both instances of me perhaps acting out the hurt and pain that existed in Dan's inner and outer world. In our last session he hurt me by stabbing me in the eye, then he left with no goodbye and I felt like weeping. He had symbolically finished the whole roll of tape, showing me perhaps that he understood that our time together had finally run out.

Conclusion

During my work with Dan I attempted to provide a safe setting where he could express his messy, angry, violent feelings with someone who would try to understand him and also, importantly, who would survive and not be destroyed. I did not criticize, punish, or reject him in the way he expected. Dan began to manage the process of internalizing aspects of a healthy relationship where someone cared and thought about him within the context of a boundaried therapeutic context.

Winnicott (1956a) writes that, "The treatment of the antisocial tendency is not psycho-analysis. It is the provision of child-care, which can be rediscovered by the child" (p. 315). Dockar-Drysdale (1971) echoes this when she writes, "The most valuable thing we can do in such circumstances is to continue to be alive, reliable and concerned" (p. 128).

CHAPTER SIX

A little boy left alone

Clare Keogh

> "We are effectively destroying ourselves by violence masquerading as love"
>
> R. D. Laing (1990)

This chapter refers to the therapeutic work of the present author with a violent 5-year-old boy called "Sam". Sam was seen for therapy twice a week on an open-ended basis. The work that follows highlights the importance of play and containment, alongside thinking and understanding within the overall child therapeutic process. The clinical work is presented alongside a theoretical framework, which is comprised of attachment theory and psychoanalysis.

Psychotherapeutic context

Sam, who was white Irish, had been referred to see me by his group play leader. He lived with his mother and newborn baby brother. Sam's mother had left him with relatives at the age of 18 months. She had been in a mental health clinic, as she had suffered from addictions and a mood disorder. After sixteen months, she returned home, and Sam continued to live with her. Sam attended a playgroup at a community centre in inner-city Dublin. I worked with Sam therapeutically for eighteen months while he attended the centre. His behaviour was described as "non-compliant, aggressive, and sometimes violent". Sam would often attack other children in his group by hitting them. It was becoming increasingly difficult for his play leader to run the group, as much of her time was spent on ensuring Sam did not hurt other children and disrupt the group.

I worked as a psychologist/psychotherapist at the centre. Many of the children had been referred by their schools, and their parents or guardians had given consent for them to attend therapy at the centre. The children's playgroups focused on developing their social skills in groups. Children who had experienced difficulties in their lives and needed extra support for the resulting psychological issues were referred for psychotherapy. I worked with the children individually or in group therapy. A therapy room suitable for working with children was also based at the centre.

Presenting problem and assessment

In assessing Sam's emotional and developmental needs, I read from reports that he had been described by his play leader as aggressive, violent, upset, and angry. This was evident in the eight months he had spent at the play centre. The group leader punished Sam's aggressive behaviour. She scolded him for being naughty and told him to sit on a bench away from the other children until he behaved. The consequence of this exclusion was an increase in the incidences of his aggressive behaviour. Sam had experienced early separation from his mother, and there were clearly unresolved loss and separation issues alive in him. Pert, Ferriter, and Saul, (2004) describe how early separation from one or both parents can be a significant aetiological factor in patients suffering from personality disorders. Earle and Earle (1961) correlate early maternal deprivation for a period of six months or longer, in the first six years of childhood, with a later personality disorder.

In addition to the early separation that he experienced, Sam was also an observer of domestic violence, and he had also experienced emotional abuse, deprivation, and physical violence. Consequently,

Sam had very little sense of self. He also had difficulties at school with concentration, attention, and listening to and following instructions. Turn-taking and sharing resources were also difficult for him, as was planning and thinking through his actions. Sam lacked a sense of being aware of danger. Loss and the lack of a permanent attachment figure, emotional abuse, and deprivation were central to Sam's emotional and behavioural difficulties.

Disorganized attachment disorder

Sam had a disorganized attachment disorder, which was evident in his lack of emotional and psychological resources to deal with separation. Gerhardt (2004) describes disorganized attachment as existing in families that are "unable to provide the most basic parental functions of protecting the child and creating a safe base from which to explore the world" (p. 27). Gerhardt proposes that these children were lacking in "psycho feedback" (p. 25). The parents of such children had frequently experienced trauma in their own lives, which had not been processed. Carlson, Cicchetti, Barnett, and Braunwald (1989) describe disorganized attachment patterns as also existing in abused children. According to Bowlby (1969, 1973, 1980), the presence of an attachment figure enables a child to overcome fear, and the child then develops an exploratory behavioural system.

Attachment styles are hypothesized to reflect the child's internal working model (Kendall, 2000). Kendall describes the child's internal working model as a cognitive representation of the self and of others in the relational world, and of the relationship between the child and his/her primary caregiver. The child's early attachment relationships influence his or her subsequent relationships and play a key role in well-being and mental health throughout the lifespan (Allen, 2001). Bowlby (1969, 1973, 1980) refers to the instinct to attach as being linked to developing feelings of security and comfort.

Ainsworth, Blehar, Waters, and Wall (1978) have identified four attachment strategies that may be correlated with early separation and development.

1. Secure: Infants wanted to be near the caregiver on return after a separation, and they wanted to play.

2. Avoidant: Infants appeared less anxious during separation, and they stayed away from the caregiver on return
3. Anxious ambivalent: Infants displayed anxiety on separation, and they became angry and clingy when the caregiver returned, even though there was no presence of danger.
4. Disorganized–disorientated: Infants had no tactics to deal with the separation.

Gabbard (2000) describes *securely attached* children as being able to interact well with others and as displaying emotional resilience. *Avoidantly attached* children can be anxious at home, and they do not stay close to the caregiver, for fear of rejection. In addition, they may be attention-seeking and angry at school. *Ambivalently attached* children are clingy, even when there is no presence of danger. They are emotionally unstable and experience this instability in their environments. Gabbard (2000) describes these attachment styles as also extending into adulthood and as correlating with adult categories of attachment.

Swearing, shouting, and acting out violently

In Sam's case, without a secure internalized attachment object he expressed his need for attachment with aggression, anger, and violence. Sam frequently sounded like an adult when upset. He would swear, shout, and behave in an emotionally abusive way. He used projective identification (Klein, 1957), as a method of externalizing what he could not integrate, by projecting those parts of himself into others. Klein (1957) maintains that projective identification functions as a defence against primitive paranoid anxiety. He had experienced a failure in "holding" (Winnicott, 1965b) by his mother and, consequently, experienced anger towards the love object, his mother. Sam's inability to see his individuality and to achieve constancy in his internal object relations was evident. Sam was angry, aggressive, and violent. He felt he was bad, and he focused his anger on himself as well as on those around him. He lacked self-esteem and felt controlled by his feelings.

THE COURSE OF THERAPY
Beginning of therapy (Months 1–6)

Family consultation

A letter was sent to Sam's mother (mam—the Irish term for mother) inviting Sam and herself to have a consultation with me, to increase my understanding of Sam in the family and social context of which he was part (Winnicott, 1965b). Brafman (2001) proposes that there is much to be gained by having the parents present in the initial meeting with the child, as it provides an opportunity for the parents to discuss the actual experiences of the child's problem as well as providing an opportunity for the parents to discuss any relevant information of their own that may help the child. Sam's Mam could not make the consultation date, and she also found it difficult to attend for any further appointments.

A family consultation would have provided the opportunity to meet Sam's Mam and to observe the family dynamics. Brafman (2001) proposes that parents tend to treat their children according to how they perceive their child alongside how they see themselves as parents, and the child in turn relates to the actual way he is treated, which can at times develop into a vicious pattern.

How do I keep Sam safe?

In our first session, Sam ran around, roughly pulling at toys and attempting to walk on the table and cupboards. Sam's uncoordinated running around appeared to mirror his feelings and were symbolic of both his chaotic internal world and his traumatic external world, where conflict, uncontainment, and confusion abounded. His overwhelming fear and anxiety were reflected in his external behaviour, as he ran around chaotically, knocking over toys and art materials, and throwing them on the floor. Sam also exhibited a terrible fear of talking about his feelings. I was very aware of having to try to keep him safe.

I introduced the therapeutic frame to Sam. Milner (1957) describes the important containing function of the frame in a work of art, and she links this to the important containing function of the boundary conditions in therapy. I told Sam I would be there to meet him twice a week, and each session would last fifty minutes. Sam and I talked about me picking him up at his playgroup prior to sessions and then, after the session, walking back with him to the group. We also talked about the times we would not meet, during holiday breaks at the centre, and about confidentiality and privacy.

Sam was aware I wouldn't talk to others about our sessions unless I thought he was at risk. Sam knew I would talk to him about this too, should such an issue arise. Sam was also provided with a box where he could put anything he made in the sessions. This would be kept safely for him until he finished therapy. "The framework that is established in the initial consultation could be seen as a promise on the part of the therapist. It is a contract, a way of working that has been carefully thought about and put into practice because it has been found, usually, to be the best way of working" (Gray, 1999, p. 18).

The aim of the therapeutic space was to provide Sam with a secure, safe place where he could develop his sense of self and individuality. Early on, we were both to experience severe challenges to this therapeutic ideal of safety and the containing function of the "frame".

The dangerous start to therapy: safety and danger

Within minutes of our second session, Sam had jumped onto the table, with a game in his hands. I told him I didn't think it was safe for him to be up on the table and that I would help him to get down. With this, Sam became very angry and quickly and forcefully pulled the plastic bear's leg in the board game. He did not say anything and did not look at me. As he did this, a small piece of plastic became lodged in the top of his finger. I was aware he needed medical treatment and took him to first aid. Sam cried, and I was aware that he did not ask for his Mammy when he hurt himself. While Sam sat on my knee crying, we waited for his mother to come, as the school had called her and asked her to come and fetch him. She soon arrived and took him to the hospital, where the piece of plastic was removed.

I was aware that Sam's accident introduced an interruption to the therapeutic process, and I was worried about the fact that he had hurt his finger. I was also aware that Sam may have felt I couldn't keep him safe and, therefore, may have wondered how I was going to look after him and help him with all the danger that existed both inside and outside him.

Perelberg (1999) describes violence as having "a defensive function", which is "designed to prevent intrusion into the patient by a frightening object, often the analyst" (Perelberg, 1999, p. 5). Fonagy and Target (1999) describe attacks on one's own body "as an attempt to blot out intolerable thoughts or images in the patient's own mind" (p. 55).

Returning to the danger

At our next session the first thing Sam did was look at the same game. He found the box and told me "There's only other parts here." He quickly tried to repeat the same action with the game. "The game doesn't work, there are bits missing. I went to the hospital and they took out the plastic, and Mam was there." I noticed he was happy his mother was there and less concerned about his accident.

Sam tried to scribble on the cupboards and table with felt-tips and crayons. I linked this behaviour to his showing me his upset feelings, and how they felt they were running away like the crayons and pens; perhaps he was angry with me for not keeping him safe the last time we met, and there was also a part of him that wanted to leave his mark in the room. I intervened by saying I could see he wanted to write all over the walls and cupboards but I did not want him to do that, and that he could write on the paper provided on the table.

Sam then snapped a crayon in half, and I linked this to Sam wanting to tell me how dangerous things felt inside with his feelings and in the room with me and that I failed to keep him safe in the second session, and perhaps he was wondering if I was going to be any good at all at keeping him safe.

Sam would want to sit beside me when he was drawing pictures and occasionally would hug me; however, this was in contrast to his disorganized, dangerous behaviour of running around, throwing art materials on the floor, and destroying his paintings when he felt frightened.

Sam was known for asking for hugs at the play centre, and he had started ask for them in the playroom. I talked to Sam about there being two Sams—one who is a very good little boy who likes hugs, and the other little boy who was scared and frightened and unhappy. I said I wanted to understand and help the unhappy Sam—the one that wants to break things and hurt himself and others. Sam told me he did not like talking about feelings. I acknowledged that it was difficult for him to talk about his feelings and that it felt very dangerous for him.

I soon afterwards heard his Mam tell the centre manager that she did not like him talking about feelings. His Mam still did not respond to further requests to meet me to talk about how Sam was doing.

Infantile longings and rage

During our next session, Sam tried to pull apart a baby teddy bear from the mother teddy bear, by pulling at it roughly and throwing it around. I was aware that he had told me his Mam was going to have another baby and wondered with him about his feelings about his mother having another baby, and that maybe he was angry at the baby and also scared he was not going to get enough care. I wondered with him if he was worried if I would care enough for him. Sam then started to display very baby-like behaviour.

He began to use baby language and sat on my knee. He then cuddled up to me just like a baby. I wondered with him if he felt that if he were a baby he would be cared for more. He then proceeded to get off my lap and wanted to play a board game. He soon began to cheat. I wondered with him about the difficulty he was having because I made the rules in the playroom, especially the one about how long and how often he could see me for sessions. He told me one of the cards in the game had an angry face. I said that perhaps he was very angry with me for being the one who made the rules in the playroom, about when we see each other and how much time we spend together, and also angry that his Mam was having another baby.

Early work with Sam seemed to be characterized by his attempts to break things, or by him actually breaking things, showing his poor sense of having any clear idea of boundaries and especially showing his "broken" internal world, where nothing good or whole seemed to remain that way for long.

Early on in the therapy, the end of the sessions became increasingly difficult for Sam to manage. He would cling to me and desperately try to stay in the room or would remain physically attached to me like a little baby. I talked with him about how hard it was to leave and that he wished I would stay and hold him all day long, not just physically, but also in my mind. He would respond by clinging to me and wrapping his arms around my neck. I would wonder with him if he was afraid that I was not going to keep him in a safe place in my mind, a place where he would be remembered.

Sam displayed this extreme dependent behaviour alongside an angry, controlling sadistic side. A pattern became observed whereby there was an extreme oscillation between his dependent "merging" behaviour and his violent sadistic side. Sam would shout in the sessions, screaming instructions about what I was to do. He would shout things like: "Go get that paint! Why you so slow? Look at me! You stupid or something? What's your problem?"

Glasser's (1979) concept of the "core complex" describes an infant's yearning for union with the mothering object, while at the same time linking this union with a "fear of annihilation" when the developmental process has been effected. Sam's aggressiveness was a defence against an object that he recognized as fearful and dangerous. His aggression appeared to function as a method of finding a balance where he did not feel too enmeshed or too distant from the object (Perelberg, 1999).

Glasser (1996) focuses on what/who is attacked with the use of violence, and what in the phantasy is correlated with the aggression and violence (self-preservative violence). Glasser also describes sadism or malicious violence. Glasser (1996) maintains that the principal aim of aggression lies in negating danger, whereas sadism aims to inflict physical and emotional suffering. Sam displayed the tendency for both types of violence—self-preservative and sadistic violence.

Pooh, wee, and mess

In one of our sessions, Sam knocked over the paints and water and proceeded to try to spread the mess on the floor and table. He began singing a rhyme that he had made up, with the words, "Pooh and wee mixed together, all in heaven!"

I linked the pooh and wee to Sam's feelings of sadness and anger and to feelings that felt so scary that he wanted to flush them away like pooh. He then mixed the paints, which I linked to his feelings feeling mixed together. The colours turned from a green/blue to a brown/black which he spilled on the floor. "Maybe your feelings feel like they are spilling over inside Sam, just like the brown paint on the floor?"

He looked at me angrily and with a threatening glare on his face. He was about to throw the paint at me, but I intervened and said: "I see you want to throw the paint at me, Sam, and you perhaps want to show me how angry you are with me, and maybe angry that I say things that hurt you inside or that I get it wrong sometimes, but I would prefer that you didn't throw them." Sam refrained from throwing the paints.

It was a challenge to keep him and me safe in the room alongside the cardinal rule of psychoanalytic therapy (free association)—that is, for him to do or say anything he wanted except hurt himself or me. I did not want to interfere with him expressing the necessary anxieties and phantasies, but I was aware that issues of containment had to be managed; otherwise, both he and I would feel uncontained and I would be of little help to him. I tried to ensure I was not colluding by re-creating the situation at home. It was therefore important to keep a close watch on what he was doing.

Love, hate, and sibling rivalry

Sam displayed ambivalent feelings of love and hate towards me, the therapy, and the room. He would describe the playroom as "mine" and would be very upset if he saw me speaking to other children in the corridor outside our session times. Strengths and limitations of the setting existed. I worked with other children at the centre for psychotherapy, and some of them were aware of the other children I saw, as they would see me going to and from the playroom. This was difficult due to the layout of the centre, which had limited space, and because the playroom was in close proximity to the other areas of the centre. The issue of other children in the playroom usually presented in the sessions and was explored repeatedly during them.

In relation to Sam's ambivalence, I found that Klein's (1946, 1975) ideas about the developmental continuum that exists between the paranoid–schizoid and depressive positions helped in facilitating my understanding of this aspect of the process of therapy.

Melanie Klein

Melanie Klein worked with the fantasies of early childhood, and she maintained that in order to defend against the fear of the death instinct, the baby's ego "splits", projecting the aggression and destruction of the death instinct on to the mother. The baby then fears both retaliation from the mother and that the mother will get inside him/her and destroy the goodness that exists and that has been split off. The infant uses an intrapsychic process of splitting as a protection against his/her aggressive phantasies.

The child regards the "good" mother as the one who fulfils his/her needs, and the "bad" mother as the one who does not. Klein links these experiences to the "paranoid–schizoid position" (Klein, 1975). After the "bad" objects have been projected onto the mother, they are reintrojected in order that control is re-established. When the child begins to realize that the "good" and the "bad" part-objects are parts of the same person in his mother, he becomes fearful that the destructive phantasies have hurt the mother. Klein refers to this as being associated with "depressive anxiety" (Klein, 1975). The depressive position occurs when the child observes that the "good" and "bad" are parts of the same person, and this awareness facilitates psychical maturation and independence. During the paranoid–schizoid position, the child is concerned with being harmed by others, in contrast to the depressive position, in which the child feels guilty that his/her destructive aggressive phantasies may hurt others. The child through "reparation" tries to repair the damage he/she has done, whether through his/her phantasies or in reality (Klein, 1991). Klein (1946) emphasizes the importance of a good early environment in helping a child to overcome early, paranoid anxieties.

Months 6–12 of therapy

On not wanting to say goodbye

Sam found holiday breaks at the centre very difficult, as we would not be seeing each other. He usually responded by telling me he didn't want to go to the playroom. In one session he lifted a chair above his head ready to throw it. I linked this to him experiencing his feelings as dangerous, especially when we were not going to see each other over the break. He told me he would put the chair down, but when I stood back he raised it again.

At times Sam showed very little distinction between reality and fantasy. He began playing with a fire engine and placed a man on the end of the engine's ladder. I asked him if the fireman felt any danger being at the end of the ladder, just as Sam may feel danger and sadness, as we wouldn't see each other until after the holidays. "No! Not Sam!" he replied, throwing the engine.

I asked him if it might feel less scary if it was not Sam. Sam then sat on my knee and held my hand, leaning back towards the floor and giggling. He asked me to tell him a story and began prodding my breasts. I sat back and said to Sam, "Are you afraid your Mam will give more to the baby when she feeds him and, by hitting my breasts, you are asking me if I have enough time for you, or if I can feed you like your Mam feeds your brother?"

I realized later that I could have talked about how difficult the break felt, especially when he felt like a little baby that needed lots of breast milk to keep it going, and that that milk (the therapy) was not going to be available over the break.

Sam displayed difficulty and confusion with boundaries of the self and body, sometimes clinging to me like a baby and also trying to look down my jumper and trying to hit my breasts. He disliked the idea of his mother breastfeeding his little brother, just like he disliked me seeing other children for therapy, and at times he also showed a dislike for my breasts, by trying to hit them. He appeared to love me and hate me at the same time. Sam seemed to be slowly coming to terms with the loss he felt over losing his mothers attention, and the feeding of the new baby, and over losing me at the end of the sessions.

Boobies, footballs, and danger

In a later session, Sam said he wanted a story, but "No story about a horrible man kicking Mam's boobies like footballs then banging her head." I asked him what happened next. He replied by knocking over an art box.

It seemed that dangerous and violent images appeared in Sam's mind around issues of separation. In my mind I questioned whether Sam had actually witnessed a man hurt his Mam, as it was also possible that Sam was trying to tell me what he had seen at home when there was violence against the mother. Depending on a mother who couldn't keep herself safe would raise painful issues about survival and safely for Sam's own existence—both physically and psychologically.

I asked him if the story of the footballer and the hurt boobies was scary for him, making his feelings spill over, like the box. He demanded paper in a grown-up voice. I asked him about the voice. He punched holes in the paper. I asked him if his feelings felt like the paper, punched with holes. He began to ignore me when I spoke about feelings. He banged a tambourine loudly and told me to march in time to the tambourine, depending on whether the music was loud or soft. This play seemed to be very significant, as Sam was the one in control—telling me what he needed, as opposed to a parent telling him what to do.

When I asked him if his feelings felt loud and angry and at other times soft, and then all mixed up together, he sang louder and tried to hit his head with the tambourine. I quickly stopped him. I asked him if he was trying to get rid of his angry, scary, and sad feeling by hitting his head. He looked at me and nodded in agreement. This sense of acknowledgement and understanding was a significant achievement for him.

Dreams and bad feelings not stopping

Sam proceeded to say, "It keeps banging Sam, it does! Won't stop!" He threw away the tambourine, perhaps an action to show how he himself felt thrown away and hurt by his mother and myself.

He told me he had had a bad dream about birds, and he asked me if I was scared in the playroom. I answered him by saying maybe he felt scared by his sad and angry feelings in the playroom, and by talking about them they may feel less scary and may hurt less.

I realized that rather than talking about the scariness and trying to reassure him, I should have asked him more about his dream. I identified my need to reassure him, which Sam may have experienced as a mother-therapist being unable to help him with his scary dream/feelings. By attempting to reassure Sam, I was probably adding to him feeling uncontained.

Sam's dream had come from a deep, less defended part of his personality. His dream had represented symbolic situations, individuals, and impulses in his life. Sam's dream was based on impressions of his infantile experiences as well as on current events (Freud, 1900a).

Sam had shown me that he did possess a capacity to distinguish between the dream and the reality. I thought he could use therapy very well, but we both had to learn a language together symbolically of what Sam was trying to tell me. When symbolic functioning broke down for Sam, acting out would begin and he would use a behavioural solution such as attacking the dolls or me, or attempting to leave the room.

It was the end of the session, and he clung to me and cuddled me as we left the playroom. I said to him: "Even though I'm holding you because you are scared, we need to talk and think about feelings too. In my heart, I hold onto Sam, like I'm holding onto you now, even when we don't see each other." I asked Sam if he could create a place in his heart like that.

Trying to understand Sam's violence

I questioned in my mind the actual meaning of the violence for Sam in relation to development and to communication. The violence seemed to be a complex way of communicating, and it was a communication method that had already been used by his mother to communicate with him.

Object relations theory

Object relations theory helped to conceptualize aspects of Sam's developmental problems and violence. Fonagy and Target (1996) describe the classification of developmental disturbances and how they are worked with therapeutically, and they consider the link between attachment theory (Bowlby, 1973) and object relations theory. Cashdan (1988) maintains that within object relations theory, the psychic structures of the mind are a result of the human need to develop and preserve relationships (Cashdan, 1988).

From an object relations perspective, it is the need for contact with others that is important, and the theory considers how internal and external objects (people) are related and, in turn, affect relationship dynamics. Objects may be external real people or internal objects—which may be real or imaginary—in the psyche. How an individual attaches is dependent on object introjects of attachment relationships in early infancy (Buelow, McClain, & McIntosh, 1996).

Attachment is necessary to be in relationship with important objects, as object introjection is necessary for attachment (Buelow, McClain, & McIntosh, 1996). Object relations theory focuses on the relationship between child and parent, and the objects introjected by the child, which will affect the child's thoughts, emotions, and behaviour in childhood and adulthood. The theory focuses on both inter-psychic and interpersonal relationships and acknowledges the difference "between actual and psychic reality" (Fonagy & Target, 1995b).

Early determinants of behaviour and personality

Sam spoke of "dog poohs" and of "poohs everywhere". According to Freud's (1905d) psycho-sexual theory of development, the anal stage focuses on the time the child gains sphincter control and directs his attention to this new skill. Sam had full control over holding or expelling the contents of his bladder and rectum. Sam could not, however, control events at home and in his life.

He played games where he wanted to be the adult and would tell me what to do, just as he was being told what to do in his own life. In the therapeutic relationship, Sam experienced a power struggle. His aim was to control his mother, and to control me, in correlation with controlling the anal sphincter. Abraham (1924) proposes that the anal-sadistic stage consists of two phases, depending on the individual's behaviour. In the first stage, anal erotism is linked to the sadistic tendency to harm the object and is also linked to evacuation. In the second phase, it is linked to the instinct to control, and to retention. Abraham proposes that the move from the first to the second stage is a move towards object love, yet between these two stages neurotic and psychotic regressions may occur.

Sam often wanted to play a guessing board game, in which he cheated, showing me that he wasn't listened to and didn't have consistency in his life. Things would often change for him when he least expected it. He liked to put his hands into paint and mix the colours around, and he was happy that I associated the colours with his emotions depending on the colours he used. He found it difficult to leave at the end of sessions and would continue painting and playing. Sam was worried I would leave him like his mother had, and he experienced love and hate simultaneously, one often triggering the other in sessions. Sam had experienced emotional deprivation, and attachments had been made and broken in his life, which explained his rage. I encouraged his group leader to talk about his anxieties with him if an appropriate situation arose, and I also advised the centre that it would be good for him to have a box of toys that he could play with between the group time and our sessions, to help with the transition.

Symbolic play—playing butterflies

Sam began to include me in his play, which was a huge achievement for him. Sam still struggled verbally to express his emotional feelings and experiences. He was, however, now expressing them indirectly in his play as feelings, fears, and conflicts. Sam's use of fantasy and displacement in his play functioned as a way to communicate with me as well as a way to "master anxieties" (Winnicott, 1991, p. 144). I was also aware that if I responded too promptly while working with Sam, it could prevent him reaching the understanding he needed. Winnicott (1969) proposed that at times the use of prompt interpretations may actually stop the patient thinking for him herself and may also mask the underlying problem.

One game that Sam liked to play was pretending to be butterflies. In one session he made paper wings for both of us and wanted me to lift him up, so it would be like flying. He told me he wanted me to be a mammy butterfly. He was about to hit my breasts, but then stopped. He looked at me with acknowledgement in his face that this was wrong. He told me he wanted his Mam and Dad to go away, and he wanted to be a butterfly. Sam's facial expression was one of relief. Sam's butterfly was perhaps a symbolic communication about his need to fly away from his family and leave his anxieties behind. Sam was beginning to acknowledge my understanding of his experiences, phantasies, anxieties, and feelings through the medium of his play (Klein, 1932).

When it was time to go, we left the playroom and walked towards the play centre. Sam told me he had had a scary dream the night before and that he wanted to go back to the playroom. When we reached the centre, he ran back to the playroom and hid behind the door, where he told me he was so scared. This was a huge achievement for Sam, as he was using words to tell me he was afraid.

He had a toy sword in his hand. I told him we could talk about the scary dream next time, and I acknowledged that it was also scary to say goodbye when he had so many scary feelings inside. I felt his sadness, anger, and disappointment. I also felt an intense countertransference feeling of not wanting to let him go, as I knew how scared he was.

Infantile and childhood rage continues at separation

Sam continued hugging me when I met him before each session, and he still wanted me to carry him like a baby to and from sessions. His language in sessions changed from silent aggression to use of words like "shut up", "shut your face", "are you stupid or something", and sometimes "shut up I'm talking". These injunctions would appear when I attempted to make links to his feelings and his play. He wanted me to know what it was like for him when he was spoken to like that. It appeared that my interpretations were causing a lot of anxiety.

In one session Sam began to wrap a roll of paper around his feet and the chair when the session was finished. Sam was afraid I would forget him and our time together. I worked with the deficit. I acknowledged it was difficult for him to leave. He then put his arms out for me to hug him and carry him back to his playgroup.

Sam's behaviour represented how he was looked after—how he was close to a caregiver and then rejected. I spoke to him about the mixed feelings he had for me, liking me and disliking me at the same time, and how he was showing me the way he was treated.

There was a thin line between his displays of aggression and affection. Sam wrestled with a large, soft toy tiger, throwing it around similarly to the way he wanted to wrestle with his sad feelings and throw them away. As time progressed, and Sam knew I was not going to leave him, he would listen to me when I spoke about his feelings or linked them to what he was doing. He appeared relieved when this occurred.

He would, however, suddenly try to scribble on tables and walls, then stop as quickly as he had begun. He would come towards me wanting to hug me and sit on my knee, acknowledging that I understood that what he was doing in the therapy room reflected what he was feeling inside. When I asked Sam if what he needed was attention and hugs, he looked at me half angrily and half surprised. I acknowledged that his running around and climbing was a way of telling others and me what he felt inside, but it was hard for him sometimes to tell me or them. Sam acknowledged what I said by hugging me tightly.

I asked him if he wanted me to be like a Mammy, and he told me: "Not like my Mammy!" This was a major achievement for Sam. Sam was telling me that what he got in psychotherapy was different from what he got at home. What he got from his Mam at home did not always bring him relief. This sequence conveyed Sam's feelings of loss: he was mourning the loss of the Mammy he wished to have and did not, and it was a frightening experience for him, this realization. I thought there was also hope that I could hold him through this mourning. I had not left Sam, despite his anxieties, phantasies, aggression, and violence. There followed an improvement in Sam's emotional development and in his ability to relate to me.

Winnicott and the "good-enough mother"

Winnicott (1958, 1965) emphasized the importance of relationships within the overall development of the child, and he particularly stressed the importance of the mother–child relationship. He referred to the "good-enough mother" (Winnicott, 1965) as a mother who provided optimal care, and he coined the term "there is no such thing as a baby" to emphasize that babies essentially needed an optimal relationship and that whenever you have a baby you have a mother/carer for the baby (Winnicott, 1958).

Winnicott (1958) described the reflective function of the mother (i.e. the mother as a mirror reflecting the baby's emotions) and how, if this experience was optimal, it could later lead the baby to think and reflect. Winnicott (1971a) proposed the concept of "When I look I am seen, so I exist" (Winnicott, 1971a, p. 114) to emphasis the link between being seen and being found by the mother to the development of the self. Winnicott (1958) emphasized the effect of the environment on the mother–child relationship, and the importance of "holding" by the mother in the attachment relationship.

Winnicott (1953) also proposed the concept of "transitional objects", which help the baby adjust to the experience of himself as an individual away from the mother, with the transitional object representing the mother who is not present. This then helps the child to process the separation intra-psychically. The transitional object is also exposed to aggression from the child. Winnicott proposed a "true self" whose development could be enhanced or hindered depending on responses from the mother and others in the child's environment. Winnicott (1956a) also regarded destructiveness and aggressiveness to be essential processes that enabled the child to separate from the mother. Winnicott (1956a) also differentiated between aggressive behaviour and antisocial behaviour by proposing that while aggression is an essential part of development, antisocial behaviour results from environmental and emotional deprivation.

Use of objects

Sam related to the soft toy tiger in the room as his unhappy feelings and to a teddy bear as his happy feelings. He still experienced a huge dichotomy of experience between his happy and unhappy feelings. He occasionally went to the game he had hurt his finger on, and this usually occurred when he was angry and wanted to break toys. I asked Sam if he felt the only way he would get attention for his feelings was to hurt himself, but he told me, "no feelings, not talking about it!" I challenged him, saying not talking about feelings can make him feel unhappy. Sam listened but did not respond, and he appeared to be searching for something.

Sam had a favourite book, about a little dog that was unhappy, yet later found happiness. He told me he liked it when the dog became happy. Sam got upset when I asked him if he felt like the little dog in the story and wanted to be happy like him. He threw paper and pencils around and then sat on my knee, hugging me. I felt a maternal countertransference as Sam sat on my knee. He wanted me to take away his anxieties and fears and to behave like a Mammy for him.

Sam was coming to terms with his internal and external world through his symbolic play (Klein, 1932). I was still trying to find the correct balance between playing and staying in the metaphor with him and moving to make an interpretation about his symbolic play. It seemed that Sam was not always ready for a verbal interpretation, and at times it seemed more appropriate to stay "in the play" with his painful experience.

Sam would often order me to read him stories and play games with him, in a raised adult-like voice, almost afraid I would not want to play with him if he did not speak to me like this. He was "identifying with the aggressor" (Freud, 1936b) in an attempt at trying to control the fear of a "dreaded, external object" (Freud, 1936b).

Months 12–18 of therapy: endings

In one session Sam ran to the room and showed me how angry he was. He told me he was angry at his Mam and new baby brother. He threw feathers around, putting one on his tongue, and telling me it was "yuck". In his angry raised voice, he told me to put away games. "What are you waiting for, you? Hurry up!" He was perhaps telling me how angry he was with me as a result of having to wait for me and our session time.

He looked at me angrily and scattered a box of coloured feathers. If the different coloured feathers were feelings, I asked, what might those feelings be? He chose colours for "angry" and "nice". He then began spitting on the table and rubbed the spit away with the "angry feather". He made up music with a toy drum, shouting without words or making words up.

We then played hide-and-seek, which showed a developmental achievement, expressing his need to be found—particularly "found in mind" (Fonagy, 2001a). Fonagy posits the importance for the child of being found in the mind of the carer, and how this is a fundamental emotional need for every child. He proposes that this process of "being found in mind" is aided by the capacity of the parent/carer/therapist to "mentalize".

Fonagy (2001a) describes mentalization as a "specific symbol function" (p. 165) that is important in both attachment and psychoanalytic thinking. On the basis of empirical observations and theoretical elaboration, Fonagy and Target have developed the argument that the capacity to understand interpersonal behaviour in terms of mental states is a key determinant of self-organization and affect regulation, and that it is acquired in the context of early attachment relationships. This capacity is referred to as mentalization and is operationalized for research as a reflective function (Fonagy & Target, 2003, p. 270).

Fonagy (2001a) maintains that the capacity to "mentalize" helps us to distinguish between internal and external reality and that this capacity is seen as a developmental achievement. The level of the child's achievement to mentalize is connected to the experience of his/her earliest relationships, and, in turn, the development of the child's internal world is reflected in his/her ability to mentalize.

Fonagy (1998) strengthens the long-established psychological position that behaviour is clearly connected to internal states like feelings and thoughts. As the child and caregiver interact, the child begins to learn about this interconnectivity in him/herself and others, as he/she slowly perceives how thoughts and feelings help to determine behaviour.

Sam did not have a mother, a "container", who could tolerate and hold his painful feelings (Bion, 1962). The therapeutic relationship functioned as a container for Sam's chaotic and painful experiences. Sam was slowly able to find his feelings and himself in his mind, as I was simultaneously able to find him in my mind. The hide-and-seek game enabled him to look for his feelings, find them, and tolerate them. During the hide-and-seek game, I told him I found him just like I found him in my mind when we were not together.

Sam was calmer in sessions. He had been staying with relatives for a month, as his Mam needed to be hospitalized for an operation. Sam began bringing his homework to sessions and taking pride in his work. He told me his aunt helped him with his homework. This was something he had not experienced previously.

Sam would now often talk to me about his unhappy and angry feelings, which he said he felt inside. In one session he wanted to know if I had a baby, and he was insistent about asking me this again and again. I asked him if he thought I would not be able to look after him properly if I had a baby. He hugged me. Sam continued wanting to be hugged and carried like a baby to and from sessions. He used fight games with animals to express the confusion, anger, difficulties, and internal conflicts he experienced. He told me his happy feelings lived inside him, and that was their home. He drew pictures of a car, telling me his Mam had left him, and then he started swearing at her.

Sam projected his feelings onto me. At times he showed me what it was like to be shouted at and not listened too. He displayed confusion with body boundaries by trying to touch my breasts when he was behaving like a baby. I asked him if he thought I had to feed him to look after him the way Mams look after babies.

I had hurt my back doing sports and could not continue carrying Sam to the room, so I asked him if he wanted to hold my hand instead. I told him I had hurt my back. He listened, then wrapped his arms around my leg as we walked, so I had to walk slowly. Sam pointed to a picture of a woman in a book, pointing to her "boobies" for babies to suck. I asked him if that's what he thought when he tried to touch my "boobies", and when he wanted me to carry him and look after him like a Mammy looks after a baby. He ran away and hid behind a cupboard outside the room. I followed him and asked him if it was difficult to talk about things like unhappy feelings and feeling like a baby. He held onto my leg and told me he loved me. He looked both scared and sad. I felt a sadness that Sam had so much fear and confusion, which was so mixed up with his experience of love.

Physical proximity was easier for Sam than was psychological proximity. He worried that if I did not carry him and hug him, I did not care for him. He sometimes ran around the room, or ran off before or after sessions, so I would have to run after him. He wanted to make sure I would find him physically and mentally, in various attempts aimed to master his very painful separation anxiety.

During holidays, and sometimes at the end of a session when he found it difficult to leave, we would paint or draw a picture together, which he would take with him, as it was difficult for him to hold me in mind or to believe that I would not forget him.

Story telling

In one session Sam asked me to choose a story to read to him. I told him the story was about a little boy, and, because his feelings had become very hurt, he had to make his heart hard to protect himself because he was frightened (Sunderland, 2000). Sam grabbed the book and threw it across the room. He began spilling beakers of water. He had made paper hearts for his family, which he wanted to look at. I asked him if he wanted us, while in the playroom, to make his family's hearts feel better. He ignored the hearts and took out his paintings. It was difficult for him to think about his family. He cuddled me and clung to me as I took him back to the centre. He found it very difficult to say goodbye, and he clung desperately to me—extending the time we had together.

It was difficult for him to keep me in mind when we did not meet, and so he clung to me, so I wouldn't leave him, thus showing me how insecurely attached he was. He also ignored me on occasions, showing me what it felt like for him feeling thrown away.

As sessions progressed, Sam would sometimes pretend to be asleep and to snore. I asked him why he was sleeping. He told me he was frightened of the "scary, angry inside". He wanted to go to sleep so he did not have to think about these anxieties, fears, and inner conflicts. He sometimes spoke in a deep croaky voice. When I asked the "croaky voice" to come out and go away (the scary feelings), the scary feelings would tell me in the same voice that they lived inside Sam and wouldn't go away. Sam said the happier ones would be happier. He was almost reluctant to let his scary feelings out, almost in a protective way. I thought about what he was protecting in his family.

On one occasion he sat on my knee cuddling me and pretending to be asleep. He played with the bin liner, and I asked him if the sad feelings had gone into the bin. He looked happy and smiled, and he handed me a book about hugs. He sat happily as I read him the story. I linked this to Sam feeling safe and happy when he was hugged. He smiled and looked into the bin. Sam was becoming more articulate. He would ask me if I was angry with him when he swore, and also at the end of sessions when he felt I was sending him away. I would acknowledge that I was not angry but that it was time to go. When I told him I knew he was feeling angry and upset, he would say, "Yea scary", and then he would hug and cuddle me for long periods in the session.

Sam would show various fluctuations in his insecure behaviour by climbing on the table and then changing to sitting at the table and wanting to play a game. He would tell me that he was a good boy, and when I made a link to Sam being a good boy, but that his scary, angry feelings were making him scared, he was able to acknowledge this and agree with me. Sam would wrestle with a large tiger in the playroom, showing me how difficult his scary feelings were. He would say "shut up, Mam". When I asked him the name of the scary feelings, he called them "Smelly, horrible!" I tried to join his external and internal worlds by telling him that sometimes it was hard for him to find words for his feelings inside.

Increasingly, Sam would tell me when he felt happy or sad. After a holiday at the centre, when we did not meet for four weeks, he told me he was annoyed with me. He felt I had left him, but he spoke about the picture we had made together and which he had taken home with him—a transitional object, which reminded him of our time in the playroom.

Sam drew pictures of himself, his mother, his sisters, and his baby brother. In the pictures he drew himself as a pig. I asked him if he felt different to the other members of his family. Throughout the session he had been making pig noises. He told me the pig noises were his unhappy feelings. I asked him if the unhappy feelings hurt him so much that it was hard to see what he looked like and sounded like. I asked Sam if I, too, had made him unhappy by going away during the centre's holidays. He then drew another person in the family picture holding hands with the other family members.

Sam became increasingly open with his anxieties, fears, and sadness as the sessions progressed. He was happy to see me, and he called the chair he liked to sit on in the playroom, "The chair where nice things happened". He laughed and played, but when he wanted to show me how he was feeling, it was usually through the medium of play. He told me he heard party-poppers one day, and then he wrapped a roll of paper around the room so that he and I were in the middle of the paper. When I asked him if his feelings felt messy and tangled inside, like the paper, he began to swear, imitating an adult voice. He wrapped himself in the paper, ran around the room, and said, "This is so cool—look, paper everywhere!"

I asked Sam if it was cool because we could see what he felt like inside. He smiled and skipped around. Sam was finally using his play to speak and to master his anxieties (Winnicott, 1991). I could then use interpretations, through which Sam would gain further relief from his conflicts and anxieties and also begin to understand our therapeutic work together (Klein, 1945).

In one session Sam had asked me to play Mammy's and Daddy's with him, and when I asked him what we would do to play, he looked upset and ignored me and ran out of the playroom, and he told me he wanted to go to the toilet. I asked him if he felt scared and wanted to flush his scary feelings down the toilet. Sam's playgroup leader later told me he had urinated on another child.

Sam then played a fighting game with toy monster figures. He told me it was his happy feelings and his sad feelings fighting. He said his happy feelings lived inside him. He told me two of the monsters were people in his family and the other two were Mammy and Daddy. The Mammy and Daddy killed the other monsters, and then they started fighting and killed each other.

When I linked this to his feelings hurting him, he pretended to be asleep. I linked this to Sam feeling tired of these feelings and fights. He showed me a truck with him and his Mam in it, and then he began swearing at her. When I asked him where his

Mammy was, he said, "Gone away without me". He then tried to put his hands down inside my jumper. I sat back and asked him, "What was happening now? Suddenly you've tried to put your hand under my jumper." I asked him if he was trying to show me something that had happened to him.

He had tried to cross body boundaries, and I also thought he had regressed to wanting to be breastfed, like his sibling was. He was showing me things that happened in his mind, and in his reality. He was communicating being left as a baby that needed to be breastfed by the mother.

Sam was projecting onto me a confusion between self and other as safe versus an other that appears safe and is not (Klein, 1991). This object is confusing for him, which he projects onto me. He pointed to a picture of a woman in a storybook, "Look, boobies!" When I asked him what boobies were for, he told me they were for babies to suck. He cuddled me and then asked me to name animals in a book, which he did not recognize. I linked this to him wanting to talk about boobies and about other things that might be difficult for him to understand and name. Sam ran off, out of the room, and down the corridor.

When I caught up with him he was hiding, and I asked him if it was difficult to talk about things like boobies. He hugged me, and he held on to my leg. He replied, "I love you." He looked up at me sadly.

Sam wanted to make sure I would find him when he hid. Physically and mentally, he was testing the physical boundaries. He liked playing hide-and-seek, in further attempts to master separation anxiety. He was still afraid I would leave him. It was time to go back to his playgroup. I felt protective over Sam; he hugged me and said, "See you next time."

Sam wanted me to carry him to the next session; instead, I offered him my hand, which he took. In the playroom, I asked him if he felt I had to carry him and look after him with my boobies, to take care of him. I told Sam I could still look after him without carrying him or feeding him with my boobies.

He began making pictures with glitter and coloured paper and started showing a sense of pride in his work, telling me how good he thought his pictures were. In subsequent sessions, Sam would run around when he was upset, sometimes throwing toys. He told me when he did this people thought he was naughty. I asked him if people like teachers, and Mammy, and other children thought this because they did not understand he was unhappy. He told me his Mammy was bad, and he began swearing at me when I asked him why. I had become the bad mother-therapist.

We talked about him telling people when he felt unhappy, so they would not think he was naughty. Sam quickly went to the art materials and carefully drew a picture he wanted to give to his Mammy. I linked this to Sam wanting to show his Mammy how clever he was. Sam smiled and continued drawing his picture. Sam began speaking to his group leader, telling her how unfair he thought it was that his Mammy had previously left him and had gone away for a while.

In a subsequent session Sam regressed slightly, wanting to crawl to the playroom, telling me that his (phantasy) sisters looked after his Mam, and his baby brother looked after him. I asked him if it was very difficult at home, especially with a baby looking after him. He threw dolls and jumped on them, telling me they were his scared, sad feelings. When I asked him if he thought the dolls were hurt, he began swearing. He then wanted to draw a picture, telling me his picture was stupid. When I told him it was a clever picture like the other clever pictures he had drawn, Sam kissed me on the cheek. He found it difficult to leave the session. Sam knew it was a holiday break for two weeks. I told him I would think about him in my mind and heart when I did not see him, and we would see each other after the holiday break. Sam hugged me and kissed me on the cheek.

Sam still continued to feel abandoned at holiday times, and he felt as though I was throwing him away. Sam showed a pattern of regression when his needs were not being met. Just before one break, Sam wanted me to paint a picture with him, to have when we did not meet. Instead of taking it home, however, he put it in his box and told me it would be in his box to look at when we met the next time.

The following day I was told that Sam would be leaving the centre. The council had re-housed his family, and his mother was going to move him to a play centre nearer his new home. The new centre had a psychotherapist.

Sam's mother had told his current play leader that she would consent to further therapy there, but she did not want to meet with me before the move, which was in six weeks' time. Sam and I talked during sessions about the move and endings. Sam knew he would see a new therapist and told me that that was good, but that he really wanted to stay with me.

Containing sad goodbyes

Sam told me he was sad at having to leave, and he regressed, displaying aggression by throwing toys around the room when we spoke about endings. He said he was scared about going away. He began making "containers" out of Playdough to take home to his mother. He did this during every session for our final weeks. He also gave the same "containers" to his play leader and helpers. He wanted to know they would contain and hold him in a way he had been contained and held in sessions. I had functioned perhaps as a "container" (Bion, 1962) for Sam, as I had received his fear, chaos, internal conflicts, anxieties, violence, and pain and tried to understand them. Through the therapeutic relationship, Sam was able to understand and find meaning in both his internal and external worlds.

Through the therapeutic relationship, Sam had found a space in my mind where he was understood, which helped him to think and so find a space in his own mind. Before he left, Sam gave me a card. It was carefully made, covered with the glitter colours he liked and pieces of collage. He hugged me and kissed me on the cheek, and he smiled as he handed me the card. I gave him a card, too. I told him I would always remember him in my mind and heart. Sam's card read: "Thank you for looking after me, I'll miss you but it's okay when you're gone. Love Sam."

I knew it would be difficult for Sam adjusting to his move and meeting a new therapist. I also knew that he had begun to develop a capacity to "mentalize" (Fonagy, 2001a, 2001b) and self-reflect and to think about his aggressive and violent behaviour. Although his home environment was not favourable, therapy had perhaps given him relief to deal with difficult situations in his environment (Klein, 1932).

DISCUSSION AND EVALUATION

During therapy, I used different interventions in relation to working with Sam's past, his feelings, and our therapeutic relationship.

The therapeutic work was done mainly through the medium of play, with the added use of art and stories, which allowed him to communicate some of his internal and external chaos and pain, and to master anxieties that were in line with developmental progress (Winnicott, 1991).

I attempted to provide a holding environment for Sam in psychotherapy, which aimed to provide a space, in turn, for Sam to bring conflicts and deficits in his inner and outer world as well as his unconscious phantasies (Winnicott, 1956a). The therapeutic environment and working alliance provided a "developmentally needed" (Clarkson, 1995, p. 108) maternal, holding, environment that encouraged him to express his feelings, anxieties, fears, thoughts, and emotions through the medium of play.

Winnicott (1956a) proposed that by tolerating projections and destructive parts in the therapeutic relationship and making interpretations, as well as surviving attacks, the therapists presence would enable the establishment of an awareness of an individual that was separate and would thus facilitate necessary developmental processes. I felt that this had begun to happen with Sam.

CHAPTER SEVEN

Neutralizing terror

Rosemary Campher

This chapter explores the clinical work of the present author with a young boy over a three-year period. It explores theoretical concepts pertaining to normal and abnormal development; the development of violent tendencies; and their use as a defence against extreme vulnerability, helplessness and frightening feelings of terror. Issues of clinical technique are discussed to highlight the complexity and challenge of working psychoanalytically with a violent child in a child therapy setting.

The context

The therapeutic work took place in an inner-city school, where I was employed by the school as a psychotherapist. The therapy room, which was a fully equipped child-therapy room, was in the school and was used solely for the practice of child psychotherapy. The practice of psychotherapy in schools has its strengths and its limitations. A central primary strength is that the child's attendance at therapy is usually very high, because the therapist does not have to rely on caregivers to bring the child to the sessions. In inner cities, there appears to be a great reluctance on the part of parents to take their child to therapy in a clinic setting or, once it has begun in a clinic, for there to be a continuation of the process. The high attendance rate within the school setting not only increases the viability of the therapy, but also fosters a sense of continuity, reliability, and consistency, which are three important features that appear to be very significant in the development of a good-enough therapeutic practice.

"Tim"

Tim was referred to me for psychoanalytic psychotherapy due to his high levels of uncontained aggression, which would lead to violent outbursts in school. These violent actings-out would occur within the playground and, at times, within the classroom. Tim's emotional and psychological difficulties would also manifest in difficulties in concentrating, in learning difficulties, and in disruptive behaviour in the classroom setting. He would often be excluded from class for his disruptiveness and anger as well as from the whole school at times as a result of his violence and aggression towards other children. Tim was at risk of being permanently excluded from school on beginning therapy with me. Tim would kick, push, fight, and throw things and would seem to be unable to control these states.

Tim was from a large extended family. He was born in East Africa and arrived in the UK when he was 3 years old. His father was absent, and the school did not know his whereabouts. He was the second youngest of five children. The family struggled financially and had obvious multiple stressors as a result of this. Apart from these few facts, very little else was known about the home setting.

The start of therapy

I fetched a tall, thin, and lively 8-year-old from his classroom. He looked sheepish and a bit nervous, yet had an animated look on his face. He had been informed that I would fetch him, and he was thus expecting me. I told him my name and explained that we would be going along to the playroom. He kept his head down as we made our way to the therapy room. Once there, I explained who I was and then introduced the child therapy frame: that I would be fetching him every week to come to the room to play, talk, and think about things that he may find difficult. I explained that the session would be for fifty minutes and that we would not meet over the school holidays. I further explained that he could do whatever he liked in the room, except hurt himself or me, and that we could talk about those feelings and urges if they came up. I introduced the idea of privacy and confidentiality by saying that everything he did or said in the room was private and that I would not be talking to anyone else about what he did or what he said, but that I would need to if he told me that he was being hurt in some way and if he was in danger. I explained that I would then have to talk to another adult to try to make it safer for him. I showed him a private container that had a few toys in it that were to be just for him. I explained that he could keep anything he made during the session in the box and that the box would be kept for him until he and I finished our work together.

Discussing and clarifying the frame or boundary conditions at the onset of therapy fulfils a function of containment as well as being a communication about the reality that the therapeutic space is a very different space from other social contexts. Freud (1912e) talked about the need to provide a consistent and reliable space, which honoured and protected whatever unique and private experiences the client was to present. The therapeutic frame provides a basic structure that functions to facilitate the therapeutic work and the relationship on the one hand, and to foster containment on the other. The therapeutic work is centred on understanding the communicative value of the child's play and the part played by the therapeutic relationship. While understanding the play of the child is central to the work, a crucial element also lies in the "receptivity of the analyst's (therapist) mind" (Hoxter, 1977, p. 209).

Tim looked around the room and then asked what was in the cupboard. I told him that he could take a look, but that was where we kept all the paints and some other toys. He took a look and played around with some coloured pencils. He asked what something else was used for in the cupboard, and I interpreted that "Perhaps he was really curious about this room and me and what this is all called and how it is going to be here with me, and that perhaps he was also a bit nervous to be here, bearing in mind that we had just met."

He left the cupboard and went over to a container that had baby dolls in it and which was covered with a blanket. He then went over to a big chair and started to cuddle up in it. I asked him if he would like the blanket over him. He nodded. I carefully laid the blanket over him and decided to hold back any interpretation about him feeling like a baby. He lay very still and every now and then would open his eyes to look at me. He started to dose off. After about ten minutes, he roused and opened his eyes. I interpreted that perhaps he was wondering how I was going to be looking after him and caring for him, not just by keeping him warm, but by helping him with difficult feelings and thoughts that perhaps made him unhappy. He looked at me but did not say anything.

Tim then got up and started to play with some cars. His play with the cars contained a mixture of crashing a few cars together and then parking them in very separate parking spaces. I reflected that the cars seemed to be angry at each other at times and that they all seemed to need their very own space. After this he drew a picture of a figure alone on the page. The drawing was similar in style to a 4-year-old's drawing. Tim found it difficult to leave the room when the session came to an end; I told him that I could see that it was difficult to leave and that he wanted to stay, but that we had to finish for today. He still struggled to leave but finally did so after a minute or two.

This first session highlights the need to establish clear boundaries and to introduce the idea of the importance of thinking about experiences as opposed to action-orientated behaviour that attempts to obliterate thinking or feeling. Anna Freud (1965) succinctly states the importance and developmental value that lies at the centre of child therapy by referring to the implicit value of transforming emotionally undigested experience into symbolic experience (thoughts, words) and thus replacing acting out with thinking through. She maintains that

> The ego of the young child has the developmental task to master on the one hand orientation in the external world and on the other hand the chaotic emotional states, which exist within himself. It gains its victories and advances whenever such impressions are grasped, put into thoughts or words, and submitted to the secondary process. [A. Freud, 1965, p. 32]

Difficulties in thinking

While the first session was relatively contained, I wondered about the possible split within Tim. On the one hand, he was showing me an extremely vulnerable and needy child, who was able to use symbolic play to communicate some of his inner world to me, yet I also knew that he had been referred for very disruptive and violent behaviour. From the second session onwards I was able to see more of the disturbed part of Tim, and the next few months showed that Tim had difficulty in thinking and reflecting on his behaviour; it seemed much easier for him to be engaged in "action-orientated behaviour" rather than to be reflective or even begin to think things through. The same difficulty pertained to his sense of awareness of his emotions and how to express these in a healthy way. What became evident was the painfulness of thinking for Tim and the attendant anxiety that occurred. When my words, contained in an interpretation, resulted in him feeling anxious and afraid, he would increase his attacks on me with words, accusations, or attempts to throw things at me. He would attempt to attack and destroy all thinking—in me and in himself. Fonagy and Target (1999) discuss Britton's (1989) views about the importance of the father in helping the child to develop a capacity to think by the child having to come to terms with the presence of the father, thus introducing a third person into the oedipal situation. Fonagy and Target further explore Britton's (1989) view that emphasizes the importance of the child being "able to accommodate the perspective of a third person, the father" (Fonagy & Target, 1999, p. 67). They also discuss Britton's view of how this triangular oedipal situation allows the child "space to think" (Fonagy & Target, 1999, p. 67).

Fonagy and Target (1999) further link Britton's views with their own on not-thinking and violence: "We follow Britton in seeing violence, and specifically destructiveness towards the analyst and analysis, as expressing a wish to obliterate unbearable thoughts, to destroy reality and to restore omnipotence" (Fonagy & Target, 1999, p. 67). Perelberg (1999) agrees that violence can be understood as an expression of there being difficulties inherent in the capacity to think. Perelberg adds that "As part of this fundamental difficulty in thinking, there is a tendency for body and mind to become confused, so that violent acts on one's own or another's body are used to get rid of intolerable states of mind" (p. 6).

Campbell (1999) discusses the importance of how the "father's gender role identity and parental Oedipal impulses" affects the process of the father "claiming his child" (p. 81). This "claiming" helps the child to "become aware that he or she occupies a place in father's mind that is separate and distinct from mother" (p. 82). Campbell further explains the importance of the child then becoming "aware of a place for mother in father's mind and a place for father in mother's mind" (p. 82).

The core complex

Tim's aggressive and anxious behaviour was shown alongside some very regressive and infantile projections. The first session seemed to show me the extreme vulnerability and dependency needs and fears that lay beneath his aggression and violence. In the initial stages of the therapy, there was thus an oscillation between violent phantasies and aggressive behaviour and very infantile behaviour based on merging phantasies. It seems possible that Tim's need to merge created a conflict in him and made conscious awful fears of perhaps being either engulfed or abandoned (Glasser, 1979). Glasser posits the notion of a "core complex" to understand these internal fears, which "includes an intense longing for indissoluble union with the object (typically the mother), which leaves the individual, at the same time, with a fear of being merged and annihilated" (Glasser, 1985, p. 409).

Glasser (1979, 1992) maintains that the "core complex" occurs throughout normal development and suggests that it begins when the child begins to have anxieties about loss which are ushered in by the child's own moves towards separation and individuation. Glasser views the infant's wish to merge with the idealized, gratifying mother as an attempt to solve these painful anxieties about loss. Glasser (1979, 1992) proposes that the success of the merging "solution" depends on the presence and availability of both a good-enough mother *and* a good-enough father—the former providing a nurturing, attuned relationship and the latter providing an alternative to the maternal fused exclusivity and also functioning in a protective way to any maternal failings (Glasser, 1979, 1992).

The following extract from an early session with Tim shows some of the above-mentioned anxieties. It is important to note that separation-anxiety issues had been expressed in many previous sessions.

> Tim had been lying in a chair, pretending to sleep. He would lie very still, but every now and then he would open his eyes to look around the room. His eyes rested on a doll that had a bonnet on its head. This was a bonnet that he had often played with and had tried to take from the room with him on many different occasions. On this particular day, he got up and picked the bonnet up and put it on his head. He said that he was going to take it today, and he started to run around the room in a manic

> way, as if I was going to chase him and take the bonnet away. I said that it seemed that he felt he needed to take something with him as it was hard to say goodbye at the end of the sessions, and especially hard when he felt like a baby that needed to be looked after by me. He stopped running around and sat on the floor near a box of toys. He started to pick up things and throw them away. I wondered with him if that was how he felt when I ended the session—that I was throwing him away. He stopped throwing things and looked at me and said that he was going now and that he was taking the bonnet with him. I said that we still had a few minutes left together and that I would prefer he stayed, but that maybe he was telling me how really hard it was to stay in the room with all these baby feelings and also very hard that I was the one who ended the session, especially when he felt that he needed more of me.
>
> He went over to the cupboard and took out a pair of scissors and cut the two strings that came down from the sides of the bonnet to tie under the neck. He put the baby bonnet back on his head. He then turned to me, looking a bit scared and yet excited, and said that he was going now—and he ran at full speed out of the room. I followed him to the door, but he had already run away down the passage. As I was standing at the door thinking, he came rushing back and threw the hat at me and then ran away again.

Tim's difficulty in separating was always evidenced by manic behaviour at the end of sessions. It seemed, however, that in this session, besides him expressing his anxiety about leaving, there was also an expression of his fear of what would happen if he stayed—that is, what would happen if he did stay all day or all the time. I felt that he was, perhaps, expressing a fear of "being engulfed", and he had showed me his need to separate or cut himself loose by cutting the ties on the baby's bonnet. His manic behaviour, however, also showed that he tried to make very sure that he didn't feel the sadness that he felt when it was time for us to say goodbye. The manic activity was a desperate attempt to flee from these feelings, and in the manic defence he found a "pathological solution" (Fonagy & Target, 1999) to these anxieties. There appeared to be a desperate conflict between the need to develop on the one hand, and the need to remain in a regressed state on the other. Neither separation nor development was easy for Tim, and each seemed to be imbued with its own sense of peculiarity and painfulness.

Tim's fears around separation also seemed to be linked to the difficulty in remembering our time together and also believing that I would remember him and hold him in my mind after we said goodbye. Tim displayed, at various times, both anxieties about being abandoned and annihilation anxieties pertaining to being engulfed. Glasser (1996) suggests that annihilation anxieties about engulfment and abandonment arise as a result of a failure to resolve the core-complex issues.

There was also a very real experience for Tim of having the feeling of there not being enough time, which was connected to the fact that I only saw him for therapy once a week. I had to manage that limitation and yet continue to think about it with Tim.

It appeared that Tim didn't trust me enough yet to be able to help him with his painful feelings or help him to manage them. He felt too overwhelmed to even think of allowing me verbally to know about these feelings. Thus they found a "container" in the manic behaviour and aggression. I would then be the one left in the room in a state of despair and helplessness and he was the one who ran out triumphantly. I found that if I didn't talk about these painful endings near the beginning of the next session, they would tend to continue in an unabated way. It was almost as if it was impossible for him to take in any interpretation while he was in that state of anxiety at the end, and thus I had to think about these feelings with him when he was more able to bear them. There would always be something in the play that I could use to make the links, and thus I continued to "analyse this resistance" until it became easier for Tim to leave without destroying what had been created between us in the session. There was a slow change in this behaviour as he was able to endure the separation and all that it meant for him.

It appeared that the more relaxed and contained I felt, it tended to influence his behaviour when in these manic states. When I was feeling anxious and desperate as a result of the incessant attacks or the manic defences and hopeless about whether I would ever be able to help him, in supervision I would think about these feelings and have them contained by my supervisor; then I felt I could contain him better. There was a slow change that became evident in the content of his play and within the process of our relationship. The attacks on thinking and symbolic play that would arise when he was anxious and feeling overwhelmed were slowly replaced by more playfulness between us and a more sustained capacity to manage feelings and difficult thoughts within each of us. Reaching that position, however, was an arduous task, which challenged me in very many ways.

Rapid oscillations

Tim could alternate rapidly between two states in the play room—playing symbolically either on his own or with me included in some way; and acting out in an angry, violent, and at times ruthless way. During the latter state he would throw or pretend to throw things at me, break things, leave the room, and swear and shout at me. At times, this behaviour would be replaced by a marked change in his emotional expression—he would sink into despair and depression and would then lose all interest in playing or with being with me in the room. At these times he would usually threaten never to come back. He would, however, always come to the next session, and never once was he resistant to attending—in other words, he would come readily with me when I fetched him from his classroom, and it was only once we were in the play room that he would actually threaten to leave. During the times when Tim would violently act out, he would appear to lose touch with any capacity he had to use transitional phenomena—his playing and use of symbols would be profoundly affected.

It seemed that there were rapid oscillations between being in the paranoid–schizoid and the depressive positions (Klein, 1946). Steiner (1992) proposes that,

> Perhaps the most significant difference between the two positions is along the dimension of increasing integration which leads to a sense of wholeness both in the self and in object relations as the depressive positions is reached. Alongside this comes a shift from a preoccupation with the survival of the self to recognition of dependence on the object and a subsequent concern with the state of the object. [Steiner, 1992, p. 46]

The achievement of being able to enter into the depressive position is also linked to the growing capacity to deal with loss.

It seemed that as Tim was able to slowly depend more on me to help him with difficult thoughts and feelings around separation, loss, helplessness, pain, and violence, some important shifts began to appear. Anna Freud (1970) proposed that separation anxiety was deeply embedded in the fear of losing the object and was often linked to excessive separations and the existence of a maternally unreliable figure. She maintained that annihilation fears and extreme feelings of helplessness were also linked to early fears of loss (of object and love) and that these could be found alongside fears of desertion, punishment, and natural disasters

Further in relation to Tim's threats to leave, I also wondered if he had been witness to experiences that involved a parent threatening to go away and never come back. If this was the case, it could be possible that the significance of the "absent father" was much more complicated. It did seem possible that the "absent father" was a very really presence in his mind, not in a helpful or a containing way but, rather, in a persecutory and painful way. Fonagy and Target (1999) review the literature pertaining to the adverse effects that the absent father has on development, and they note that "Herzog (1980, 1982) in particular highlights how absence or loss of the father during the first few years can undermine the infant's capacity to modulate aggression" (Fonagy & Target, 1999, p. 66). The father's role is also very significant in "helping the child to develop a space in which he can see himself as separate from the mother . . ." (Perelberg, 1999, p. 7). Campbell (1999) highlights at least two important functions that the father plays within the development of a child's capacity to form a mental representation of a self that is separate: "The good-enough father provides a model for identification as well as an alternative relationship to the child's regressive wish to return to a 'fusional' state with mother with subsequent anxieties about engulfment" (Campbell, 1999, p. 82).

Countertransference

The first year's therapy with Tim seemed to be focused around the difficulty in thinking and containing experience (in both Tim and myself), and sessions would frequently be characterized by him having violent outbursts in the room and engaging in manic destructive activity, as well as by his difficulty in staying in the room for the full fifty minutes. I, too, struggled at times with being able to think and thus to understand what he was trying to tell me and what was going on between us. I also became aware of strong feelings of fear within me. In the initial stages of experiencing these feelings, I found it difficult to digest them and use them; thus, the days when Tim did leave the room early, I was often left with a feeling of relief.

There seemed also to be a repetition of unresolved conflict between us. I began to find Tim very difficult to work with, and I wondered if I was going to be able to help him at all. He seemed so terrified about any emotional contact and furious at direct interpretations about his possible internal states or about what may be taking place between us. In essence, it seemed that my interpretations felt like persecutory presences in the room that roused his anger and violence even more. Perhaps my words were experienced as unbearable reminders that we were indeed separate and that I had a mind of my own. It seemed, however, that at times he experienced my interpretations as invasions into his mind and not as an experience of having his mind contained/found in mine.

Fairbairn (1954) proposes that aggression is associated with a lack of gratification and a sense of deprivation. Tim was certainly making it clear to me that he felt he was not getting what he needed and that I was often depriving him of something—especially when there were breaks, at the end of the session and over holidays. Fairbairn (1954) further maintains that violence is an attempt at finding a solution to the frightening feeling of being overwhelmed by the object. It was clear on many occasions that Tim felt overwhelmed by my words and what they represented.

As a result of my countertransference feelings of fear and the expression of anxiety and terror that I sometimes saw in Tim, I began to wonder if his impulses to be violent or his actual violent behaviour itself were functioning in a way to attempt to neutralize the terror he felt. This terror was related to many things—fear of emotional contact, fear of abandonment, fear of being understood as well as not being understood, violent feelings, and extreme helplessness. This deeper understanding of the functioning of his violence and violent tendencies gave me more insight into the terrifying place that Tim's internal world was. It also ushered in a more sustained capacity for me to be able to think in the midst of his attacks and to use this thinking in a way that was more helpful in reducing his anxious states of mind and body.

He would often throw and break things. If he was intending to throw things at me, I was able to prevent this by pre-empting the attack. I would often say: "I see that you are very angry with me now, and that my words seem to have hurt you, and you want to hurt me now, by throwing something at me." Tim would usually then stop the physical attacks on me and throw the toys down onto the floor. This behaviour would usually be followed by verbal attacks on me about how awful I was and that he was going to leave and never come back.

It took many difficult sessions, and much helpful supervision, for me to be able to contain all the attendant anxieties and fears—within both his mind and my own. I then started to use my countertransference experience of feeling how difficult it was to be in the room with him and my relief when he left. I said that it must be very hard for him to be in the room with someone he feels annoys and hurts him with words and, most of all, who he feels is not helping him with his feelings of anger and hurt. After working for a while with interpretations based upon this idea, things seemed to start to slowly change. I noticed that he was not leaving the room as often and that I was not as scared or stuck in my capacity to think, contain, and understand what was happening.

Sibling rivalry and being found in mind

This therapeutic shift seemed to usher in a phase of intense sibling rivalry. Tim had seen me walking with another boy to the room for therapy. As a result of this, he began again to launch various verbal attacks on me for seeing another child. He was clearly devastated and very angry and hurt. He once again threatened not to come, and when he did come, he would do anything and everything to attack any links that we had. He would shout and scream at me and would threaten to hurt the other child.

Although I saw more than one other child, Tim was convinced that this child had changed things in the room. These changes that he would notice would be of the very smallest nature—that is, that a car was not in exactly the same box in which he had left it, or that something had been moved to a different place. There were no big changes in the room, as it was kept in a consistent way from week to week: it was the small things that he noticed—the things that had to do with reality (i.e. time changing and Tim's absence from the room).

These changes that he was noticing seemed also to communicate his hatred of the reality of separation, and thus if the room was not exactly the same it would indicate that some time had passed since we saw each other and that various real changes had taken place in that time. I was also reminded of the play in the first session of cars crashing/fighting and then each being parked in a separate parking space. Perhaps he felt that he didn't have a special, separate space in his mother's mind as there were five other children, and the anger and pain related to earlier unresolved anxieties of not being "found in mind" were being projected onto me.

I talked with him about his feelings of feeling hurt by me because I saw other children, but I concentrated on his fear that I did not have enough space in my mind for him if I saw other children and on his terrible fear that I would forget him. I talked about how hard it was for him to imagine that I had a space in my mind that was just for him and how hard it seemed for him to imagine that I kept him safely in my mind even when we were not together.

Transitional objects

During this phase he would also try to take things from the room at the end of the session, again signifying his difficulty in saying goodbye, but also his difficulty in believing that he could be remembered and that he could remember our time together as well when we were apart. He also clearly needed more than I could offer, and his need for "transitional objects" (Winnicott, 1958, 1965c) could also be seen as his own rudimentary attempts to find an internal space that could help him with the pain and anxiety of separation. Winnicott (1958, 1965c) maintains that the transitional object is the first not-me object that helps the child to move from a state of being merged with the mother to a state of feeling and being in relation to her.

Perelberg (1999) presents Winnicott's views (1965c, 1971a) on early development in relation to aggression, love, and the creation of a transitional object, stating that, "In the beginning, aggression and love are fused with each other. In the process of creating a transitional area, if the object survives the aggression of the child, it assumes a quality of permanence, independence and reality" (Perelberg, 1999, p. 26). Perelberg continues to explain Winnicott's views (1956a) by writing that "A child or adult will have to risk a hostile, potentially destructive attack on the relationship with the loved one in order to internalize the imago of that person. The loved one must be slain metaphorically, in order to become a separate person in reality. Aggression and destructiveness are thus seen as necessary for the separation between self and object" (Perelberg, 1999, p. 26).

Mentalization

Fonagy and Target (1999) make links between understanding violence and thinking about inherent difficulties a child may have in the realm of mentalization. They refer to Fairbairn's (1952) view that "Habitual violence towards either the self or another may reflect a failure to meet the fundamental need of every infant to find his mind, his intentional state, in the mind of the object" (Fonagy & Target, 1999, p. 62).

Fonagy and Target (1995a) describe how mentalization comes about as a result of a child having the experience of his mental states being reflected on by a significant carer. Secure play with a parent could be included in this category. This process is seen as an embellishment of the complex mirroring process that is linked to infancy, and thus the "emergence of mentalizing is deeply embedded in the child's primary object relations" (Fonagy, 2001a, p. 170). There is also a significant relationship between the caregiver's capacity to understand the child's mind and the establishment of a secure attachment (Gergely & Watson, 1996).

Research also shows that a favourable consequence of good-enough mothering is the child's developing capacity to be able to cope with separation anxieties and feel that his feelings and thoughts can be contained. Bion (1962) introduces concepts of "container" and "contained" and the significance of environmental factors in containing and transforming a child's aggression. Bion proposes that during early development the mother's capacity for reverie is central to this process of containment, as reverie functions to transform unbearable anxieties into bearable experiences. Thus, Bion (1962) maintained that this process of a mother's capacity to transform ("alpha-function") the infant's unbearable experience ("beta-elements") into more tolerable forms occurred as a result of the mother's capacity for mirroring and attunement.

Tim's separation difficulties and his violent outbursts can be understood on one level to be a consequence of a failure in being able to internalize a "good-enough mother" and a difficulty in coping with representing reality. Early trauma and deprivation appear to have played a part in this failure and to have caused emotional and developmental problems for Tim. These problems would logically have a direct effect on his sense of self and would lead to a loss of autonomous development. Stern (1985) suggests that it is in investigating the effects of a child's sense of self on development that we come to understand the powerful effect of the subjectivity and the intersubjectivity involved in the caring process. When there is an early lack of a reflective relationship to work though trauma, there will be an accumulation of unbearable emotional states that will nevertheless still seek to be contained. It seemed that Tim could not tolerate the unbearable emotional and psychological states that he experienced, and perhaps the only solution—albeit a pathological solution (Fonagy & Target, 1999)—to these was violence.

Fonagy and Target (1999) show how it is possible to understand these developmental failures in relation to an absence of early mirroring and containment. The reality of "being found in mind" by the carer ushers in for the child a sense of being contained. Consequently the experience of containment is a direct function of this image becoming internalized. When there is a lack or a failure in this type of functioning, a child will embark on a "desperate search for alternative ways of containing thoughts and the intense feelings that they engender", and this may begin the search for "pathological solutions" (Fonagy & Target, 1999, p. 62).

The search for alternative solutions is thus directly related to the failure of acquiring the "reflective function", which is indelibly connected to the intersubjective process that occurs between the infant and his or her mother/father (Fonagy & Target, 1997). Without these internalized patterns, internal and external reality become much more difficult and frightening places for the child. The capacity to be aware of the relationship between internal reality and external reality is seen to be a significant developmental achievement, and not something that is universal (Fonagy & Target, 1996).

Fonagy and Target (1996) suggest that a child arrives at mentalization—a reflective mode in which mental states can be experienced as representations—by the age of 3 or 4 years. This capacity fulfils an important role in linking inner and outer reality, but not through any use of dissociation or equation (Fonagy & Target, 1995a). Tim was struggling with both inner and outer reality and often used dissociation and psychotic-like thinking.

Neutralizing terror

One of the most challenging aspects of the therapeutic process with Tim was the frustrating, fearful, and despairing feelings that were left in me when he felt manic or violent. It was imperative that I contained and understood these feelings and worked with them in the process, by slowly feeding them back to Tim in a more digestible form. According to Bion (1962), this refers to being able to transform "beta into alpha elements" and thus contain the very painful and terrifying feelings that lay underneath the violent actions and phantasies. Britton (1992a) in thinking about Bion's concepts of containing and transforming the infant's anxious states, explains that, "The mother, if she was receptive to the infant's state of mind and capable of allowing it to be evoked in herself, could process it in such a way that in an identifiable form she could attend to it in the infant" (Britton, 1992a, p. 105). Britton further explains that Bion posited that this primitive method of communication (projective identification) was seen as a "forerunner of thinking" (p. 105).

It seemed that, for Tim, his use of violence functioned in a way to neutralize the terror he felt by being overwhelmed by feelings inside him or by feeling overwhelmed by me. Thus during the potentially violent phases of the therapy, there were extremely poignant and powerful feelings of fear and terror around in the therapy room. These had to be processed and understood with Tim, in order both for his violent defences to be replaced by healthier, age-appropriate coping mechanisms and for him to begin to tolerate thinking. This terror, fear, and violence began to decrease as I was able to repeatedly contain and reflect on the unbearable feelings and experiences. This process involved reflecting Tim's experience back to him, as well as reflecting on my experience with him in supervision.

Supervision played an integral part in helping me to reflect more psychoanalytically. The more I felt contained and helped to think by my supervisor, the more I could do more of the same with Tim. It seemed that in a powerful way, Tim was making me feel like the victim he felt, while he occupied the role of the aggressor. This, however, was unconsciously purposeful and necessary in order for his painful feelings and thoughts to be transformed.

Tim's "identification with the aggressor" and his attempt to rid himself of feelings of fear, terror, and helplessness became very evident in a session that followed the tragic 9/11 terrorist attack in New York. He came into the session very excited and animated. He started to re-enact the terrorist attack and took a toy plane and flew it into part of a house. He screeched with glee and was very pleased. "Did you see it, man? Osama bin Laden—he is a hero! He is powerful man! All those people were killed and I was there. I saw it all. All the dead bodies and the buildings falling!"

Tim repeated the flying tragedy again and laughed in a manically excited way. Tim clearly identified with the terrorist's role and was not in any way interested in the effects of the tragedy. He could in no way identify with the feelings of pain and helplessness in the victims and the carnage, as that would bring him dangerously close to his own feelings of pain.

I reflected that he seemed very excited and happy at all the deaths and that maybe he felt a bit relieved that there was somebody out there more violent than him. I added that it seemed easier to think about the attackers and not those people who were attacked and in pain or dead. "No, its good, man—all those people dead! I was there you know, I saw it all happen!"

I mentioned something about perhaps him seeing it all on the TV, but he interrupted me and said emphatically that he was there. He then became annoyed with me for mentioning the TV and not believing him. It seemed that in some way this destruction and violence reflected his most violent phantasies and that his excitement was linked to the fact that he could participate in the destruction through proxy, and thus also escape any punishment. It also meant that he could escape coming into contact with his extreme vulnerability. It is also possible that the scenes of death that he saw may have in some way reflected all the "dead internal objects" inside him. It is also possible that he had a dream after seeing the tragic event on TV, and thus for him he really was there.

Again, it was only in subsequent sessions that he could bear to listen to thoughts about his helplessness and terror that he tried so desperately to get rid of. This point highlights Freud's notion of psychic reality. For Tim, he really was there in New York—it was very real for him in his mind, and it was this psychic reality I had to understand and work with and that was in some way being communicated via the vehicle of the terrorist attack. The concept of "neutralizing terror" again became evident to me while I tried to think about his actions and the thoughts and fantasies he was expressing. It seemed that, for Tim, violence functioned in a psychic way to neutralize the terror he felt. The violence, or identification with the violent act, seemed to be the only way he could find relief from the torment of the inner terror. This inner terror seemed to be related to the fear of being inhabited by "bad, invasive and frightening objects", which is the opposite of feeling contained and having good internal objects that help in times of crisis. I was also very conscious of experiencing some of that terror and fear myself, especially while he was enacting violence or talking about it.

These feelings were, I felt, part of the projective-identification process. Tim was doing things that resulted in me feeling things that he felt he couldn't bear. It became clearer as time went on that beneath his aggression and violent tendencies lay an extreme vulnerability comprised of fear, terror, and hopelessness and a fear of psychic collapse and invasion. There seemed to be a dialectical relationship between the two states: the more violent he was, the more afraid and vulnerable he really felt. The violent phantasies and actions were an attempt to neutralize the terror and the fear, and in some way this resulted in a temporary numbing of his painful mental and affective states. The mindless activity and detached mode (dissociation) seemed to secure him some partial relief from the terrors he felt. The "pathological solution" (Fonagy & Target, 1995a) seemed, however, to function like an addictive object: he was too afraid to do without it, despite knowing that it (the violence), too, ultimately let him down. The neutralizing effects of engaging in violence provided only temporary relief.

It is important to again note that often just prior to or after engaging in violence, Tim would lose the capacity to use his transitional capacity in a healthy way—that is, playing (transitional-object phenomena) would cease completely for a while. This made me wonder about how Tim would use violence in a transitional way, when all other healthier transitional-object phenomena had been lost. The violence would often be related to separation difficulties—either emotionally experienced or actually experienced in reality by Tim.

Sustaining feeling and not-knowing

All these feelings were also felt in the transference, and it seemed that it was only the slow feeding back of these states and attempts to understand them that resulted in some changes. It was at times very difficult not only experiencing not-knowing or not understanding, but also not knowing how to help. Thinking about this despair in me made me realize that Tim, too, perhaps had a fear that nothing could really help. There were times that I even felt I didn't want to see him, as the sessions seemed so chaotic and difficult. I was also aware that my interpretations were not always helpful and I would get it wrong and that sometimes they unconsciously functioned in a way for me to rid myself of difficult feelings. There seemed to be a parallel process at times in my not wanting to be there and his not wanting to hear what I had to say. Tim would often ridicule what I said. The fact of owning my own destructive capacity and coping with these feelings helped me in a fundamental way to help Tim in a more organized and contained way. Despite all Tim's attempts to destroy the good we had or to attack emotional links, he still had difficulty in saying goodbye at the end of sessions. This I viewed, however, as a hopeful sign—a sign that he was struggling with his dependency on me and not completely destroying his need for me.

On being able to play

After many months of trying to think with him about these vulnerable feelings and thoughts and of reflecting his behaviour and the process between us, I started to notice a change in his aggression towards me. There seemed to be fewer aggressive attacks made on me, and instead I was seeing this aggression and violence reflected in the content of his play. I was also told that he had not been excluded since he had started therapy with me and that he was doing much better both socially and academically. It seemed that he was bringing all that he needed to be dealt with to the therapy room, and thus he was able to function in a less aggressive way in his social arena. It seemed also that the use I made of my countertransference in attempting to understand his feelings—as opposed to getting rid of them by using quick or clever interpretations—facilitated the creation of a transitional space where Tim could both play and be engaged in fundamental, psychological work (Winnicott, 1971a).

Symbolic play

Slowly, symbolic play was able to capture Tim's thoughts and feelings and contain them. This seemed to have a parallel process in relation to my capacity to contain his extreme emotional states.

This change made it much easier for me to follow him emotionally and think with him about his difficulties. There were still, however, many times of not knowing and not understanding. I had to tolerate that "not-knowing" and the anxiety that related to this absence of knowledge. Sessions did, however, change with this new sense of containment, and the early difficulties of staying in the room or needing to end the session early because of violence in the room or towards me decreased. My countertransference feelings of finding Tim very difficult, and at times wanting to avoid him, were replaced by a sense of enjoyment of working with him and looking forward to seeing him.

Absence of knowledge and the absent father

I thought about the times that I didn't understand Tim and how it sometimes took me longer to understand experiences with him in therapy. It appeared that during these times, I could not access my own intelligence. What became evident was that Tim was a very clever child, but that this intelligence was under attack from the violent parts of him. Tim also acknowledged that he had to hide his intelligence. As his aggression decreased, I saw more of this intelligence in the room. This was evidenced in his choice of playing some complicated board games. I also began to wonder if there was some link to the actual absence of his father and my absence of knowledge and his attempt to get rid of his knowledge. I knew nothing about the father and why he was not with Tim, and it seemed that Tim was in a similar place in relation to knowledge about his father. I began to think that it was not just perhaps the missing father that was significant in some way, but also the fact that there was no information about him. The lack of knowledge about the father's absence seemed in some way to compound the various psychological absences that were a feature of Tim's development and, at times, of my psychological states within the sessions.

Issues of technique

Tim's difficulty in dealing with internal and external reality would also manifest itself in a distortion of reality, and at times he said or did things that had no basis in reality. His attacks with words fell into this category. I had found that when I interpreted this reality distortion in a classical way —that is, linking it to the transference and to his repressed feelings—he would only get more and more angry and I would lose him. I discussed this in supervision, and my supervisor suggested that I try a different technique in the way I talked to Tim. I was to try to relate to the information by "using his own language" (A. Brafman, personal communication, 2004). The change to this use of language and intervention was quite remarkable in its effects.

In one session Tim accused me of being a rapist who raped a woman teacher in the school. This accusation came completely out of the blue while he was playing quietly on the floor. I responded by saying "What on earth do you mean and what is happening? You have been playing quietly on the floor and now suddenly these thoughts come out about accusing me of being a rapist. What do you mean?"

Instead of getting angry, he was rather taken aback and looked relieved and laughed, but not in a defensive way. It seemed to be a laugh of relief. Did he feel that I was meeting him on his own "ground"? The accusations also gave us an opportunity to think about his fears about rape and sex, and his confusion between the two.

I used the same technique for another repetition of behaviour that had been going on for a while. At times when he painted or drew, he would aggressively order me to get things for him. While in the past I would interpret this behaviour in various ways ("perhaps you want me to help you with feelings", "you want me to know what it's like to be told what to do", etc.) and sometimes possibly get the paint, this time I said that he could get it himself; or, when we were playing a game, I would tell him to fetch various things that we needed. He laughed at this and went ahead happily to get the things. He appeared more relaxed and at ease when this occurred. Previous interpretations around interpersonal and intrapsychic dynamics moved to include more direct interpersonal ones between Tim and me. I changed the content of the interpretation, yet kept the focus around very real interpersonal dynamics. This seemed to work better at certain times.

Getting inside: feeling the need to get inside something good

Tim's curiosity and confusion about sex and intimacy and being contained in mind became evident in play, which involved him putting a blanket over me. He insisted I close my eyes, and while I did he would come very close with his face to mine. It seemed that he was trying to almost get inside me and that he wanted to kiss me. I interpreted this, and he laughed but insisted we carry on playing the game. I didn't feel very comfortable with the rules, and I told him that I didn't want to keep my eyes closed and that I would prefer not to play this game. I wondered what it was he was trying to tell me, and I wondered if he might be saying that something had happened to him that he didn't like. There was a manic quality to his behaviour, and he was not able to think about what I said. When I told him I didn't want to play this game any more, he was angry and disappointed, but he did not insist we continue.

When I interpreted that perhaps he wanted to get inside me and make sure he was inside me so that I would not forget him, he calmed down and was able to represent his need to feel contained in a special place in my mind by playing with the dolls' house. He arranged every room in an organized way and placed people in strategic places in the rooms. What appeared to me to be central to this play was the positioning of a little child on a mother's lap. This seemed to be the first indicator that he could believe that I could perhaps keep him safe, not only in mind, but also in body, by establishing clear boundaries and thinking with him. By repeatedly thinking with him about his feelings and thoughts, I was unconsciously communicating the fact that I did actually have him in my mind and that I could sustain having him as a presence in my mind.

There seemed to be a change in him from being ruthless to being more concerned with the room, with the toys, and with me. Previous uncontained destruction of the room and toys were replaced by more concern and order. He still, however, found it very hard to tidy up at the end of the sessions, and there seemed to be a need to leave me to sort out the mess. I discussed this with him as his way, perhaps, of letting me know that he felt he couldn't sort out the mess in his head when he left and that he wanted me to do all of it for him. I suggested that we could do it together, both the cleaning up *and* the making things easier inside where his thoughts and feelings were. He slowly began to participate in the cleaning up of the mess he made, and eventually the need to make a mess decreased considerably.

Tim also started to develop more of a concern for the toys and for his works of art that were kept in his box. Up until halfway through the therapy, there was very little that he had made and kept in his own private box. For a long time the only remnants in his box were two pieces of string and bits of paper that were disorganized and messy. The messy room and the empty, messy box appeared to reflect parts of his internal (and perhaps external) world that were deprived and vacant.

Calling the spirits!

During the last year of the therapy Tim began to communicate more easily, and he started to use musical instruments to express himself. Tim would play the drums in a very loud way that seemed to be designed initially as an obstacle to any real communication or enjoyment. The drums would get beaten louder and louder if I tried to talk or make an intervention. A new form of interaction subsequently replaced this play. He would play the drums, and he would then tell me to play the guitar. At the start of this new pattern, he would be very clear on how I should play and when I should play. I was to start and to stop playing when he indicated to me with his drumstick. This I did. I felt that he felt an enormous sense of relief that he could tell someone when to accompany him and when not to. I also felt a sense of relief that finally there seemed to be more points of contact between us that were based on a creative, healthy element as opposed to a destructive one. In the initial stages of the dual-instrument play, he still did not want me to speak. Perhaps there was something in just the "process of playing" together (Winnicott, 1971a) that was important to him. The loudness of his drum playing, however, also indicated that he didn't want me to think. In actuality, it was very hard to think when he was making such a noise. Classical and interpersonal interpretations, however, did not seem to work, and I was not sure at all what he might be trying to tell me.

I said that perhaps I had been a bit slow at understanding what he was trying to tell me and that maybe he could help me to understand. It seemed then that the drum playing became less about being used as an obstacle to communication and more as a form of communicating an idea. Tim then told me that they played drums at his church. I asked him what they were used for, and he replied, with cultural certainty, that they were for "calling the spirits".

I realized then that he was using the drums to represent both an element of his own cultural experience and an internal phantasy.

I asked if the spirits were here yet, and he replied that they were not. In a moment of silence between the drumming, I wondered with him if he may be worried that I was not there for him, and that while I was sitting there physically with him, he may be worried that my mind was somewhere else. This did actually happen on certain occasions when he was playing the drums in a repetitive way.

Tim's drum playing got louder and louder. It was as if he was calling me into the room and making sure I was there. The drums were being played in such a way, that my mind could not be anywhere else. I told him that I was there in the room with him, but that perhaps he really was afraid that I didn't have him in my mind. With that comment the drum playing stopped, and there seemed to be a new sense of being connected. I had finally understood. Following this interpretation, Tim started to look at objects around the room. The following extract is what took place after this:

Tim: "Where do you get these strange ideas?"

Rose: "You think they are strange ideas?"

Tim: "Yes. Where do they come from, man?"

Silence.

Rose: "They come from my head—the place in my head where I think about you and hold you in my mind. The place I have for you even when we do not meet, like holidays and the days that we don't see each other."

He remained quiet, and then proceeded to get two games.

He read a bit of the paper that had the rules of the game on it. (This was new, as he usually made up the rules!) He then turned and looked at me.

Tim: "You read how to play—the rules—what to do."

I read the rules. It was a board game that involved a dice and markers and using subtraction and turn taking. I explained the rules to him that I had read. We played, each taking our turn. He then asked if he could throw for me. I said that he could. Amid this interaction, what emerged was the importance to him of winning. One game I won, and one game he won.

After he had won on one occasion, he told me that he had cheated. I said that I saw that it was very important for him to

> win and that he didn't like losing and coping with the feelings of loss. Despite the cheating and his desire to win, I felt that there was something much more important about the fact that we were playing a game together and in a fairly reciprocal way. There also seemed to be something very important to him about sitting close to me while we were playing and about feeling contained by sitting next to me.

Although he would occasionally cheat and want to be in control, it seemed to be secondary to his desire for us actually to do things together. The process between us was characterized by much more reciprocity and interaction. Tim generally seemed more contained and less tormented, and I was able to think with him in a way that he found less threatening. Tim seemed to have finally arrived in a mental space where he was less afraid of his dependency needs and also had less need to use violence as a defence.

Tim's violent and aggressive behaviour inside and outside the room had stopped. He was still prone to get angry when he felt frustrated, yet this did not lead him to act out any of his aggression in a violent or dangerous way. He was doing much better in class and had made some good friends. The therapy came to an end after three years, when Tim had to move on to secondary school. I arranged for Tim to continue to have therapy if it was needed when he was in secondary school. Tim was also eager to have somebody to talk to and who could help him with any difficulties that he might experience.

CHAPTER EIGHT

Finding abused children's voices: junior-school living nightmares

Valerie Sinason

It is the familiar moment in the horror film. The innocent child or adult hears or sees something. She walks along a corridor anxiously searching. Suddenly we hear the familiar, yet distorted sounds of a child's nursery rhyme. The tune remains the same, but the notes are stretched and distorted deliberately, in order to convey a sense of eeriness and fear.

How do we know this sound and this moment deep in our preverbal selves? What does it draw on? And what happens when the sound heard draws on current rather than old memories?

A parent leaves the room and the tiny baby cries—a baby only a couple of months old. "I won't be a moment, " says the cheerful loving voice. However, the baby does not know that: for following the mother's cheerful exit, the baby is thrown into a timeless universe of terror—the terror of never ever being near the possibility of "being found" or "finding again".

The baby does not understand that the parent will only be gone a few seconds. For the baby, the parent has gone forever. We know that, for the baby, out of sight really is out of mind—and out of mind is a terrible, all-encompassing place for the lost to be in. Bion (1962) called it "nameless dread". We are all unconsciously drawn to that sound, for we recognize it from deep known and unknown places within ourselves. The loving parent/carer also knows those places, for the "reassuring" talk is an attempt to cross the unbridgeable divide of absence.

However, by 6–9 months the baby who has had a "good-enough experience" of early maternal care (Winnicott, 1949) will have some preliminary sense of "object permanence". The baby will slowly come to know, as a result of continuous, consistent, and reliable care, that a parent will return after leaving, and thus managing to survive a little while on his/her own resources becomes the necessary challenge and the adaptable task.

At the same time as this sense of permanence is being developed, the capacity to communicate is also being developed and is growing within the intimate emotional human matrix. The capacity to smile begins to develop after 8 weeks and is linked with extra babbling. At 9 months a baby can find a hidden object if he/she has seen it being hidden (Stern, 1985). Emotionally and physically, a huge, incredible journey is being undertaken. The seeking-and-finding system is hardwired into us as a species (Schore, 1994), but it can go painfully wrong.

With very small children and with mothers and babies, we experience the beginnings of humour linked to seeking. The peek-a-boo game played between mother and baby elicits a smile of pleasure as well as a giggle. Where a mother tickles a baby slightly too much or gives the visual equivalent of a punchline at the wrong time, she is a failed comedienne, with devastating results (Sinason, 1996).

Perhaps the reason why we find a failed joke or an unsuccessful comedian so unbearable is because it takes us back to the feeling of betrayal when mother mistimed/misattuned (Winnicott, 1949). Perhaps, too, that is why we are so grateful to brilliant comic writers/performers, because we can trust we will not be betrayed in the vulnerable act of giving ourselves over to laughter. Where the mistiming is more serious or even intentional, we hear the distorted music of the horror-film nursery rhyme.

Playing peek-a-boo, using a jack-in-the-box, lifting up beakers to see what is hidden inside—all this can only be done if there is enough safety and pleasure in permanence to test out in play the experiences of loss. Where loss is occurring all the time or where the object is cruel over finding or being found, how can there be pleasure in seeking and finding? What happens to those who face a Scylla and Charybdis of terrible abandonments (which make a presence) and abusive presences? The distance–closeness alternation leads to a borderline diagnosis—a further hiding from the original meaning of symptoms.

What happens when the voice that goes "Boo!", the hand that says "I've found you!" and lifts the covers, is the hand and voice of abuse? What happens when the face that finds your face is a mask or a face of hatred or of sadism?

The voices below are those of children whose finding, seeking, and attaching experiences were distorted through trauma. They smear, wet, fight, self-harm, cannot concentrate, sexualize, cut off their voices, and scream. They are excluded, moved on and on, and thrown to the vagaries of the care system. All of the children written about here were referred for violence to the self or to others. (For reasons of confidentiality, all children's names used in this chapter are not their real names.)

Sarah, aged 8:
abuse included "games" of treasure hunts

It was the school end-of-term spring party, and the children were told there would be a treasure hunt. The staff had hidden tiny chocolate Easter eggs with a name on them for each child. They had spent weeks planning this, with different clues to follow. All the children were excited, but Sarah aged 8 was in a state of terror. Frozen with terror she stayed on her classroom seat, holding tightly on to her best friend's hand. The friend wanted to join the hunt, but Sarah was in such terror at letting her go that a classroom assistant stayed with both of them.

Steve, aged 10:
physically abused in a punitive fundamentalist family

"Quick hide!" whispered Johnny excitedly to his friend Steve. "The girls are coming to find us." Steve did not move. He sat down despairingly. "God can find you wherever you are. There is no hiding place."

Susan, aged 9:
sexually abused by her father

"You can't play hiding. It's a bad game," said Susan. "Daddy told me to suck his lollipop and I said no and ran away to hide and he said I was a bad girl and he'd give me a good hiding."

Individual or group psychotherapy, as in the examples below, can help children like this to find themselves and bring them to consider the health-giving reality that they are themselves worth seeking for.

John, aged 11

John has a severe learning disability, is physically violent, and was emotionally, physically, and sexually abused in early childhood. He was excluded from two nurseries, three infant schools, and two junior schools before finding a place in a specialist unit. While there he faced suspensions for violence to female teachers.

After three months of individual therapy

John covered himself with a blanket on the couch in the therapy room. "*Find me*" he calls. It is the first time he has tried to play hide-and-seek.

"I wonder where John is?" I say wonderingly, as if to a baby. I am aware of speaking slowly and softly, so that he can regulate his affect.

"Is he under the table? No. He is not there."

I start slowly with the table furthest away from him. I walk softly so as not to frighten him. I speak very slowly, being aware of his terror.

I am at the opposite side of the room to him.

"I'm here!" he suddenly screams, crying desperately, flinging the blanket off himself and throwing himself onto the floor sobbing uncontrollably.

I wait a moment until his crying has quietened. A touch would have been an intrusion to him. Then I said, "You found it hard to be found and hard to hide."

He put the blanket over his head.

"Blah blah blah," he shouts.

I am quiet.

He is quiet.

"You're alive. I can hear you breathe," he says.

It is such a painful moment.

"We are both alive," I say. "We are both breathing."

There is a strangled sob from under the blanket.

"Blah blah blah," he shouts.

He throws the blanket off and throws toys in all directions.

"Kill kill kill!"

After six months of therapy

He picked up a jack-in-the-box for the first time and nervously pressed the button. The jack sprung up and John cried. It was a loud and angry cry, with tears pouring down his face.

Still crying, he pushed the figure down and closed the lid, and then he threw the box away.

"Blah blah blah!"

"It's frightening," I say.

He nods.

He picks up the jack-in-the-box, and says:

"Poor Jack. He is locked away."

After one year of therapy

He tries hiding under the blanket again.

" Find me," he asks.

Again, I begin slowly. "Where is John? He is not under the table."

This time I am allowed to play for longer.

"He is not on the chair; he is not under the chair. He is not behind the curtain. He is not at the side of the cupboard."

I go slowly and softly but nowhere near him.

Once again John screamed and cried, "I'm here."

He is panting, breathless, eyes widened in terror.

I stay absolutely still.

John's breathing slowly quiets.

We are both standing still.

"We are both alive," he says.

"Yes," I agree.

After two years of therapy

John said, "Can I try again?"

He picked up the jack-in-the-box warily and pressed the button. He gazed with shock as Jack came out, and he closed the lid slowly.

"Jack—are you crying? It's alright. I won't let them hurt you."

He pressed the button and Jack came out. He stared at Jack and touched him all over. "No bruises. They didn't hurt him this time."

"We are all alive and no one is hurt," I said.

"They don't do that where I am now," he tentatively said. He was then immediately shocked by his disclosure.

"Blah blah blah!" he shouted, throwing chairs and tables over.

After three years of therapy

John looked round the therapy room. "Where is that Jack?" He covered the jack-in-the-box with a blanket on the couch.

"Where are you?" he asked.

He walked round the room with slow soft steps and a slow soft voice. He had introjected my voice. Slowly he approached the couch. He lifted the blanket up.

"I'm here, Jack. You're alright."

He pressed the button.

"Hello Jack. I didn't forget you."

By the time he left therapy, John could still not play hide-and-seek, but he managed to deal with his terrified and terrifying feelings around exclusion and trauma. Teachers did not exclude him again. It became clear that when frightened he expected to be violently assaulted and locked away. It emerged he was locked in a cupboard under the stairs by both his parents. This meant that the response by staff to exclude him when he revealed this state actually fell into a re-enactment of the original trauma and abuse done to him.

Maria

Here is Maria after three years of therapy in a specialist unit for emotionally disturbed children before moving on to a mainstream school. When she first came to therapy she found it very frightening to open her toy drawer and look inside. She was worried the different little animals would bite her. All her feelings about secret abuse in her family were projected onto the animals, and that made the toy drawer—the container—a dangerous one. As therapy moved on, she was able to explore and search, and it slowly became more obvious how this container, something that could be opened and looked in and have things taken from it, also represented, for her, her own dirtied inner space.

The following extract involves a session with Maria that took place after three years of therapy and was in its closing stages as she was being helped to prepare to start in a mainstream school.

(Maria came straight to the table and took out her toys.)

Maria: "Here is the Daddy bull. He is quiet in the day, but in the night if someone wakes him up he charges."

Me: "The night-time Daddy bull is different to the daytime one."

Maria: "Yes. Because he is very peaceful in the daytime."

Me: "So something wakes him up at night."

Maria: "Yes. He does not want to wake up and charge."

Me: "So he feels quite bad he can't stop himself from doing it."

Maria: "That's right. The poor Daddy bull can't stop himself, and it's so tiring for him. He doesn't want to. But if the people wake him—especially someone bad—he can't help it. There are two calves. One little calf loves her mummy best and wants to grow up to be a cow, and the other little calf wishes she could grow up and be a bull."

Me: "One little female calf wants to grow up and be a cow, but the other wishes she could be a male."

Maria: "Yes. Because then she would grow into a strong bull and she could charge instead of being a calf or a cow."

Me: "So the little calf feels it is so helpless being a female and little that she wishes she could be strong and she thinks only bulls are strong and then she would charge."

Maria: "Yes."

Me: "Perhaps the little calf would especially like to be a bull now it is time to leave the Unit"

Maria: "Yes. I would like to be a bull and I will take him with me, but all the other wild animals I want to leave in my drawer."

Me: "You would like me to look after the wild Maria after you go."

Maria: "Yes. I will take the tame animals and the bull but you can keep the lions and tigers, all the wild Marias."

Me: "You really are worried about being a wild schoolgirl in your new school."

Maria: "I can't be. I have to be tame. They won't have me there otherwise."

Me: "Perhaps you worry I will only look after the wild Maria animals after you have gone. Perhaps you worry I would not feel safe or strong enough to let you be wild while you were still here in the room with me."

Maria: "But I am! Remember when I stamped my feet and splashed the water. Splash! I made a great sound. And I cried last week and did not want to come. That was wild."

Me: "So you have been wild here and in the Unit, but not wild at night-time."

Maria (sadly): "No, only the bull is wild at night-time. The baby is tame and quiet."

Me: "That seems very hard. You love the wild Daddy bull so much and perhaps you love your Daddy so much too."

(Total silence: Maria wriggled on her chair.)

Maria: "I love the Daddy bull when he is tame."

Me: "That's really hard then, especially as you will be leaving the Unit soon and I won't be able to hear what the bull is doing."

Maria: "Perhaps the little calf and the little piglet will be able to tell the new teacher and the new therapist."

Me: "I hope they will. Because otherwise the new teacher and new therapist might not understand why a little piglet is so tired and frightened and doesn't want to be a female."

Maria: "And if the little piglet wants to grow up and get bigger, like I am, she might need someone to tell."

Me: "Yes. Because you have got bigger in the three years I have known you."

Maria: "Yes. I have got bigger and the piglets and the calf have got bigger. Only the bull has stayed the same. One day I will be bigger than him."

Me: "You will get taller and he will stay the same, but you might never get taller than him or stronger. But you can keep yourself safe better."

Maria: "Because the mummy cow doesn't want the bull to charge. She thinks she wants the baby to grow up. The baby thinks she wants to grow up. Maybe the bull only likes babies. Maybe he won't charge at big piglets."

Me: "Maybe you are feeling I am letting you go and leave the Unit because I don't want big Marias, only little ones, and you feel sad as well as relieved that the bull seems to like little ones best."

Maria: "Yes. But I think I am more relieved—because I really am getting bigger, Mrs Sinason. Do you remember when you first saw me? I was tiny. I was only a tiny little piglet. Anyone could have killed me. I hate the piglet. I hate the stupid female piglet. I never want to see her."

Me: "Why?"

Maria: "Because she is so stupid and I'm sick of her."

Me: "Perhaps you are worried the female piglet would feel angry at being left behind in the room."

Maria: "She might, because I took the male. The male piglet is no problem. He is just easy. But the female isn't. I can't bear the female. I can't, and I won't play with her ever again and I won't go near her."

I asked why.

No reply.

I commented that last session she had been painting the female piglet as if she did not like her colour.

Maria: "I don't like the female piglet's colour. She is dirty and horrid and the wrong colour."

Me: "Your Daddy and I are white and you and your sister and Mummy are black and perhaps you worry about that."

She nodded.

Maria: "I don't like my stupid vagina. I hate its colour."

Me: "Maybe you feel your vagina has to be stupid so it would not know something difficult."

Thoughtful silence.

Maria: "It is stupid and greasy."

Me: "When is it greasy?"

Silence.

Me: "Is it greasy when you touch it or if someone else does?"

There was a pause. She moved nearer to me.

Maria: "It is not my vagina that's greasy. It is another girl's."

Me: "Another girl's?"

Maria: "Yes. It is greasy."

Me: "Which girl's?"

She snapped ferociously

Maria: "Don't say it is my mother's."

We certainly had concerns about her mother abusing her but I said nothing. She then looked awful and pale.

Maria: "I hate the colour of my vagina."

Me: "I wonder if you worry that you and your mother are different—that your vaginas were not just a different colour on the outside but different on the inside too."

She looked interested.

Maria: "It is—is it different from your one?"

She then quickly added:

Maria: "But my one is stupid. It does nothing. It is dirty and it only causes trouble and I wish I didn't have one. I wish I was nothing. I wish I didn't have it."

Me: "You and the little piglet both feel it is very hard to be a girl."

Maria: "Yes. It is horrid to be a female. It is so easy for the male piglet. It is easier for males."

Me: "Do you wish you were a male?"

Maria: "No. It's, I don't want anything down there at all."

Me: "You don't want anything sexual down there, you've had enough."

Maria: "That's right. Nothing. I'm tired of greasy cows and night-time Daddy bulls."

She put the male piglet down and picked up the female piglet.

Maria: "She doesn't bite. She is only a little toy and she is dirty and needs a wash. Poor piglet—she is so dirty between her legs."

I said she felt the female had been left all unwashed and dirty between her legs. She washed the piglet in the sink, wiping off the discolouring paint that was still there. She dried her very carefully, showing she was cleaning between the piglet's legs.

Then she carefully stood up holding the piglet tenderly and went to her drawer. She opened the drawer carefully with one hand and put the piglet in.

Maria: "Now she is content."

Then she carefully explored the rest of the drawer commenting on what she saw.

Maria: "I like looking here."

I reminded her of how frightened she had been at the beginning to look in her drawer.

She smiled brightly.

Maria: "Yes. When I was very tiny, so tiny I could not look in the drawer because I might find big things, giant things, like Daddy bulls. But now I have got bigger here with you and the Daddy bull only stays the same."

The group voice

Within a group setting, the sounds and behaviours of children are louder. The violence can be startling. And through it children can slowly find themselves in others and hide themselves in others.

The following two extracts are taken from two children's groups—one of children with extreme emotional and behavioural disturbances, the other of children with learning disabilities.

The children with extreme emotional and behavioural disturbances were seen in a specialist therapeutic day unit that included schooling. The children with learning disabilities were seen in a once-weekly outpatient child and family department. In both groups there were two staff members as co-facilitators, and the membership ranged from six to eight children.

If we consider the meaning of the lived experience behind these brief descriptions of group members, we can understand why violence had become the key expression to be used by these children.

Children with extreme emotional and behavioural disturbances

The members of the group

Adrian, aged 9 years, lived with his single, physically disabled mother. His violent, sexually abusive father was removed from the home when he was 3 years old, and he spent the next few years shunted between his grandparents and his mother. In his play he was split between a "boss", who was all-powerful and comforting when agreed with but lethal when opposed, and a victim. He asked what would happen in the group if his "boss" said he should climb out of the window and go down the fire escape. I said the boss could hope what he liked but we would not let that happen. "But how will you stop him?" insisted Ken. I said he wondered if we were strong enough to deal with his boss. He agreed.

Brian was a small 10-year-old who had required resuscitation at birth and continued to present with feeding and weight problems. He needed further hospitalization for iron-deficiency anaemia. He is the youngest of five. His brothers are homosexual, and his father is worried he will be. He has been sexually abused by two different people—one a neighbour, and a brother's boyfriend. In his assessment meeting, his conversation was full of violent and sexual undertones. He spoke of fear of being bullied, of how an abusing neighbour invited him to watch a circumcision but he didn't want to watch.

Caroline was a dark-skinned, dark-haired 9-year-old, with an expressive face and a tendency to fix people with a stare that other children called "the evil eye". She is the second child of three in her family. The eldest died as a baby, and the mother was accused of poisoning her. The parents believe Caroline is "evil" and have had her exorcized by a priest on several occasions. They have reported that her play with her younger brother is very sexualized. In her assessment session she oscillated between moments of being a frightened child and moments of being murderous.

Darla, a 9-year-old, was of mixed parentage. She is the eldest of three children, all born to an alcoholic mother who never felt close to her. Mother went to work when Darla was aged 3½ months, and she went to a child minder. She was abused by the child-minder's son and rejected after disclosure by her mother.

The sessions

The group therapy room is a large room with windows overlooking the street, covered with a wire mesh as a security precaution. There is a sink, two cupboards, sofa, tables, and chairs. It is a pleasantly spacious room.

In the first twenty sessions a window in the therapy room was smashed, an armchair was slashed, a sofa was broken, a glass-framed picture on the stairs was smashed, a wooden cupboard was pierced, a fireplace was nearly ripped from the wall, and one child had received a nosebleed.

After five sessions the therapists (the author, and educational psychologist Lesley Holditch) had given up on a toy drawer and had kept the cupboards locked, in addition to turning the water taps off tight and removing the plastic washing-up bowl and metal dustbin. By Session 20 both therapists noted that having a chair to sit on was no longer considered possible. One therapist needed to be standing near the window and one by the door. "There would not be enough time to get to a standing and running position quickly enough." At the same time the children were slowly yet dramatically transforming.

The first session revealed themes that continued to be central throughout the group work. The first important theme that emerged was that there was no ability to play. An embryonic version of hide-and-seek quickly corrupted into seeking to lock each other in a cupboard, with open comments of the sexual abuse that could follow. The nature of both the absences and presences that they had experienced had clearly affected their capacity to play. Second, anything that anybody picked up or touched was spoiled or stolen by someone else. No one could own anything, and no one could share. Third, the only possible way of gaining peer attention was by doing something dangerous, and, finally, crying from having been hurt was the only possible way of ending a difficult situation. In this way the group affect-regulation showed the way that the abused child's ability to calm down after overwhelming premature stimulation is compromised.

There was an internal constellation being reflected where attachment was perverse and cruel but clung to because there was no other object available to depend on. The mafia boss granted security only to a total slave. In return for being allowed to survive, the slaves have to give up all hope of any possession or individuality. This boss was especially strong after the horror of a long holiday, where children were in dangerous homes.

To find us again and to find them again after each break meant facing the terrifying places they lived in externally and internally when school was closed.

Most painfully, on Fridays and before holidays there was no attempt to even pretend to be glad that school was closing for a weekend or holiday break.

Children with learning disabilities

A group of children with learning disabilities who had emotional and behavioural problems following abuse were seen once-weekly at an outpatient child and family department. Membership of the group varied between six and eight children and there was a co-facilitator.

The members of the group

Anne, aged 9 years, was in a residential home following abuse by her father.

Ewan, aged 10 years, who was physically handicapped and violent, had been abused by his father and by a paedophile ring. He was still at home with an unsafe mother.

Brenda, aged 8 years, was in a residential unit following neglect and abuse.

Karen, aged 10 years, lived with her mother, who disbelieved her account of abuse by her ex-partner.

John, aged 10 years, lived with an alcoholic father. His mother had been physically abusive, and he had been abused by one of her lovers.

Julie, aged 11 years, had three sisters who were in and out of care and a mother who had a succession of abusive partners.

The session

The meeting followed a half-term break. The children rushed into the room. Anne threw a paper cup noisily into the dustbin and announced with very great energy and pride that she had been stealing with Tony, a boy in her residential home. She said it was easy. They went into a shop, and it was really exciting. It was because he pushed her and then he slipped bubblegum into his pocket, and they had lots of bubblegum afterwards. It was wonderful, and he stole a pussycat from a little kid.

Brenda had gone to the toy house and checked the saucepans. "Erch! They are filthy. Look what happens when I am not here." Karen hid under a large soft blanket: "I haven't come in yet. You can't see me." Ewan had rushed to the giant teddy bear in the corner of the room: "Here you are. I missed you". He started wrestling with the teddy bear. "Stealing is wrong," he said, while simulating anal sex with the teddy. "You missed me," he said to the bear. "You missed that."

I said they were just back from half-term and perhaps it felt I had stolen from them, didn't keep the place properly, didn't know if they were here or away, and didn't care for their feelings at all.

Ewan looked at me really sadly and intently. "What happened at my case conference?" I said that everyone said they were worried he was not safe at home and thought he would be safest in a boarding school. Brenda asked what his Mum said: "Does she believe him?"

I asked Ewan what he thought. He did not reply. I said, no she didn't. Brenda looked sad. I asked John and Karen if their Mums believed them now. Karen said yes: "I haven't seen my Dad for ages. I miss him."

"What did your Dad do?" asked John. Karen pretended not to hear. "What did he do?" repeated Ewan, falling down on the bear and not looking at her. He came to the table and sat down gently and said to her very seriously "What did your Dad do to you?"

Anne looked very sad. "Is it hard for you to tell? Does it hurt you to think of it?" asked John. "You tell", said Ann to me. I said he pulled her hair and hurt her and tore her clothes. "He raped her, didn't he?" said Ewan. "That too", I said. Anne looked sad.

"I will kick your Dad when I see him" said Ewan and he went to kick the teddy bear and jump on him. Anne gave a thumbs up sign and looked sparky and excited. "I will see him at Easter, and I am stronger now." I agreed.

Ewan carried on simulating anal sex with the teddy bear, and Anne went back to talking of stealing. "I wasn't stealing. Tony was." "You were with him," said Ewan. I said Ewan was also showing us with the teddy how he could not stop being part of something exciting, even though he knew it did not help him.

Julie walked in. "Hello," said Ewan and John. Julie said hello. She said she had been in a school photo yesterday and did we like the way she had combed her hair. She said she was in love with her boyfriend and wanted to marry him and she also said her sister was going to hospital. She had poured with blood all over the sofa. Anne said "How disgusting." John thrust his book in my face. Ewan meanwhile had a sudden fit and sat on an armchair near the doll's house. Anne was terrified and furious and started throwing things. John said, "Calm down, don't be a bully." Anne carried on trying to hurt Ewan. I restrained her and said she was very frightened and furious with Ewan for doing that.

John went to her when she tried to throw something hard and said she mustn't. "It won't hurt," she said, picking up something softer. Then they all rushed to where the teddy was, each simulating sex in turn. I said they were frightened Ewan had had a fit and were trying to hide that fear with a bad sexy feeling. Brenda said she was Sleeping Beauty and would go to sleep. She lay down and pretended to sleep, as did John.

Ewan started to emerge from his fit, and Anne shouted at him that he had frightened her. John said she was frightened Ewan would die and that was why she was shouting. Brenda agreed. I said the group really cared for Ewan and wondered if Anne could try something different now she understood. "How?" she asked. I asked what the others thought. No reply. I said she could speak quietly to him." Show me how." I knelt next to him and spoke quietly, and then she did, and she did bring him round gently saying "Good boy—it is alright. You are back here. We have found you. The group has started again."

In the group, after the fearfulness of the half-term break, it slowly became possible for the group to find each other and their true voice.

Conclusion

In this chapter I have wanted the subjects to speak: small children from primary school aged 6–11 years, children with learning or physical disabilities, children with emotional problems from trauma—they all struggled to find their true voices in therapy. Seen within a day unit, a clinic, and schools for emotionally and behaviourally disturbed children, they all show the enormity of the task they have been faced with. Instead of secure attachments and the excitement of birthdays and Christmas, their world consists of a Dickensian underworld that few of the adults who look after them could cope with living in.

Small and helpless, they hide their pain by waiting to be big, by adopting the sexual and delinquent armour of lost teenagers, by finding excitement to liven the deadness.

And yet, within the rare resource of on-site psychotherapy, they have a chance of unpicking some of the experiences they have faced. Lacking parents capable of providing a mentalizing function (Target & Fonagy, 1996), they can slowly internalize small aspects of their therapy. There is no six-month treatment to provide a lasting change. These children require long-term intensive treatment if we wish them to become adults capable of finding themselves.

REFERENCES

Abraham, K. (1924). A short study of the development of the libido. Viewed in the light of mental disorders. In: *Selected Papers of Karl Abraham*. London: Hogarth Press, 1927. Reprinted London: Karnac, 1988.

Abram, J. (1996). *The Language of Winnicott*. London: Karnac.

Acquarone, S. (1992). How shall I stop him crying. *Journal of Child Psychotherapy, 18* (1): 33–56.

Acquarone, S. (2004). *Infant–Parent Psychotherapy: A Handbook*. London: Karnac.

Affleck, G., Tennen, H., Rowe, J., Roscher, B., & Walker, L. (1989). Effects of formal support on mothers' adaptation to the hospital-to-home transition of high-risk infants: The benefits and costs of helping. *Child Development, 60*: 488–501.

Aichhorn, A. (1951). *Wayward Youth*. London: Imago.

Ainsworth, M. D., Blehar, M. C., Waters, E., & Wall, S. (1978). *Patterns of Attachment: A Psychological Study of the Strange Situation*. Hillsdale, NJ: Lawrence Erlbaum.

Allen, J. G. (2001). *Traumatic Relationships and Serious Mental Disorders*. Chichester: Wiley.

Alvarez, A. (1992). *Live Company*. London/New York: Routledge.

Anderson, C. A., & Bushman, B. J. (2002). Human aggression. *Annual Review of Psychology, 53*: 27–51.

Anderson, R. (Ed.) (1992). *Clinical Lectures on Klein and Bion*. London: Routledge.

Arnsten, A. F. T. (1998). The biology of being frazzled. *Science, 280*: 1711–1712.

Arnsten, A. F. T., Mathew, R., Ubriani, R., Taylor, J. R., & Li, B.-M. (1999). Alpha-1 noradrenergic receptor stimulation impairs prefrontal cortical cognitive function. *Biological Psychiatry, 45*: 26–31.

August, G. J., Realmuto, G. M., Hektner, J. M., & Bloomquist, M. L. (2001). An integrated components preventive intervention for aggressive elementary school children: The early risers program. *Journal of Consulting and Clinical Psychology, 69* (4): 614–626.

Badcock, C. (2000). *Evolutionary Psychology: A Critical Introduction*. Cambridge: Polity Press.

Balbernie, R. (2001). Circuits and circumstances: The neurobiological consequences of early relationship experiences and how they shape later behaviour. *Journal of Child Psychotherapy, 27* (3): 237–255.

Barkley, R. A., Shelton, T. L., Crosswait, C. C., Moorehouse, M., Fletcher, K., Barrett, S., et al. (2000). Multi-method psycho-educational intervention for preschool children with disruptive behavior: Preliminary results at post-treatment. *Journal of Child Psychology and Psychiatry, 41*: 319–332.

Baron-Cohen, S., Wheelwright, S., Hill, J., Raste, Y., & Plumb, I. (2001). The "Reading the Mind in the Eyes" Test revised version: A study with normal adults, and adults with Asperger syndrome or high-functioning autism. *Journal of Child Psychology and Psychiatry, 42* (2): 241–251.

Barth, R. P., Blythe, B. J., Schinke, S. P., & Schilling, R. F. (1983). Self-control training with maltreating parents. *Child Welfare, 62*: 313–324.

Barth, R. P., Fetro, J. V., Leland, N., & Volkan, K. (1992). Preventing adolescent pregnancy with social and cognitive skills. *Journal of Adolescence Research, 7*: 208–232.

Barth, R. P., Hacking, S., & Ash, J. R. (1988). Preventing child abuse: An experimental evaluation of the Child Parent Enrichment Project. *Journal of Primary Prevention, 8*: 201–217.

Bateman, A., & Fonagy, P. (2004). *Psychotherapy for Borderline Personality Disorder: Mentalization Based Treatment*. Oxford: Oxford University Press.

Bell, D. (2004). Reflections on the death drive: Commentary on "The So-Called Death Drive" by Jean Laplanche. *British Journal of Psychotherapy, 20* (4): 485–491.

Belsky, J. (1999). Modern evolutionary theory and patterns of attachment. In: J. Cassidy & P. R. Shaver (Eds.), *Handbook of Attachment: Theory, Research and Clinical Applications* (pp. 141–161). New York: Guilford Press.

Belsky, J., & Fearon, R. M. (2002). Infant–mother attachment security, contextual risk, and early development: A moderational analysis. *Development and Psychopathology, 14*: 293–310.

Bick, E. (1968). The experience of the skin in early object relations. *Psychoanalytical Journal, 49*: 484.

Bion, W. (1962). *Learning from Experience*. London: Heinemann.

Black, D. (2001). Mapping a detour: Why did Freud speak of a death drive? *British Journal of Psychotherapy, 18* (2): 185–198.

Blackman, N., Weiss, J., & Lamberti, J. (1963). The sudden murderer,

III: Clues to preventative interaction. *Archives of General Psychiatry, 8*: 289–294.

Blair, R. J. (2001). Neurocognitive models of aggression, the antisocial personality disorders, and psychopathy. *Journal of Neurology, Neurosurgery, and Psychiatry, 71* (6): 727–731.

Blair, R. J., & Cipolotti, L. (2000). Impaired social response reversal: A case of "acquired sociopathy". *Brain, 123* (Pt. 6): 1122–1141.

Blair, R. J., Morris, J. S., Frith, C. D., Perrett, D. I., & Dolan, R. J. (1999). Dissociable neural responses to facial expression of sadness and anger. *Brain, 1222*: 883–893.

Blumenthal, S. (2000). Developmental aspects of violence and the institutional response. *Criminal Behaviour and Mental Health, 10* (3): 185–198.

Bollas, C. (1987). *The Shadow of the Object*. New York: Columbia University Press.

Bonnet, C. (1992). Adoption at birth: Prevention against abuse and neonaticide. *Child Abuse & Neglect, 17* (4): 501–513.

Boston, M., & Szur, R. (1983). *Psychotherapy with Severely Deprived Children*. London: Routledge. Reprinted London: Karnac, 1990.

Boswell, G. (2000). *Violent Children and Adolescents: Asking the Question Why*. London/Philadelphia, PA: Whurr.

Bott Spillius, E. (1992). Clinical experiences of projective identification. In: R. Anderson (Ed.), *Clinical Lectures on Klein and Bion* (pp. 59–73). New Library of Psychoanalysis, Vol. 14. London: Routledge.

Bowlby, J. (1969). *Attachment and Loss, Vol. 1: Attachment*. London: Hogarth Press & The Institute of Psychoanalysis; New York: Basic Books.

Bowlby, J. (1973). *Attachment and Loss, Vol. 2: Separation: Anxiety and Anger.* London: Hogarth Press & The Institute of Psychoanalysis.

Bowlby, J. (1980). *Attachment and Loss, Vol. 3: Loss: Sadness and Depression*. London: Hogarth Press & The Institute of Psychoanalysis.

Brafman, A. H. (2001). *Untying the Knot: Working with Parents and Children*. London: Karnac.

Brazelton, T. B., & Greenspan, S. I. (2000). *The Irreducible Needs of Children: What Every Child Must Have to Grow, Learn and Flourish*. New York: Perseus.

Britton, R. (1989) The missing link: Parental sexuality in the Oedipus complex. In: J. Steiner (Ed.), *The Oedipus Complex Today* (pp. 83–102). London: Karnac.

Britton, R. (1992a). Keeping things in mind. In: R. Anderson (Ed.), *Clinical Lectures on Klein and Bion* (pp. 102–113). London: Routledge.

Britton, R. (1992b). The Oedipus situation and the depressive position. In: R. Anderson (Ed.), *Clinical Lectures on Klein and Bion* (pp. 34–45). London: Routledge.

Britton, R. (2003). *Sex, Death and the Superego: Experiences in Psychoanalysis*. London: Karnac.

Broidy, L. M., Nagin, D. S., Tremblay, R. E., Bates, J. E., Brame, B., Dodge, K. A., et al. (2003). Developmental trajectories of childhood disruptive behaviors and adolescent delinquency: A six-site, cross-national study. *Developmental Psychology, 39* (2): 222–245.

Brotman, L. M., Klein, R. G., Kamboukos, D., Brown, E. J., Coard, S. I., & Sosinsky, L. S. (2003). Preventive intervention for urban, low-income preschoolers at familial risk for conduct problems: A randomized pilot study. *Journal of Clinical Child and Adolescent Psychology, 32* (2): 246–257.

Brown, K. D. (2002). "Domestic Violence and Its Effects on the Children Who Witness it." Paper presented at conference on Violence in Children and Parents, Centre for Child Mental Health (28 September).

Browne, K. D., & Hamilton, C. E. (1999). Police recognition of the links between spouse abuse and child abuse. *Child Maltreatment, 4* (2): 136–147.

Browne, K. D., & Herbert, M. (1997). *Preventing Family Violence*. Chichester: Wiley.

Browning, D. (1974). Patient's reactions to their therapist's pregnancy. *Journal of the American Academy of Child Psychiatry, 13*: 468–482.

Bruner, J., Jolly, A., & Sylva, K. (1976). *Play: Its Role in Development and Evolution*. New York: Basic Books.

Buelow, G., McClain, M., & McIntosh, I. (1996). A new measure for an important construct: The attachment and object relations inventory. *Journal of Personality Assessment, 66* (3): 604–623.

Burch, G., & Mohr, V. (1980). Evaluating a child abuse intervention program. *Social Casework: The Journal of Contemporary Social Work*: 90–99.

Burgess, A. (1962). *A Clockwork Orange*. London: Penguin.

Calkins, S., & Fox, N. (1994). Individual differences in the biological aspects of temperament. In: J. E. Bates & T. D. Wachs (Eds.), *Temperament, Individual Differences at the Interface of Biology and Behaviour* (pp. 199–217). Washington, DC: American Psychological Association.

Campbell, D. (1995). The role of the father in a pre-suicide state. *International Journal of Psychoanalysis, 76*: 315–323.

Campbell, D. (1999). The role of the father in a pre-suicide state. In: R. J. Perelberg (Ed.), *Psychoanalytic Understanding of Violence and Suicide* (pp. 75–86). New Library of Psychoanalysis. London/New York: Routledge.

Campbell, D. (2000). Violence as a defence against breakdown in adolescence. In: I. Wise (Ed.), *Adolescence* (pp. 11–20). Psychoanalytic Ideas Series. London: The Institute of Psychoanalysis.

Campbell, D. (2004). Mervin Glasser's contributions to psychoanalysis. *Bulletin of the British Psychoanalytical Society, 40* (1).

Carlson, V., Cicchetti, D., Barnett, D., & Braunwald, K. (1989). Finding order in disorganization: Lessons from research on maltreated infants' attachments to their caregivers. In: D. Cicchetti & V. Carlson (Eds.), *Child Maltreatment: Theory and Research on the Causes and Consequences of Child Abuse and Neglect* (pp. 494–528). New York: Cambridge University Press.

Cases, O., Seif, I., Grimsby, J., et al. (1995). Aggressive behavior and altered amounts of brain serotonin and norepinephrine in mice lacking MAOA. *Science, 268*: 1763–1766.

Cashdan, S. (1988). *Object Relations Theory: Using the Relationship*. New York: W. W. Norton.

Caspi, A. (2000). The child is father of the man: Personality continuities from childhood to adulthood. *Journal of Personality and Social Psychology, 78* (1): 158–172.

Caspi, A., McClay, J., Moffitt, T. E., Mill, J., Martin, J., Craig, I. W., et al. (2002). Role of genotype in the cycle of violence in maltreated children. *Science, 297* (5582): 851–854.

Cavadino, P., & Allen, R. (2000). Children who kill: Trends, reasons and procedures. In: G. Boswell (Ed.), *Violent Children and Adolescents: Asking the Question Why* (chap. 1). London: Whurr.

Chamberlain, D. B. (1995). What babies are teaching us about violence. *Pre- and Perinatal Psychology Journal, 10* (2): 57–74.

Chess, S., & Thomas, A. (1984). *Understanding the Withdrawing Child with High Sensitivity or High Intensity*. Van Nuys, CA: Kaiser Permanente, Child Development Media.

Clarkson, P. (1995). *The Therapeutic Relationship*. London: Whurr.

Conduct Problems Prevention Research Group (2002a). Evaluation of the first 3 years of the Fast Track Prevention trial with children at high risk for adolescent conduct problems. *Journal of Abnormal Child Psychology, 30*: 19–35.

Conduct Problems Prevention Research Group (2002b). The implementation of the Fast Track Program: An example of a large-scale prevention science efficacy trial. *Journal of Abnormal Child Psychology, 30*: 1–17.

Conduct Problems Prevention Research Group (2002c). Predictor variables associated with positive fast track outcomes at the end of the third grade. *Journal of Abnormal Child Psychology, 30*: 37–52.

Correia, I. (1994). *The Impact of Television Stimuli on the Prenatal Infant.*

PhD dissertation, University of New South Wales, Sydney, Australia.

Cote, S., Tremblay, R. E., Nagin, D., Zoccolillo, M., & Vitaro, F. (2002). The development of impulsivity, fearfulness, and helpfulness during childhood: Patterns of consistency and change in the trajectories of boys and girls. *Journal of Child Psychology and Psychiatry and Allied Disciplines, 43* (5): 609–618.

Cowie, H. (2000). Aggressive and bullying behaviour in children and adolescents. In: G. Boswell (Ed.), *Violent Children and Adolescents: Asking the Question Why* (chap. 9). London: Whurr.

Cuipers, P. (2003). Examining the effects of prevention programs on the incidence of new cases of mental disorders: The lack of statistical power. *American Journal of Psychiatry, 160*: 1385–1391.

Davis, C. H., MacKinnon, D. P., Schultz, A., & Sandler, I. (2003). Cumulative risk and population attributable fraction in prevention. *Journal of Clinical Child and Adolescent Psychology, 32* (2): 228–235.

Daws, D. (1985). Sleep problems in babies and young children. *Journal of Child Psychotherapy, 11* (2): 87–95.

De Bellis, M. D., Keshavan, M. S., Spencer, S., & Hall, J. (2000). N-Acetylaspartate concentration in the anterior cingulate of maltreated children and adolescents with PTSD. *American Journal of Psychiatry, 157*: 1175–1177.

Decker, S., Kirby, S., Greenwood, A., & Moore, D. (Eds.) (1999). *Taking Children Seriously*. London: Cassell.

Dermen, S. (2002). The work of Mervin Glasser: Violence. *Bulletin of the British Psychoanalytical Society, 38* (6): 29–34.

de Waal, F. B. M. (2000). Primates—a natural history of conflict resolution. *Science, 289*: 586–590.

de Zulueta, F. (1993). *From Pain to Violence. The Traumatic Roots of Destructiveness*. London: Whurr.

Diamond, N., & Marrone, M. (2003). *Attachment and Intersubjectivity*. London/Philadelphia, PA: Whurr.

Dockar-Drysdale, B. (1971). The management of violence in disturbed children. In: B. Dockar-Drysdale, *Therapy and Consultation in Child Care* (pp. 123–136). London: Free Association Books, 1993.

Dockar-Drysdale, B. (1993). *Therapy and Consultation in Child Care*. London: Free Association Books.

Earle, A. M., & Earle, B. V. (1961). Early maternal deprivation and later psychiatric illness. *American Journal of Orthopsychiatry, 31*: 181–186.

Eckenrode, J., Zielinski, D., Smith, E., Marcynyszyn, L. A., Henderson, C. R., Jr., Kitzman, H., et al. (2001). Child maltreatment and the early onset of problem behaviors: Can a program of nurse home visitation break the link? *Developmental Psychopathology, 13* (4): 873–890.

Emery, R. E., & Laumann-Billings, L. (2002). Child abuse. In: M. Rutter & E. Taylor (Eds.), *Child and Adolescent Psychiatry: Modern Approaches* (4th edition, pp. 325–339). Oxford: Blackwell Scientific.

Erickson, M. T. (1993). Rethinking Oedipus: An evolutionary perspective of incest avoidance. *American Journal of Psychiatry, 150* (3): 411–416.

Erikson, E. (1950). *Childhood and Society*. New York: W. W. Norton.

Erikson, E. (1959). *Identity and the Life Cycle, Vol. 1. Selected Papers: Psychological Issues*. New York: International Universities Press.

Erikson, E. (1977a). *Childhood and Society*. London: Paladin.

Erikson, E. (1977b). *Toys and Reasons: Stages in the Ritualization of Experience*. New York: W. W. Norton.

Fairbairn, W. R. D. (1952). *An Object-Relations Theory of the Personality*. New York: Basic Books.

Fairbairn, W. R. D. (1954). *Psychoanalytic Studies of the Personality*. London: Routledge, 1990.

Farrell, A. D., Meyer, A. L., Sullivan, T. N., & Kung, E. M. (2003). Evaluation of the Responding in Peaceful and Positive Ways (RiPP) seventh grade curriculum. *Journal of Child and Family Studies, 12*: 101–120.

Farrington, D. P. (1995). The Twelfth Jack Tizard Memorial Lecture. The development of offending and antisocial behaviour from childhood: Key findings from the Cambridge study in delinquent development. *Journal of Child Psychology and Psychiatry and Allied Disciplines, 36*: 929–964.

Farrington, D. P. (2003). Conduct disorder, aggression and delinquency. In: R. M. Lerner & L. Steinberg (Eds.), *Handbook of Adolescent Psychology*. New York: Wiley.

Farrington, D. P., Loeber, R., Yin, Y., & Anderson, S. J. (2002). Are within-individual causes of delinquency the same as between-individual causes? *Criminal Behaviour and Mental Health, 12* (1): 53–68.

Fenster, S., Phillips, S. B., & Rapoport, E. R. G. (1986). *The Therapist's Pregnancy: Intrusion in the Analytic Space*. Hillsdale, NJ: Analytic Press.

Field, T. M., Widmayer, S., Greenberg, R., & Stoller, S. (1982). Effects of parent training on teenage mother and their infants. *Pediatrics, 69*: 703–707.

Flaxman, S. G. (2000). Play: An endangered species. *Scholastic Inc, 110* (2): 39–41.

Fonagy, P. (1991). Thinking about thinking: Some clinical and theoretical considerations in the analysis of borderline patients. *International Journal of Psychoanalysis, 72* (4): 639–656.

Fonagy, P. (1998). *An Open Door Review of Outcome Studies in Psycho-*

analysis. Draft report by the Research Committee of the International Psychoanalytical Association (12 December).

Fonagy, P. (1999). *An Open Door Review of Outcome Studies in Psychoanalysis*. London: International Psychoanalytical Association.

Fonagy, P. (2001a). *Attachment Theory and Psychoanalysis*. New York: Other Press.

Fonagy, P. (2001b). Treatment of borderline personality disorder with psychoanalytically oriented partial hospitalisation: An 18-month follow-up (with A. Bateman). *American Journal of Psychiatry, 158* (1): 36–41.

Fonagy, P. (2003a). The development of psychopathology from infancy to adulthood: The mysterious unfolding of disturbance in time. *Infant Mental Health Journal, 24* (3), 212–239.

Fonagy, P. (2003b). Towards a developmental understanding of violence. *British Journal of Psychiatry, September, 183:* 190–192.

Fonagy, P., Gergely, G., Jurist, E., & Target, M. (2002). *Affect Regulation, Mentalization and the Development of the Self*. New York: Other Press.

Fonagy, P., & Target, M. (1995a). Towards understanding violence: The use of the body and the role of the father. *International Journal of Psychoanalysis, 76*: 487–502.

Fonagy, P., & Target, M. (1995b). Understanding the violent patient: The use of the body and the role of the father. *International Journal of Psycho-Analysis, 76*: 487–502.

Fonagy, P., & Target, M. (1996). Playing with reality: 1. Theory of mind and the normal development of psychic reality. *International Journal of Psycho-Analysis, 77*: 217–233.

Fonagy, P., & Target, M. (1997). Attachment and reflective function: Their role in self-organisation. *Development and Psychopathology, 9*: 679–700.

Fonagy, P., & Target, M. (1999). Towards understanding violence: The use of the body and the role of the father. In: R. J. Perelberg (Ed.), *Psychoanalytic Understanding of Violence and Suicide* (pp. 51–72). New Library of Psychoanalysis. London/New York: Routledge.

Fonagy, P., & Target, M. (2003). *Psychoanalytic Theories: Perspectives from Developmental Psychopathology*. London: Whurr.

Fonagy, P., Target, M., Steele, M., & Steele, H. (1997). The development of violence and crime as it relates to security of attachment. In: J. D. Osofsky (Ed.), *Children in a Violent Society* (pp. 150–177). New York: Guilford Press.

Fonagy, P., Target, M., Steele, M., Steele, H., Leigh, T., Levinson, A., et al. (1997). Morality, disruptive behavior, borderline personality disorder, crime, and their relationships to security of attachment. In: L.

Atkinson & K. J. Zucker (Eds.), *Attachment and Psychopathology* (pp. 223–274). New York: Guilford Press.

Fraiberg, S., Adelson, E., & Shapiro, V. (1975). Ghosts in the nursery: A psychoanalytic approach to the problems of impaired infant–mother relationships. *Journal of the American Academy of Child Psychiatry, 14* (3): 387–422.

Freud, A. (1927). The methods of child analysis. In: *The Writings of Anna Freud, Vol. 1* (pp. 50–70). New York: International Universities Press, 1974.

Freud, A. (1936a). *The Ego and the Mechanisms of Defence.* London: Hogarth Press. Reprinted London: Karnac, 1993.

Freud, A. (1936b). Identification with the aggressor. In: *The Ego and the Mechanisms of Defence* (pp. 117–131). London: Hogarth Press. Reprinted London: Karnac, 1993.

Freud, A. (1949). Aggression in relation to emotional development: Normal and pathological. *Psychoanalytic Study of the Child, 3/4*: 37–42.

Freud, A. (1965). *Normality and Pathology in Childhood: Assessments of Development.* London: Karnac, 1989.

Freud, A. (1970). The symptomatology of childhood: A preliminary attempt at classification. *The Writings of Anna Freud, Vol. 7: Psychoanalytic Psychology of Normal Development 1970–1980* (pp. 157–188). London: Hogarth Press & The Institute of Psychoanalysis.

Freud, S. (1900a). *The Interpretation of Dreams. SE,* 4/5.

Freud, S. (1905d). *Three Essays on the Theory of Sexuality. SE,* 7, pp. 125–245.

Freud, S. (1905e). Fragment of an analysis of a case of hysteria. *SE,* 7, pp. 7–122.

Freud, S. (1907c). The sexual enlightenment of children. *SE,* 9, pp. 129–140.

Freud, S. (1911–1915). Papers on technique. *SE,* 12, pp. 85–174.

Freud, S. (1912e). Recommendations to physicians practising psychoanalysis. *SE,* 12, pp. 109–120.

Freud, S. (1914c). On narcissism: An introduction. *SE,* 14, pp. 67–104.

Freud, S. (1920g). *Beyond the Pleasure Principle. SE,* 18, pp. 3–64.

Freud, S. (1930a). *Civilization and Its Discontents. SE,* 21, pp. 57–146.

Freud, S. (1940a [1938]). *An Outline of Psycho-Analysis. SE,* 23.

Gabbard, G. O. (2000). *Psychodynamic Psychiatry in Clinical Practice* (3rd edition). Washington, DC: American Psychiatric Press.

Garmezy, N., & Masten, A. (1994). Chronic Adversities. In: M. Rutter, E. Taylor, & L. Hersov (Eds.), *Child and Adolescent Psychiatry: Modern Approaches* (pp. 191–208). Oxford: Blackwell Scientific.

Garvey, C. (1977). *Play.* The Developing Child Series, ed. J. Bruner, M. Cole, & B. Lloyd. Cambridge, MA: Harvard University Press.

Gergely, G., & Watson, J. S. (1996). The social biofeedback theory of parental affect-mirroring: The development of emotional self-awareness and self-control in infancy. *International Journal of Psycho-Analysis, 77*: 1181–1212.

Gerhardt, S. (2004). *Why Love Matters: How Affection Shapes a Baby's Brain*. Hove: Brunner Routledge.

Gilliom, M., Shaw, D. S., Beck, J. E., Schonberg, M. A., & Lukon, J. E. (2002). Anger regulation in disadvantaged preschool boys: Strategies, antecedents, and the development of self-control. *Developmental Psychology, 38*: 222–235.

Glasser, M. (1979). From the analysis of a transvestite. *International Journal of Psychoanalysis, 6*: 163.

Glasser, M. (1985). The weak spot: Some observations on male sexuality. *International Journal of Psychoanalysis, 66*: 405–414.

Glasser, M. (1992). Problems in the psychoanalysis of certain narcissistic disorders, *International Journal of Psychoanalysis, 73*: 493–503.

Glasser, M. (1996). Aggression and sadism in the perversions. In: I. Rosen (Ed.), *Sexual Deviation* (3rd edition). Oxford: Oxford University Press.

Glasser, M. (1998). On violence: A preliminary communication. *International Journal of Psychoanalysis, 79*: 887–902.

Glover, E. (1960). *The Roots of Crime*. London: Imago.

Golding, W. (1954). *Lord of the Flies*. London: Penguin.

Gray, A. (1999). *An Introduction to the Therapeutic Frame*. London: Routledge.

Gray, J., Cutler, C., Dean, J., & Kempe, C. H. (1979). Prediction and prevention of child abuse and neglect. *Journal of Social Issues, 35*: 127–139.

Greenson, R. (1968). Dis-identifying from mother: Its special importance for the boy. *International Journal of Psychoanalysis, 49*: 370–374.

Grinberg, L. (1962). On a specific aspect of countertransference. *International Journal of Psychoanalysis, 43*.

Hardy, J. B., & Streett, R. (1989). Family support and parenting education in the home: An effective extension of clinic-based preventive health care services for poor children. *Journal of Pediatrics, 115*: 927–931.

Harrington, R., Fudge, H., Rutter, M., Pickles, A., & Hill, J. (1991). Adult outcomes of childhood and adolescent depression: II. Links with antisocial disorders. *Journal of the American Academy of Child and Adolescent Psychiatry, 30*: 434–439.

Hartmann, H., Kris, E., & Lowenstein, R. M. (1949). Notes on the theory of aggression. *Psychoanalytic Study of the Child, 3/4*: 9–36.

Herzog, J. M. (1980). Sleep disturbance and father hunger in 18- to 28-

month-old boys: The Erlkönig Syndrome. *Psychoanalytic Study of the Child, 35*: 219–233.

Herzog, J. M. (1982). On father hunger: The father's role in the modulation of aggressive drive and fantasy. In: S. W. Cath, A. R. Gurwitt, & J. M. Ross (Eds.), *Father and Child* (pp. 163–174). Boston: Little, Brown.

Hofer, M. A. (2004). The emerging neurobiology of attachment and separation: How parents shape their infant's brain and behavior. In: S. W. Coates, J. L. Rosenthal, & D. S. Schecter (Eds.), *September 11: Trauma and Human Bonds*. New York: Analytic Press.

Holmes, J. (2001). *The Search for the Secure Base*. Hove: Brunner-Routledge.

Howell, J. C. (1997). *Juvenile Justice and Youth*. Thousand Oaks, CA: Sage.

Hoxter, S. (1977). Play and communication. In: D. Daws & M. Boston (Eds.), *The Child Psychotherapist and Problems of Young People*. London: Wildwood House. Reprinted London: Karnac, 2004.

Humphreys, J., Sharps, P. W., & Campbell, J. C. (2005). What we know and what we still need to learn. *Journal of Interpersonal Violence, 20* (2): 182–187.

Hurry, A. (1998). *Psychoanalysis and Developmental Therapy*. London: Karnac.

Ianniruberto, A., & Tajani, E. (1981). Ultrasonographic study of fetal movements. *Seminars in Perinatology, 5* (2): 175–181.

Infante-Rivard, C., Filion, G., Baumgarten, M., Bourassa, M., Labelle, M., & Messier, M. (1989). A public health home intervention among families of low socio-economic status. *Children's Health Care, 18*: 102–107.

Jaffee, S. R., Caspi, A., Moffitt, T. E., & Taylor, A. (2004). Physical maltreatment victim to antisocial child: Evidence of an environmentally mediated process. *Journal of Abnormal Psychology, 113* (1), 44–55.

Johnson, J. G., Cohen, P., Brown, J., Smailes, E. M., & Bernstein, D. P. (1999). Childhood maltreatment increases risk for personality disorders during early adulthood. *Archives of General Psychiatry, 56*: 600–605.

Kagan, J., & Snidman, N. (1991). Infant predictors of inhibited and uninhibited profiles. *Psychological Science, 2* (11): 40–44.

Karr-Morse, R., & Wiley, M. S. (1997). *Ghosts from the Nursery: Tracing the Roots of Violence*. New York: Atlantic Monthly Press.

Kasen, S., Cohen, P., Skodol, A. E., Johnson, J. G., Smailes, E., & Brook, J. S. (2001). Childhood depression and adult personality disorder: Alternative pathways of continuity. *Archives of General Psychiatry, 58* (3): 231–236.

Kellam, S. G., Ling, X., Merisca, R., Brown, C. H., & Ialongo, N. (1998). The effect of the level of aggression in the first grade classroom on the course and malleability of aggressive behavior into middle school. *Development and Psychopathology, 10* (2): 165–185.

Kellam, S. G., Rebok, G. W., Mayer, L. S., Ialongo, N., & Kalodner, C. R. (1994). Depressive symptoms over first grade and their response to a developmental epidemiologically based preventive trial aimed at improving achievement. *Development and Psychopathology, 6*: 463–481.

Kendall, P. C. (2000). *Child and Adolescent Therapy: Cognitive Behavioural Procedures*. London: Guildford Press.

Klein, M. (1932). *The Writings of Melanie Klein, Vol. 2: The Psycho-Analysis of Children*. London: Hogarth Press, 1975.

Klein, M. (1940). Mourning and its relation to manic-depressive states. In: *The Writings of Melanie Klein, Vol. 1: Love, Guilt and Reparation and Other Works* (pp. 344–369). London: Hogarth Press, 1975. Reprinted London: Karnac, 1992.

Klein, M. (1945). The Oedipus complex in the light of early anxieties. In: *The Writings of Melanie Klein, Vol. 1: Love, Guilt and Reparation and Other Works* (pp. 370–419). London: Hogarth Press, 1975. Reprinted London: Karnac, 1992.

Klein, M. (1946). Notes on some schizoid mechanisms. In: *The Writings of Melanie Klein, Vol. 3: Envy and Gratitude and Other Works* (pp. 1–24). London: Hogarth Press, 1975.

Klein, M. (1952). Some theoretical conclusions regarding the emotional life of the infant. In: *The Writings of Melanie Klein, Vol. 3: Envy and Gratitude and Other Works* (pp. 61–93). London: Hogarth Press, 1975.

Klein, M. (1957). Envy and gratitude. In: *The Writings of Melanie Klein, Vol. 3: Envy and Gratitude and Other Works* (pp. 176–235). London: Hogarth Press, 1975.

Klein, M. (1975). *Love, Guilt and Reparation and Other Works*. London: Hogarth Press. Reprinted London: Karnac, 1992.

Klein, M. (1991). *The Selected Melanie Klein*. London: Penguin.

Klein, M. (1997a). *Envy and Gratitude and Other Works, 1946–1963*. London: Vintage.

Klein, M. (1997b). *The Psychoanalysis of Children*. London: Vintage.

Klinteberg, B. A., Andersson, T., Magnusson, D., & Stattin, H. (1993). Hyperactive behavior in childhood as related to subsequent alcohol problems and violent offending: A longitudinal study of male subjects. *Personality and Individual Differences, 15*: 381–388.

Kochanska, G., Gross, J. N., Lin, M.-H., & Nichols, K. E. (2002). Guilt in young children: Development, determinants, and relations with a broader system of standards. *Child Development, 73*: 461–482.

Kohut, H. (1977). *The Restoration of the Self*. New York: International Universities Press.

Laing, R. D. (1990). *The Politics of Experience and the Bird of Paradise*. London: Penguin.

Larson, C. P. (1980). Efficacy of prenatal and postpartum home visits on child health and development. *Pediatrics, 66*: 191–197.

Lax, R. F. (1969). Some considerations about transference and countertransference manifestations evoked by the analyst's pregnancy. *International Journal of Psychoanalysis, 50*: 363–372.

Lealman, G. T., Haigh, D., Phillips, J. M., Stone, J., & Ord-Smith, C. (1983). Prediction and prevention of child abuse—an empty hope? *Lancet, 1* (8339): 1423–1424.

Leowald, H. W. (1969). Freud's conception of the negative therapeutic reaction, with comments on instinct theory. In: *Papers on Psychoanalysis* (pp. 315–325). New Haven, CT/London: Yale University Press, 1980.

Lipsey, M. W., & Derzon, J. H. (1998). Predictors of violent or serious delinquency in adolescence and early adulthood: A synthesis of longitudinal research. In: R. L. Loeber & D. P. Farrington (Eds.), *Serious and Violent Juvenile Offenders: Risk Factors and Successful Interventions* (pp. 86–105). Thousand Oaks, CA: Sage.

Liszkowski, U., Carpenter, M., Henning, A., Striano, T., & Tomasello, M. (2004). Twelve-month-olds point to share attention and interest. *Developmental Science, 7*: 297–307.

Lochman, J. E., & Wells, K. C. (2002). The Coping Power program at the middle-school transition: Universal and indicated prevention effects. *Psychology of Addictive Behaviours, 16* (4, Suppl.): S40–S54.

Loeber, R., Burke, J. D., & Lahey, B. B. (2002). What are adolescent antecedents to antisocial personality disorder? *Criminal Behaviour and Mental Health, 12* (1): 24–36.

Loeber, R., Farrington, D. P., & Waschbusch, D. A. (1998). Serious and violent juvenile offenders. In: R. Loeber & D. P. Farrington (Eds.), *Serious and Violent Juvenile Offenders: Risk Factors and Successful Interventions* (pp. 13–29). Thousand Oaks, CA: Sage.

Loeber, R., Green, S. M., & Lahey, B. B. (2003). Risk factors for antisocial personality. In: D. P. Farrington & J. W. Coid (Eds.), *Early Prevention of Adult Antisocial Behaviour* (pp. 79–108). Cambridge: Cambridge University Press.

Loeber, R., Stouthamer-Loeber, M., Farrington, D. P., Lahey, B. B., Keenan, K., & White, H. R. (2002). Editorial introduction. Three longitudinal studies of children's development in Pittsburgh: The Developmental Trends Study, the Pittsburgh Youth Study, and the Pittsburgh Girls Study. *Criminal Behaviour and Mental Health, 12* (1): 1–23.

Lorenz, K. (1966). *On Aggression.* New York: Bantam Books.

Losel, F., & Bender, D. (2003). Protective factors and resilience. In: D. P. Farrington & J. W. Coid (Eds.), *Early Prevention of Adult Antisocial Behaviour* (pp. 130–204). Cambridge: Cambridge University Press.

Lucas, P. (1994). Episodic dyscontrol: A look back at anger. *Journal of Forensic Psychiatry, 5*: 371–407.

Lutzker, J. R., & Rice, J. M. (1984). Project 12-ways: Measuring outcome of a large in-home service for treatment and prevention of child abuse and neglect. *Child Abuse and Neglect, 8*: 519–524.

Maenchen, A. (1984). The handling of overt aggression in child analysis. *Psychoanalytic Study of the Child, 39*: 393–405.

Mahler, M. (1968). *On Human Symbiosis and the Vicissitudes of Individuation, Vol. 1: Infantile Psychosis.* New York: International Universities Press.

Mahler, M., Pine, F., & Bergman, A. (1975). *The Psychological Birth of the Human Infant.* New York: Basic Books.

Main, M., & Cassidy, J. (1988). Categories of response to reunion with the parents at age six: Predictable from infant attachment classification and stable over a one month period, *Developmental Psychology, 24*: 415–426.

Main, M., & Solomon, J. (1990). Procedures for identifying infants as disorganized/disorientated during the Ainsworth Strange Situation. In: M. Greenberg, D. Cicchetti, & E. Cummings (Eds.) (pp. 121–160). Chicago: University of Chicago Press.

Mäki, P. (2003). *Parental Separation at Birth and Maternal Depressed Mood in Pregnancy: Associations with Schizophrenia and Criminality in the Offspring.* Dissertation, University of Oulu, Oulu, Finland.

Marchenko, M. O., & Spence, M. (1994). Home visitation services for at-risk pregnant and post-partum women: A randomized trial. *American Journal of Orthopsychiatry, 64*: 468–478.

Maughan, B., & Rutter, M. (2001). Antisocial children grown up. In: J. Hill & B. Maughan (Eds.), *Conduct Disorders in Childhood and Adolescence* (pp. 507–552). Cambridge: Cambridge University Press.

Mayes, L. C. (2000). A developmental perspective on the regulation of arousal states. *Seminars in Perinatology, 24*: 267–279.

Mayes, L. C. (2002). A behavioral teratogenic model of the impact of prenatal cocaine exposure on arousal regulatory systems. *Neurotoxicology and Teratology, 24* (3): 385–395.

McGuigan, W. M., Katzev, A. R., & Pratt, C. C. (2003). Multi-level determinants of retention in a home-visiting child abuse prevention program. *Child Abuse & Neglect, 27* (4): 363–380.

Meaney, M. J., & Szyf, M. (2005). Maternal care as a model for experience-dependent chromatin plasticity? *Trends in Neurosciences, 28* (9): 456–463.

Meins, E., Ferryhough, C., Fradley, E., & Tuckey, M. (2001). Rethinking maternal sensitivity: Mothers' comments on infant's mental processes predict security of attachment at 12 months. *Journal of Child Psychology and Psychiatry, 42*: 637–648.

Meloy, J. R. (1992). *Violent Attachments.* Northvale, NJ/London: Jason Aronson.

Metropolitan Area Child Study Research Group (2002). A cognitive-ecological approach to preventing aggression in urban settings: Initial outcomes for high risk children. *Journal of Consulting and Clinical Psychology, 70*: 179–194.

Migone, P., & Rabaiotti, C. (2003). The psychoanalytic concept of aggressive drive: Freud's theories and some suggestions of theoretical revision (second part). *Rivista Sperimentale di Freniatria: La Revista della Salute Mentale, 127* (3): 121–136 (in database: Psyc INFO 2004, Part A).

Miller, L. (1992). The difficulty of establishing a space for thinking in the therapy of a 7-year-old girl. *Psychoanalytic Psychotherapy, 6* (2): 121–135.

Milner, M. (1957). *On Not Being Able to Paint.* London: Heinemann. (First published 1950 under the pseudonym Joanna Field.)

Moffitt, T. E. (1993). The neuropsychology of conduct disorder. *Development and Psychopathology, 5*: 135–151.

Moffitt, T. E., & Caspi, A. (2003). Preventing the inter-generational continuity of antisocial behaviour: Implications of partner violence. In: D. P. Farrington & J. W. Coid (Eds.), *Early Prevention of Adult Antisocial Behaviour* (pp. 109–129). Cambridge: Cambridge University Press.

Moffitt, T. E., Caspi, A., Harrington, H., & Milne, B. J. (2002). Males on the life-course-persistent and adolescence-limited antisocial pathways: Follow-up at age 26 years. *Development and Psychopathology, 14* (1): 179–207.

Moosajee, M. (2003). Violence: A noxious cocktail of genes and the environment. *Journal of the Royal Society of Medicine, 96* (5): 211–214.

Murray, L., Cooper, P., Wilson, A., & Romaniuk, H. (2003). Control trial of the short and long term effect of psychological treatment of post-partum depression: 2. Impact on the mother–child relationship and child outcome, *British Journal of Psychiatry, 182*: 420–427.

Nadelson, C., Notman, M., Arons, E., & Feldman, J. (1974). The pregnant therapist. *American Journal of Psychiatry, 131*: 1107–1111.

Nagin, D. S., & Tremblay, R. E. (2001). Parental and early childhood predictors of persistent physical aggression in boys from kindergarten to high school. *Archives of General Psychiatry, 58* (4): 389–394.

Neil, A. S. (1968). *Summerhill.* London: Penguin.

Olds, D. L., Henderson, C. R., Chamberlin, R., & Tatelbaum, R. (1986). Preventing child abuse and neglect: A randomized trial of nurse home visitation. *Pediatrics, 78*: 65–78.

Olds, D. L., Henderson, C., Kitzman, H., Eckenrode, J., Cole, R., & Tatelbaum, R. (1998). The promise of home visitation: Results of two randomized trials. *Journal of Community Psychology, 26* (1): 1–21.

Olweus, D. (1993). *Bullying at School: What We Know and What We Can Do.* Oxford: Blackwell.

Panksepp, J. (1998). *Affective Neuroscience: The Foundations of Human and Animal Emotions.* Oxford: Oxford University Press.

Parens, H. (1987). *Aggression in Our Children.* Northvale, NJ/London: Jason Aronson.

Patterson, G. R., Reid, J. B., & Dishion, T. J. (1992). *Antisocial Boys.* Eugene, OR: Castalia.

Perelberg, R. (1995). Violence in children and young adults. *Bulletin of the Anna Freud Centre, 18*: 89 –122.

Perelberg, R. (Ed.) (1999). *Psychoanalytic Understanding of Violence and Suicide*. New Library of Psychoanalysis, Vol. 33. London: Routledge.

Pert, L., Ferriter, M., & Saul, C. (2004). Parental loss before the age of 16 years: A comparative study of patients with personality disorder and patients with schizophrenia in a high secure hospital's population. *Psychology and Psychotherapy: Theory, Research, and Practice, 77*: 403–407.

Peterson, L., Tremblay, G., Ewigman, B., & Saldana, L. (2003). Multilevel selected primary prevention of child maltreatment. *Journal of Consulting and Clinical Psychology, 71* (3): 601–612.

Phillips, A. (1999). *Saying No: Why It's Important for You and Your Child.* London: Faber & Faber.

Piaget, J. (1945). *Play, Dreams and Imitation in Childhood.* New York: W. W. Norton.

Pollock, P. H., & Percy, A. (1999). Maternal antenatal attachment style and potential fetal abuse. *Child Abuse and Neglect, 23* (12): 1345–1357.

Posner, M. I., & Rothbart, M. K. (2000). Developing mechanisms of self-regulation. *Development and Psychopathology, 12*: 427–441.

Quinton, D., Gulliver, L., & Rutter, M. (1995). A 15–20 year follow-up of adult psychiatric patients: Psychiatric disorder and social functioning. *British Journal of Psychiatry, 167*: 315–323.

Raine, A. (2002). Biosocial studies of antisocial and violent behavior in children and adults: A review. *Journal of Abnormal Child Psychology, 30* (4): 311–326.

Raine, A., Lencz, T., Bihrle, S., LaCasse, L., & Colletti, P. (2000). Reduced prefrontal gray matter volume and reduced autonomic activity in antisocial personality disorder. *Archives of General Psychiatry, 57* (2): 119–127.

Raine, A., Stoddard, J., Bihrle, S., & Buchsbaum, M. (1998). Prefrontal glucose deficits in murderers with psychosocial deprivation. *Neuropsychiatry, Neuropsychology and Behavioural Neurology, 11*: 1–7.

Raphael-Leff, J. (2003). On wild things within: An introduction to psychoanalytic thinking. In: J. Raphael-Leff (Ed.), *Parent–Infant Psychodynamics: Wild Things, Mirrors and Ghosts* (pp. xvii-xix). London: Whurr.

Rashid, S. P. (2000). Comparing studies of youth and violence: Towards an integrated approach. In G. Boswell (Ed.), *Violent Children and Adolescents: Asking the Question Why*. Philadelphia, PA: Whurr.

Reid, J. B., Eddy, J. M., Fetrow, R. A., & Stoolmiller, M. (1999). Description and immediate impacts of a preventive intervention for conduct problems. *American Journal of Community Psychology, 27* (4): 483–517.

Renn, P. (2000). The link between childhood trauma and later offending: A case study. In: G. Boswell (Ed.), *Violent Children and Adolescents: Asking the Question Why* (chap. 5). London: Whurr.

Resnick, G. (1985). Enhancing parental competencies for high risk mothers: An evaluation of prevention effects. *Child Abuse and Neglect, 9*: 479–489.

Ridley, M. (1993). *Nature via Nurture: Genes, Experiences and what makes us Human*. New York: Harper Collins.

Rutter, M. (2000). Psychosocial influences: Critiques, findings and research needs. *Development and Psychopathology, 12*: 375–405.

Rutter, M., Giller, H., & Hagell, A. (1998). *Antisocial Behaviour by Young People*. Cambridge: Cambridge University Press.

Ryan, G. (2005). Preventing violence and trauma in the next generation. *Journal of Interpersonal Violence, 20* (1): 132–141.

Salzberger-Wittenberg, I., Williams, G., & Osborne, E. (1983). *The Emotional Experience of Learning and Teaching*. London: Karnac.

Sanders, M. R., Markie-Dadds, C., Tully, L., & Bor, B. (2000). The Triple P-Positive Parenting Program: A comparison of enhanced, standard and self-directed behavioral family intervention for parents of children with early onset conduct problems. *Journal of Consulting and Clinical Psychology, 68*: 624–640.

Schore, A. N. (1994). *Affect Regulation and the Origin of the Self: The Neurobiology of Emotional Development*. Hillsdale, NJ: Lawrence Erlbaum.

Schore, A. N. (1996). The experience-dependent maturation of a regulatory system in the orbital prefrontal cortex and the origin of developmental psychopathology. *Development and Psychopathology, 8*: 59–87.

Schore, A. N. (2000). Attachment and the regulation of the right brain. *Attachment and Human Development, 2*: 23–47.

Schore, A. N. (2003a). *Affect Dysregulation and Disorders of the Self.* New York: W. W. Norton.

Schore, A. N. (2003b). The human unconscious: The development of the right brain and its role in early emotional development. In: V. Green, *Emotional Development in Psychoanalysis, Attachment Theory and Neuroscience.* Hove: Brunner-Routledge.

Scott, K. G. (2003). Commentary: Individual risk prediction, individual risk, and population risk. *Journal of Clinical Child and Adolescent Psychology, 32* (2): 243–245.

Segal, M., & Adcock, D. (1981). *Just Pretending: Ways to Help Children Grow Through Imaginative Play.* Englewood Cliffs, NJ: Prentice-Hall.

Sendak, M. (1963). *Where the Wild Things Are.* London: Picture Lions, 1992.

Shaw, D. S., Gilliom, M., Ingoldsby, E. M., & Nagin, D. S. (2002). *Trajectories Leading to School Age Conduct Problems.* Unpublished manuscript, University of Pittsburgh.

Shengold, L. (1991). *Father, Don't You See I'm Burning?* New Haven, CT: Yale University Press.

Shengold, L. (1999). Foreword. In: R. Perelberg (Ed.), *Psychoanalytic Understanding of Violence and Suicide.* New Library of Psychoanalysis, Vol. 33. London: Routledge.

Shonk, S. M., & Cicchetti, D. (2001). Maltreatment, competency deficits, and risk for academic and behavioral maladjustment. *Developmental Psychology, 37* (1), 3–17.

Sinason, V. (1996). "But psychotherapists don't laugh, do they?" *Psycho-analytic Psychotherapy in South Africa, 4*: 19–31.

Sluyter, F., Arseneault, L., Moffitt, T. E., Veenema, A. H., de Boer, S., & Koolhaas, J. M. (2003). Toward an animal model for antisocial behavior: Parallels between mice and humans. *Behavior Genetics, 33* (5): 563–574

Smith, C. A., & Farrington, D. P. (2004). Continuities in antisocial behavior and parenting across three generations. *Journal of Child Psychology and Psychiatry, 45* (2): 230–247.

Smyke, A. T., Dumitrescu, A., & Zeanah, C. H. (2002). Attachment disturbances in young children. I: The continuum of caretaking casualty. *Journal of the American Academy of Child and Adolescent Psychiatry, 41* (8): 972–982.

Spitz, R. (1953). Aggression: Its role in the establishment of object relations. In: R. M. Lowenstein (Ed.), *Drives, Affects, Behaviour.* New York: International Universities Press.

Spitz, R. (1965). *The First Year of Life.* New York: International Universities Press.

Stein, H., Koontz, A. D., Fonagy, P., Allen, J. G., Fultz, J., Brethour, J. R., Jr., et al. (2002). Adult attachment: What are the underlying dimensions? *Psychology and Psychotherapy, 75* (Pt. 1): 77–91.

Steiner, J. (1992). The equilibrium between the paranoid–schizoid and the depressive positions. In: R. Anderson (Ed.), *Clinical lectures on Klein and Bion* (pp. 46–58). London. Routledge.

Stern, D. N. (1985). The Interpersonal World of the Infant: A View from Psychoanalysis and Developmental Psychology. New York: Basic Books.

Stoolmiller, M., Eddy, J. M., & Reid, J. B. (2000). Detecting and describing preventive intervention effects in a universal school-based randomized trial targeting delinquent and violent behavior. *Journal of Consulting and Clinical Psychology, 68* (2): 296–306.

Sunderland, M. (2000). *A Wibble Called Bipley (and a Few Honks).* Oxford: Winslow.

Sunderland, M. (2002). "The Power of the Genetically Ingrained Rage Circuit in the Human Brain." Paper presented at a conference on Violence in Children and Parents, The Centre for Child Mental Health (28 September).

Target, M., & Fonagy, P. (1994). The efficacy of psychoanalysis for children with emotional disorders. *Journal of the American Academy of Child and Adult Psychiatry, 33*: 361–371.

Target, M., & Fonagy, P. (1996). Playing with reality: II. The development of psychic reality from a theoretical perspective. *International Journal of Psychoanalysis, 77*: 459–479.

Thompson, R., Briggs, E., English, D. J., Dubowitz, H., Lee, L. C., Brody, K., Everson, M. D., & Hunter, W. M. (2005). Suicidal ideation among 8-year-olds who are maltreated and at risk: Findings from the LONGSCAN studies. *Child Maltreatment 10* (1): 26–36. [Juvenile Protective Association.]

Tolan, P. H., & Gorman-Smith, D. (2002). What violence prevention research can tell us about developmental psychopathology. *Development and Psychopathology, 14* (4): 713–729.

Tomasello, M. (1999). *The Cultural Origins of Human Cognition.* Cambridge, MA: Harvard University Press.

Tomasello, M., & Haberl, K. (2003). Understanding attention: 12- and 18-month-olds know what is new for other persons. *Developmental Psychology, 39* (5): 906–912.

Tremblay, R. E. (2000). The origins of violence. *ISUMA* (Autumn): 19–24.

Tremblay, R. E., Japel, C., & Perusse, D. (1999). The search for the age of onset of physical aggression: Rousseau and Bandura revisited. *Criminal Behavior and Mental Health, 9*: 8–23.

Twemlow, S. W., Fonagy, P., & Sacco, F. C. (2004). The role of the bystander in the social architecture of bullying and violence in schools and communities. *Annals of the New York Academy of Science, 1036*: 215.

Twemlow, S. W., Fonagy, P., Sacco, F. C., Gies, M. L., Evans, R., & Ewbank, R. (2001). Creating a peaceful school learning environment: A controlled study of an elementary school intervention to reduce violence. *American Journal of Psychiatry, 158* (5): 808–810.

Twemlow, S. W., Fonagy, P., Sacco, F. C., O'Toole, M. E., & Vernberg, E. (2002). Premeditated mass shootings in schools: Threat assessment. *Journal of the American Academy of Child and Adolescent Psychiatry, 41* (4): 475–477.

Vitaro, F., Brendgen, M., Pagani, L., Tremblay, R. E., & McDuff, P. (1999). Disruptive behavior, peer association and conduct disorder: Testing the developmental links through early intervention. *Development and Psychopathology, 11*: 287–304.

Vygotsky, L. S. (1933). Play and its role in the mental development of the child. In: J. S. Bruner, A. Jolly, & K. Sylva (Eds.), *Play: Its Role in Development and Evolution*. New York: Basic Books, 1976.

Vygotsky, L. S. (1978). *Mind in Society: The Development of Higher Psychological Processes*. Cambridge, MA: Harvard University Press.

Walker, H., Irvin, L. K., & Sprague, J. R. (1997). *Violence Prevention and School Safety: Issues, Problems, Approaches, and Recommended Solutions*. Eugene, OR: Institute on Violence and Destructive Behaviour, University of Oregon.

Webster-Stratton, C. (1996). Early intervention with videotape modelling: Programmes for families of children with Oppositional Defiant Disorder or Conduct Disorder. In: E. S. Hibbs & P. S. Jensen (Eds.), *Psychosocial Treatments for Child and Adolescent Disorders: Empirically Based Strategies for Clinical Practice* (pp. 435–474). Washington, DC: American Psychological Association.

Webster-Stratton, C. (1998). Preventing conduct problems in Head Start children: Strengthening parenting competencies. *Journal of Consulting and Clinical Psychology, 66*: 715–730.

Webster-Stratton, C., Reid, M. J., & Hammond, M. (2001). Preventing conduct problems, promoting social competence: A parent and teacher training partnership in head start. *Journal of Clinical Child Psychology, 30* (3): 283–302.

Weiss, J., Lamberti, J., & Blackman, N. (1960). The sudden murder: A comparative analysis. *Archives of General Psychiatry, 2*: 669–678.

Welldon, E. (1988). *Mother, Madonna, Whore: The Idealization and Denigration of Motherhood*. London: Free Association Books.

Wellman, H. M., Cross, D., & Watson, J. (2001). Meta-analysis of theory-of-mind development: The truth about false belief. *Child Development, 72* (3): 655–684.

Wellman, H. M., & Liu, D. (2004). Scaling of theory-of-mind tasks. *Child Development, 75* (2): 523–541.

White, H. R., Bates, M. E., & Buyske, S. (2001). Adolescence-limited versus persistent delinquency: Extending Moffitt's hypothesis into adulthood. *Journal of Abnormal Psychology, 110* (4): 600–609.

WHO (2002a). *World Report on Violence and Health*, ed. E. G. Krug, L. L. Dahlberg, J. A. Mercy, A. B. Zwi, & R. Lozano. Geneva: World Health Organization.

WHO (2002b). *World Report on Violence and Health: Summary*. Geneva: World Health Organization.

Widom, C. S. (1989). Does violence beget violence? A critical examination of the literature. *Psychological Bulletin, 106*: 3–28.

Willock, B. (1990). From acting out to interactive play. *International Journal of Psychoanalysis, 71*.

Winnicott, D. W. (1946). Some psychological aspects of juvenile delinquency. In: *Deprivation and Delinquency* (pp. 113–119). London: Tavistock, 1984.

Winnicott, D. W. (1947). Hate in the countertransference. In: *Through Paediatrics to Psychoanalysis: Collected Papers* (pp. 194–203). London: Karnac, 1992.

Winnicott, D. W. (1949). Mind and its relation to the psyche-soma. In: *Through Paediatrics to Psychoanalysis: Collected Papers* (pp. 243–254). London: Karnac, 1992.

Winnicott, D. W. (1953). Transitional objects and transitional phenomena. *International Journal of Psychoanalysis, 34*: 89. In: *Through Paediatrics to Psychoanalysis: Collected Papers* (pp. 229–242). London: Karnac, 1992.

Winnicott, D. W. (1956a). The antisocial tendency. In: *Through Paediatrics to Psychoanalysis: Collected Papers* (pp. 306–315). London: Karnac, 1992.

Winnicott, D. W. (1956b). Primary maternal preoccupation In: *Through Paediatrics to Psychoanalysis: Collected Papers* (pp. 300–305). London: Karnac, 1992.

Winnicott, D. W. (1958). *Collected Papers: Through Paediatrics to Psychoanalysis*. London: Tavistock. Reprinted as *Through Paediatrics to Psychoanalysis Collected Papers*. London: Hogarth Press & The Institute of Psycho-Analysis, 1975. Reprinted London: Karnac Books, 1992.

Winnicott, D. W. (1962). Ego integration in child development. In: *The*

Maturational Processes and the Facilitating Environment (pp. 56–63). London: Karnac, 1990.

Winnicott, D. W. (1963). The development of the capacity for concern. In: *The Maturational Processes and the Facilitating Environment* (pp. 73–82). London: Hogarth Press, 1965.

Winnicott, D. W. (1965a). Failure of expectable environment on child's mental functioning. *International Journal of Psychoanalysis, 46*: 81–87.

Winnicott, D. W. (1965b). *The Family and Individual Development*. London: Tavistock.

Winnicott, D. W. (1965c). *The Maturational Processes and the Facilitating Environment*. London: Hogarth Press & The Institute of Psycho-Analysis. Reprinted London: Karnac, 1990.

Winnicott, D. W. (1968). Playing: Its theoretical status in the clinical situation. *International Journal of Psychoanalysis, 49*: 591–599.

Winnicott, D. W. (1969). The use of an object. *International Journal of Psychoanalysis, 50*: 711–716. Also in: *Playing and Reality*. London: Routledge, 1991.

Winnicott, D. W. (1971a). *Playing and Reality*. London: Routledge.

Winnicott, D. W. (1971b). *Therapeutic Consultations in Child Psychiatry*. Hogarth Press & The Institute of Psycho-Analysis. Reprinted London: Karnac, 1996.

Winnicott, D. W. (1991). *The Child, the Family and the Outside World*. London: Penguin.

Wise, I. (Ed.) (2000). *Adolescence*. Psychoanalytic Ideas Series. London: The Institute of Psychoanalysis.

Wolfe, D. A., Edwards, B., Manion, I., & Koverola, C. (1988). Early intervention for parents at risk of child abuse and neglect: A preliminary investigation. *Journal of Consulting and Clinical Psychology, 56*: 40–47.

Yoshikawa, H. (1994). Prevention as cumulative protection: Effects of early family support and education on chronic delinquency and its risk. *Psychological Bulletin, 115*: 28–54.

Yoshikawa, H. (1995). Long-term effects of early childhood programs on social outcomes and delinquency. *Future of Children, 5*: 51–75.

Zuckerman, M. (1994). Impulsive unsocialized sensation seeking: The biological foundations of a basic dimension of personality. In: J. E. Bates & T. D. Wachs (Eds.), *Temperament: Individual Differences at the Interface of Biology and Behaviour* (chap. 9). Washington, DC: American Psychological Association.

INDEX